# European Union Law for International Business

## An introduction

Written specifically for exporters and those without legal training, *European Union Law for International Business* is an introduction to the essential business laws of the European Union (EU). It is a practical guide to the regulatory and procedural issues of which exporters and businesses need to be aware.

While providing a general overview of how the EU operates as a governing body, the book specifically addresses the key matters that exporters will face during their business transactions. Topics covered include:

- direct export transactions to the EU
- exporting via an agent or distributor
- customs laws and procedures
- franchising
- resolving international business disputes
- how to establish a permanent business presence within the EU.

For each of these transaction types the book uses case studies to illustrate how they can be applied to real-world business dealings.

This book is an essential resource for anyone involved in international business with customers in the EU.

**Bernard Bishop** is Senior Lecturer in the Department of International Business and Asian Studies at Griffith Business School, Griffith University. He is co-author of *Australian Export: A Guide to Law and Practice* (CUP, 2006).

# European Union Law for International Business

## An introduction

Bernard Bishop

CAMBRIDGE
UNIVERSITY PRESS

CAMBRIDGE UNIVERSITY PRESS
Cambridge, New York, Melbourne, Madrid, Cape Town, Singapore, São Paulo, Delhi

Cambridge University Press
477 Williamstown Road, Port Melbourne, VIC 3207, Australia

Published in the United States of America by Cambridge University Press, New York

www.cambridge.org
Information on this title: www.cambridge.org/9780521881449



First published 2009

Cover design by Rob Cowpe
Edited by Angela Damis
Typeset by Aptara Corp.
Printed in Australia by Ligare

*A catalogue record for this publication is available from the British Library*

*National Library of Australia Cataloguing in Publication data*
Bishop, Bernard.
European Union Law for international business : an introduction
9780521881449 (pbk.)
Commercial law – European Union countries.
International business enterprises//Law and legislation – European Union Countries
346.407

ISBN 978-0-521-88144-9 paperback

*For*
*My parents*
*Leo and Donna Bishop*

# Contents

# Figures and tables

## FIGURES



## TABLES

# Case studies

# Preface

THIS BOOK IS written for small and medium exporters, their advisers, students and others with an interest in engaging in international business transactions with a firm in a member country of the European Union (EU). It seeks to provide an introduction to some of the more significant EU-wide laws and procedures of which business firms outside of the EU need to be aware before embarking upon their business venture. It is impossible to canvass all of the relevant laws and procedures because, not only is the volume of EU legislation extensive, but also much business activity still remains regulated at the individual EU member state level. Thus, the book is introductory and contains references to other sources, including internet sites that the reader can use to obtain more information on the particular legal issue being discussed.

In each chapter of the book an attempt has been made to place the legal issues in an international business context. The aim is to provide readers with information not only on relevant EU laws but also on how those laws might apply in an international business transaction. There are case studies in each chapter to provide examples of this. While every effort has been made to ensure that the information provided is up to date and accurate, readers should always obtain legal advice from locally qualified lawyers with regard to any particular transaction that they may be contemplating. This is stressed throughout the book along with the reasons for it.

The book commences in Chapter 1 with an introduction to the EU itself, its institutions, their role in law making and how those laws are made. To highlight the various methods by which EU laws are made, this introductory chapter concludes with a case study that shows the process that was involved in enacting the Mediation Directive.

Chapters 2–5 of the book deal with matters that need to be considered in an export of goods to an EU member country. Thus, the basics of the initial contract of sale, transport of the goods including within the EU, EU customs requirements, and payment mechanisms are discussed. The transport chapter contains a case study showing the steps taken by a freight forwarder in arranging a consignment to an EU destination. This chapter also provides information about internal transport alternatives within the EU and the relative significance of each. The customs chapter sets out the steps that are involved in dealing with customs formalities in the EU and contains two case studies that show the very detailed requirements that the EU has for goods that are exported to it. The payments chapter not only details the well-known mechanisms for payment in international business transactions and their frequency of use by importers but also seeks to point out ways in which the risk of non-payment can be minimised. There is a case study of a worldwide company that engages in credit risk insurance to show how this can be used by exporters to guard against credit risk.

Chapters 6 and 7 deal with exporting to the EU via an agent or distributor or via franchising. In the case of agents and distributors, all of the material introduced in Chapters 2–5 will also be relevant because exporters of goods via intermediaries will necessarily involve customs clearances, transport arrangements, payment mechanisms and contracts of sale. The chapter on agents and distributors includes a discussion of the EU commercial agent's directive and its influence on contracts with agents as well as EU competition laws and how they affect distribution agreements. There is a case study that shows how an exporter has made use of an EU distribution company to get goods onto supermarket shelves. The franchising chapter not only canvasses the various regulatory requirements that some countries within the EU have regarding franchising agreements but also sets out the basics of registering intellectual property rights within the EU. There is some information about the growth of franchising within the EU as well as a case study on a successful franchise operation there.

Chapter 8 canvasses the issues that an outside business person needs to consider if establishing a separate business presence within an EU country. Many exporters of goods and service providers find that to best service the burgeoning EU market, a permanent presence of some kind is eventually required. Five alternatives are canvassed. These are a private limited liability company, a branch, a public company, a European public company and acquisition of an existing company. The chapter describes law at the EU level that affects the establishment of each of these various forms. Case studies are used to show the procedures required to set up a private company and a branch using individual countries' procedures as examples. The chapter also contains information on licensing requirements for businesses and incentives that might be available to those establishing new businesses.

Chapter 9 concludes the book by examining the alternatives for resolving disputes should they arise in the course of doing business with an EU firm. The alternatives of litigation, arbitration and mediation are considered along with the main issues that arise in a European context. Two case studies are provided – one of an arbitral institution and one of an institution that is well known for its work in mediation.

# Acknowledgements

I WOULD FIRST like to acknowledge the support of the following businesses who agreed to have their firm profiled as a case study and then provided the necessary information for the compilation of that case study: Bartercard, Ozkleen, Atradius and a.hartrodt. Other businesses and organisations also provided assistance. In particular I would like to thank the Queensland Government Department of State Development (Brisbane and London offices); Austrade (Brisbane and London offices); Australian Business (London); Advance (London); Minter Ellison (London office); the Excess Baggage Company (London); and the European Australian Business Council (Sydney). I would also like to thank the very helpful staff at the Institute of Advanced Legal Studies library (University of London) and the Queen Mary University of London Intellectual Property Archive for their assistance with my enquiries and use of their library facilities.

# Abbreviations

| | |
|---|---|
| AQIS | Australian Quarantine Inspection Service |
| CHIEF | Customs Handling of Import and Export Freight |
| CIM Rules | Uniform Rules Concerning the Contract of International Carriage of Goods by Rail |
| CISG | United Nations Convention on Contracts for the International Sale of Goods |
| CMNI Convention | Budapest Convention on the Contract for the Carriage of Goods by Inland Waterway |
| CMR Convention | Convention on the Contract for the International Carriage of Goods by Road |
| COTIF Convention | Convention on International Carriage of Goods by Rail |
| CPC | Customs Procedure Code |
| EC | European Community |
| ECB | European Central Bank |
| ECC | European Commercial Cases |
| ECJ | European Court of Justice |
| EC Treaty | Treaty establishing the European Community |
| EPC | European Patent Convention |
| EPO | European Patents Office |
| EU | European Union |
| EU Treaty | Treaty on European Union |
| FIATA | Federation Internationale des Associations Transitaires et Assimiles (International Federation of Freight Forwarders) |
| GSP | Generalized System of Preferences |
| ICC | International Chamber of Commerce |
| IPR | intellectual property rights |
| ISO | International Organization for Standardization |

| | |
|---|---|
| MRA | mutual recognition agreement |
| NAFTA | North American Free Trade Association |
| OHIM | Office for the Harmonization of International Marks |
| PCT | Patent Cooperation Treaty |
| SDR | Special Drawing Rights |
| SE | Societas Europaea (European Company) |
| SPE | Societas Privata Europaea (European Private Company) |
| TURN | Trader's Unique Reference Number |
| UKHL | United Kingdom House of Lords |
| UNCITRAL | United Nations Commission on International Trade Law |
| UNCTAD | United Nations Conference on Trade and Development |
| WCO | World Customs Organization |
| WTO | World Trade Organization |

# 1 EU institutions and law making

## INTRODUCTION

THE EU HAS its origins in the European Coal and Steel community formed by France, Germany, Italy, Belgium, Luxembourg and the Netherlands by the Treaty of Paris in 1951. This treaty transferred the power over the coal and steel industries of those states signing it to a central authority. The objectives of the treaty are important because they signalled what were to become central aims of the EU. The primary objective was to have the coal and steel industry controlled centrally rather than at the individual nation state level for industry efficiency. Underlying this, however, was the view that such central control would contribute to peace within Europe by preventing any of the major powers from rearming and thereby avoiding the devastation that occurred in the previous decade in World War Two.

The formal beginnings of the EU occurred in 1957 when the same six nations to the Treaty of Paris signed the Treaty of Rome and created the European Economic Community, now the European Community (EC).[1] This treaty laid the foundations for the major institutions of the EU that exist today – the Council of Ministers, the European Parliament, the European Commission and the European Court of Justice. In addition, the EC Treaty moved beyond the aim of central regulation of a single industry to a much broader role of integration of the economies of the member countries. The treaty has been amended several times since 1957, most notably by the Single European Act of 1986; the Maastricht Treaty of 1992 that created an additional treaty to the original EC Treaty entitled the

[1] The resulting treaty is officially entitled the Treaty establishing the European Economic Community, Rome, 25 March 1957. It was later renamed the EC Treaty, when the EEC became the EC.

Treaty on European Union ('EU Treaty')[2] and laid the groundwork for the introduction for a common European currency; the Treaty of Amsterdam in 1997 that reformed many of the institutional arrangements of the EU; the Treaty of Nice in 2000 that was necessary in view of the impending enlargement of EU membership; and finally the Treaty of Lisbon in 2007 that, if ratified by all member states, will streamline administrative and governance arrangements within the EU.

The embryonic EU took some time to persuade other European nations to join. However, since the early 1970s there has been a gradual expansion so that today, most European nations are either members, or if not members, have largely integrated their economies with the EU bloc. Great Britain, Denmark and Ireland joined in 1973 followed by Greece in 1981; Spain and Portugal in 1986; Austria, Finland and Sweden in 1995; Estonia, Latvia, Lithuania, the Czech Republic, Slovakia, Hungary, Poland, Slovenia, Malta and Cyprus in 2004; and finally Bulgaria and Romania in 2007, bringing total membership to 27 countries.

The increase in membership has been accompanied by a gradual increase in the areas of responsibility that have been transferred to central authorities by the member states. From the point of view of a businessperson from a country not part of the EU, the issues that are of most significance are those relating to freedom of movement of goods; freedom of movement of capital; freedom of establishment; and freedom of movement of persons. All of these central freedoms have the objective of creating a truly single market within the EU area. Thus, freedom of movement of goods aims to have no barriers when goods are moved across national boundaries within the EU. Freedom of movement of capital likewise refers to the absence of boundaries between members for the movement of capital. Freedom of establishment, accompanied by the freedom to provide services to citizens in another member state, aims to have minimal restrictions on any person anywhere in the EU establishing a business or providing a service in any part of the EU. Freedom of movement of persons is significant because a firm needs to have the flexibility to move managers between countries to oversee the operations of the firm in those countries. Of course, freedom of movement of persons also has importance in that workers should be free to move within Europe to take advantage of work opportunities in other states.

However, as will become apparent throughout this book, the attainment of the single market objective and the four freedoms is a work in progress. While the EU has the aim of freedom of movement of goods, this only

[2] Treaty on European Union, Maastricht, 7 February 1992.

applies to internal movement of goods. Businesspersons from outside of the EU must still negotiate initial customs barriers and regulations that apply to the type of good they are exporting to an EU member country. In addition, some barriers remain to the internal movement of goods. Chapter 3 discuses the various regulations that apply for internal transport of goods within the EU and details some of the difficulties in having a truly integrated transport system within the EU area. Some of these difficulties can be traced to the underlying legal conventions relating to the international transport of goods. Chapter 4 deals with customs procedures and formalities within the EU and makes it clear that while many goods are free to move, individual countries still have room to lay down their own conditions for the entry of some goods into their territories in some circumstances.

Similarly, the freedom to establish a business presence is confined to persons and entities from within the EU. However, as will be made clear, most European countries have extended the freedom to establish a new business to persons or firms from outside of the EU as well. Chapter 8 discusses the establishment of a business in an EU member country and notes that regulation over business establishment is still split between central European institutions and individual nation states, thereby making it necessary for the businessperson wanting to establish a business within an EU member country to take account not only of central EU regulations but also those of the member states where the business is to be set up.

Freedom of movement of persons is not dealt with in detail in this book. The reason here is that an external businessperson may face very different barriers in having a manager from their home country run a business within the EU to those that apply to managers moving between countries within the EU. This is because the EC Treaty specifically provides for freedom for persons to take up offers of employment in any member state subject to any legitimate limitations of the host state on public policy, public health or public security grounds.[3] On the other hand, the outsider cannot take advantage of this freedom and accordingly more restrictions might apply to outsiders when attempting to obtain a visa and work permit.

Likewise freedom of movement of capital within the EU is not considered in any detail. Article 56 of the EC Treaty abolishes all restrictions on capital movements between member states and between member states and third countries. However, Article 57 of the EC Treaty allows for some restrictions to remain. These exist primarily in real estate investment, the

[3] EC Treaty Article 39(3)(a).

financial services sector and the admission of securities to capital markets. However, for the outside businessperson who seeks to establish and operate a business in an EU member country, the associated capital flows between their home state and the EU member state will pose few problems provided that any requirements for establishment and operation of the business are met.

It is not only the attainment of the four freedoms and the single market that are a work in progress. The EU itself is evolving both in terms of its membership and its institutional arrangements. As at the end of 2008, both Turkey and Croatia are applicants for membership. In addition, free trade agreements between the EU and third countries have the effect of expanding the EU market beyond the current 27 member states. The EU has extensive free trade agreements with Switzerland and with Norway, Iceland and Liechtenstein. These are discussed in more detail in Chapter 4.

The way in which laws are made by the EU is also the subject of evolution. Thus, while this chapter details the roles of the various institutions of the EU and how law is made at the EU level, these processes will no doubt be subject to change over the coming decades. However, an understanding of EU institutions, their role in law making, the types of laws that exist and how the laws themselves are actually made is important for any person wishing to do business with a firm in any of the EU member countries. Each of these matters is now considered in turn.

## EU INSTITUTIONS AND THEIR ROLE IN LAW MAKING

There are five main institutions involved in law making at the EU level. These are the European Council, the Council of the European Union, the European Commission, the European Parliament and the European Court of Justice. In addition, there are two consultative bodies – the Economic and Social Committee, and the Committee of the Regions. Many treaty articles require that these bodies be consulted before legislation is made. The role of each of these institutions will now be discussed with particular reference to law making as opposed to other supervisory and political functions that they may exercise.

## THE EUROPEAN COUNCIL

The European Council consists of the heads of government of each of the member states. It is chaired by the head of state of one of the member states.

The position rotates among the member states every six months. While the European Council does not have a direct role in the EU's legislative process, it nonetheless exercises a significant role in EU law making by taking the lead role in treaty revisions and major changes in EU policy. As noted earlier, the two basic treaties of the EU are the Treaty Establishing the European Community that dates from 1957 and the Treaty on European Union that dates from 1992. Both of these are discussed in more detail below.

The European Council discuses major treaty changes at summit meetings. Because of the important role of both the European Commission and the European Parliament in developing legislation based on the EC Treaty, the heads of both the European Commission and the European Parliament frequently also attend summit meetings. Changes to the treaty discussed at a summit meeting are typically followed up by an intergovernmental committee that works on the detail of the changes and then finally the adoption of the changes by a further summit meeting. Because the EC Treaty is no more than an agreement between sovereign states, each member state must then adopt the treaty as the law of their own state. Each state has its own processes for doing this. Most changes to the EC Treaty have been able to have been adopted in most states by parliamentary processes alone without the need for a referendum.

There is some evidence that when states are obliged by their own constitutions to put treaty changes to a referendum in their own state, it is difficult to convince the public to support those changes. The most recent attempts to change the treaties in 2004 and again in 2007 are a case in point. Over the 2002–2004 period an ambitious attempt was made to upgrade the treaties into what was termed 'a constitution' for the EU. Voters in both France and Germany rejected this in referendums that were held in 2004. Following this, the original proposal for a constitution was abandoned and changes were made to make the revisions to the treaties more acceptable to the public. Thus, rather than a 'Constitution of Europe', the existing two treaties were retained but with significant amendments. The Council of Europe endorsed these changes at Lisbon in December 2007 with a view to having the revised treaties in force by the end of 2008 in time for the elections for the European Parliament in 2009.

The Lisbon Treaty[4] provides for both an increase in the power of EU institutions and at the same time an increase in the checks and balances

[4] Treaty of Lisbon amending the Treaty on European Union and the Treaty establishing the European Community, Lisbon, 13 December 2007 ('Lisbon Treaty').

mechanisms that member states have over the exercise of that power. In terms of increases in the power of EU institutions, the Lisbon Treaty creates an office of President of the European Union elected by the European Council for a two-and-a-half-year term renewable once and a new High Representative for Foreign Affairs and Security Policy who will represent the EU in an extended range of international matters that can be dealt with at the EU level rather than at the level of the individual nation state. However, individual nation states are given increased power to monitor EU actions; the individual rights and freedoms of citizens are enhanced; the division of legislative powers between the EU and member states is clarified and, for the first time, member states have the option of withdrawing from the EU.

As of the end of 2008, the Lisbon Treaty has been ratified by all member states except Germany, Czech Republic, Poland, and Ireland, whose constitution required a referendum to be held. That referendum was defeated in June 2008 and accordingly Ireland cannot yet ratify the Lisbon Treaty. The ratification process is well underway in the other three states. Because all nation states must ratify it for it to come into effect, it does not yet have the force of law. The European Council has taken a lead role in attempting to resolve this impasse.

The European Council exercises important functions other than revisions to the main treaties. These include the discussion of major differences between member states on key issues and the overall future direction of the EC.

## THE COUNCIL OF THE EUROPEAN UNION

The Council of the European Union[5] consists of one representative from each member state who is authorised to bind the member state. Accordingly the representative is usually a government minister. The composition of the Council is fluid depending upon the issue under discussion. Thus, for example, if immigration issues are under consideration the Council will consist of the immigration ministers from each of the member states. Because of this fluidity, the Council is supported by a committee of permanent representatives from each member state. While the ministers who formally make up the Council take the decisions, the permanent

[5] When the term 'the Council' is used, it refers to the Council of the European Union and not the European Council.

representatives play an important role in arriving at an agreed position to facilitate Council decision making.

The Council plays an important role in EU law making because it is the body that has the final say in whether legislative proposals will become EU law. The exact role that the Council will play in approving laws and the process by which the Council makes a decision depends upon the type of legislation involved. The reason here is that the EC Treaty sets out different methods for making laws depending upon which article of the treaty the law is based upon and what type of law is proposed. A more detailed explanation of the Council's role in law making is provided in the next section which discusses the types of laws and how they are made.

Council meetings are chaired by the representative from the state that currently holds the EU presidency.

## THE EUROPEAN PARLIAMENT

The European Parliament[6] consists of 732 directly elected members, with a set number being allocated to each state depending upon the state's population.[7] However, the electoral distribution system seeks not to disadvantage smaller states by giving smaller states more representatives than would apply if a strict one vote, one value system was applied uniformly across the EU.

The citizens of each state vote to elect their European Parliament representatives. However, the European parliamentarians tend to divide themselves into informal political groupings rather than according to their state of origin. Even though these informal political groupings are not yet 'political parties', the Parliament could be characterised as a truly supranational body rather than member state representatives who are simply there to represent the interests of their own constituents – as applies in many other international organisations. Of course, it would be naive to suggest that national interests do not have any bearing on decisions. Otherwise, European parliamentarians would have very short terms. Suffice it to say that on many issues pan-European interests are considered by the parliamentarians to be equally as important as national interests.

The role that the Parliament plays in legislation depends again on the provision of the EC Treaty upon which that legislation is based. The

[6] When the term 'the Parliament' is used hereafter, it refers to the European Parliament.

[7] This number will rise to 751 if the Lisbon Treaty is adopted.

different roles that the Parliament plays in enacting legislation are detailed later in this chapter when the various types of EU legislation are discussed.

## THE EUROPEAN COMMISSION

The European Commission consists of up to 27 Commissioners – one from each member state. Commissioners must take an independent role in furthering the goals of the EU. While they are nominated by each member state and approved by the European Parliament, they must take an oath swearing that they will not be influenced by representations from any member state. Each commissioner has overall responsibility for one or more areas of the EU's work – transport, energy, etc. Each of these areas is headed by a Director-General who is a full-time EU bureaucrat and who answers to the relevant commissioner for that area. Each directorate is supported by a number of full-time staff. In total, the European Commission has some 18,000 staff, most of whom are located in its headquarters in Brussels. While this seems large it is nowhere near as large as the bureaucracies in many of the member states.

The Commission is headed by a President appointed for a set term by the Council of the European Union after consultation with the European Parliament. The President has an important role in that they not only take overall responsibility for the work of the Commission but also attend meetings of the European Council and represent the EU in international negotiations. As noted, if the Lisbon Treaty is approved there will be a new High Representative for Foreign Affairs and Security who will also be a Vice-President of the Commission.

In terms of law making, the most significant role of the Commission is to draft laws that it then refers on to the Council of the European Union and the European Parliament for the relevant law making processes to take place. The Commission does not act alone is deciding what issues require legislative action. It is common for the Council, and increasingly the Parliament, to refer matters to the Commission for investigation for proposed legislative action. An example of a reference from the Parliament is the proposed European private company directive discussed in Chapter 8. In some areas, the Commission also enjoys delegated power from the Council to enact law. Examples here include the enactment of regulations relating to the customs tariff discussed in Chapter 4 and the block exemption regulation on vertical restraints discussed in Chapter 6.

The Commission also exercises considerable supervisory functions. First it is able to take member states to the European Court of Justice (ECJ) if a member state is not following EU law. Examples of this include the references by the European Commission to the ECJ of a number of countries that have failed to recover monies from the beneficiaries of state aid given by the state in contravention of the conditions allowed for the provision of state aid. This is discussed further in Chapter 8. Second, the Commission has overall responsibly for competition policy and can take direct legal action in the ECJ against firms that are in breach of the EU's competition laws. EU competition laws are discussed in more detail in Chapters 6–8.

On the other hand, the Commission is also subject to oversight by the European Parliament. The Parliament can request the Commission to reply orally or in writing to questions put to it. As a measure of last resort, the Parliament can also by a two-thirds majority require the Commission to resign. While this power has never been used it provides a safeguard in the unlikely event that the Commission acts totally contrary to law and the interests of the EU.

## CONSULTATIVE BODIES

The European Economic and Social Committee has been in existence since the commencement of the EC. It represents the various social and community interests throughout the EU. The Committee of the Regions came into being with the Treaty on European Union in 1992. Its role is to represent the interests of the various local governments in the member states. The Lisbon Treaty fixes the numbers at no more than 350 for each committee. Membership of both committees is decided by the Council after names are put forward by the member states.

Many treaty articles require that an opinion be provided by either or both of these committees at the commencement of the legislative process. The opinions are provided to either the Council or the Parliament. Consequently one finds in the preamble to many regulations and directives a statement that indicates that the legislation is being made having had regard to the opinion rendered by either or both of these committees.

## THE EUROPEAN COURT OF JUSTICE

The ECJ consists of one judge appointed by each member state for a three-year term that is renewable once. As is the case with Commissioners, judges must act independently of their home state when making decisions. The pressure that might be brought to bear on individual judges is reduced by the fact that the ECJ always delivers just one judgement as a whole rather than the individual judgement of each judge.

The process of the ECJ differs from the process used in common law countries such as the UK, the USA and Australia. Most of the submissions to the ECJ are written submissions by the parties that the ECJ itself communicates to all parties. This is followed by short oral argument at a hearing. The ECJ is assisted by an Advocate-General who also delivers an opinion on the case to the judges in addition to the various arguments put forward by the parties.

The primary role of the ECJ is to interpret treaty provisions. It does so not only in cases that are brought directly by the Commission against member states or pursuant to competition laws but also in cases where the courts of member states have referred a question to the ECJ for an opinion. An example of the latter is examined in Chapter 6 concerning choice of law in agency agreements. The ECJ can also hear cases brought directly by individuals or institutions seeking to question the validity of community legislation.

The ECJ is relieved of some of its workload by a court of first instance that is able to hear a limited range of matters. The court of first instance is appointed in a similar manner to the ECJ itself. Any decisions of the court of first instance can be appealed to the ECJ.

## TYPES OF EU LAWS AFFECTING THE INTERNATIONAL BUSINESSPERSON

The EU is able to act on behalf of all its member sates in implementing some international treaties. However, the bilateral and multilateral treaties that individual states themselves have entered into with third states often have more significance for the international businessperson. An overview of these will be provided below. From an internal point of view, there are five major types of EU legislation. These are the treaties themselves, regulations, directives, decisions and recommendations or opinions. In addition, the ECJ plays an important role not only in the legislative process but also in ensuring that legislation complies with the various treaty provisions and general principles of law.

## INTERNATIONAL AGREEMENTS

A businessperson from a state outside of the EU doing business with a firm in an EU member state needs to be aware of the various treaties that have been entered into by that person's home state with the relevant EU country and that might affect the business transaction being entered into. There are a significant number of both bilateral and multilateral treaties that came into existence either before the EU was created or before it had the power to negotiate international agreements on behalf of its member states. Even now, the EU's power in that regard is limited. Thus, one finds that many international agreements that affect such matters as, for example, the sale of goods, transport of goods, taking evidence abroad for court proceedings, enforcing judgements and arbitral awards have been entered into by the individual member states of the EU as individual sovereign nations rather than by the EU itself acting on their behalf.

Perhaps the single most important series of international agreements where the EU negotiates on behalf of the individual nation states are those administered by the World Trade Organisation (WTO). These include the General Agreement on Tariffs and Trade, and the General Agreement for Trade in Services. The General Agreement on Tariffs and Trade requires members to set tariff rates for goods imported into their territories and to notify the WTO of those rates. The General Agreement on Trade in Services requires members to specify the range of services and the modes by which services can be exported to them. The most-favoured nation and non-discrimination principles of the General Agreement on Tariffs and Trade require member states to extend the same rates of duty to all other members. However, this agreement also allows groups of countries to form trade agreements that give lower rates of duty to goods traded between themselves than to goods coming from countries outside of the group. Those provisions allow the EU to exist as a customs union and to conclude various free trade agreements with individual member states outside of the EU. There are also certain mandatory criteria for the valuation of goods for customs duty and criteria for the imposition of anti-dumping and countervailing duties. All of these issues are discussed in more detail in Chapter 4.

## THE TREATIES

There are two treaties that provide the foundations of the EU and the exercise of its functions. The first of these is the original Treaty Establishing the European Community, or EC Treaty. It has been in force since 1957 but has undergone several major amendments as described earlier. It is this treaty that sets out the various areas in which the EU institutions are empowered to make laws. Each article sets out how a law based on that article is to be made. Consequently, it is the provisions of this treaty that will be referred to most often in the following chapters of this book. The treaty itself runs to some 300 articles divided into various parts and sub-parts. It will be renamed as the Treaty on the Functioning of the European Union if and when the Lisbon Treaty has been ratified by all member states.

The more recent of the two treaties is the Treaty on the European Union, or EU Treaty. This treaty was originally entered into in 1992 in Maastricht by the then members of the EU. Those countries joining since then have acceded to it.

The EU Treaty sets out the institutions that form part of the EU, the broad objectives of the EU and how the EU institutions and member states coexist as separate legal bodies. The main institutions of the EU that are involved in law making have been discussed above but, in addition, the EU Treaty also creates two other significant institutions – the European Central Bank (ECB) and the Court of Auditors. The ECB coordinates monetary policy throughout the EU in conjunction with the central banks of the member states. The adoption of the EU's common currency (the euro) by an increasing number of member states has resulted in the ECB playing a vital role in EU's financial system.

The objectives of the EU are first and foremost to promote the wellbeing of EU citizens, including the provision of an area of freedom, peace and security where there is social justice, absence of discrimination and respect for cultural diversity. However, for the external businessperson, perhaps the most relevant objective of the EU is to achieve a single market. This objective lays the foundation for many of the detailed provisions in the EC Treaty for laws relating to common barriers to entry of goods into the EU, freedom of movement of goods within the EU, freedom of movement of capital and persons, and freedom to establish a business presence or provide services.

The EU Treaty provides that in some areas, such as those to do with barriers to entry, the EU will have exclusive power. In other areas power is shared between the EU and member states – the achievement of a single market is a case in point. In those areas where the EU Treaty provides for shared competence, law making by EU institutions is subject to the principles of subsidiarity and proportionality.[8] Subsidiarity means that the EU should not make laws centrally when the matter under consideration can be better dealt with at the individual state level. The philosophy behind

[8] EU Treaty, Article 7.

this principle is that law should be made at the level of government closest to the citizens that those laws will affect. Proportionality means that any law made by the EU has to be both appropriate and necessary to achieve its objectives. Understandably these two principles leave plenty of room for challenge to EU laws in the ECJ by individuals and member states. Finally, if the EU Treaty does not provide for either exclusive power or shared power then competency to legislate remains with the member states. Taxation is a good example.

There are two other aspects of the EU Treaty that need comment. The first of these is that the treaty provides for the possibility of enhanced cooperation between some member states in areas where some member states are able to agree on common measures which others cannot accept. An example here is the Schengen Agreement on freedom for movement for persons within the EU area without restriction, first introduced in 1985. Most of the continental European member states have accepted this but the UK and others have decided to maintain their own immigration laws. The second aspect that requires comment is that the member states can cooperate together to achieve a common foreign policy position. This is a contentious area and attempts to strengthen the role of EU institutions in formulating common foreign policy have met with resistance from those who see it as undermining the sovereignty of the individual member states.

Many commentators on the EU Treaty describe it as having three pillars. The first relates to economic objectives such as the achievement of the single market. The second relates to relations with the outside world in the form of a common foreign and security policy, and the third to enhanced cooperation between member states.

## REGULATIONS

EU institutions are given power to enact regulations by Article 249 of the EC Treaty. Regulations are used to bring about uniformity of the law throughout the EU. Thus, in most cases, regulations have direct effect in all member states and override any existing member states' laws that may contradict them. 'Direct effect' is a term that has been subject to much discussion and interpretation but in simple terms it means that both member states and individuals in the EU are bound by the regulation and it can be enforced in national courts as well as before the ECJ. In exercising its supervisory role over the process of regulation enactment, the ECJ has continued to refine the criteria that a regulation must meet if it is to have direct effect.[9]

The process of making regulations in the EU differs from that in most individual countries. Many readers will be familiar with processes for enacting legislation that involves the initial drafting and tabling of the legislation in a lower house of Parliament; the passing of that legislation; the forwarding of the legislation to an upper house of Parliament; its passage through that house; and finally the assent being given to the legislation by the head of state (president, governor-general or monarch). Most often this procedure is used regardless of the type of legislation that is being proposed other than where power is given to agencies of the state to develop implementing regulations which are then also approved by the executive branch of government.

The process for enacting legislation by EU institutions differs in that each treaty article specifies the institutions that are to be involved in enacting the legislation and the role that each is to play. In terms of both regulations and directives (discussed below), this means that there are several ways that these types of legislation can be enacted. Successive amendments to the EC Treaty have attempted to standardise the legislative process so that most legislative action will follow the same procedure. If the Lisbon Treaty is adopted then the 'ordinary procedure' for passing legislation will be the co-decision procedure. It will apply to almost all treaty provisions. In those few treaty provisions where legislation is made other than through the ordinary procedure, it is to be made by one of the 'special procedures'. In the expectation that the Lisbon Treaty will be adopted, the following discussion describes the ordinary legislative procedure in some detail and then the special procedures.

The ordinary legislative procedure under the Lisbon Treaty will be the co-decision procedure. It already applies to the enactment of many regulations and directives under the EC Treaty. Regulations and directives almost always result from an initial proposal by the EU Commission, sometimes at the suggestion of either the Council or the Parliament. In the co-decision procedure, the draft legislation is first forwarded to both the Parliament and the Council by the Commission. The Parliament then provides an opinion on the legislation to the Council. That opinion might contain amendments to the Commission proposal. At this point the fate of the legislation can take one of four paths.

[9] For an in-depth discussion see D. Chalmers, C. Hadjiemmanuil, G. Monti and A. Tomkins, *European Union Law*, Cambridge University Press, 2006, pp. 365–90.

First, if the Council approves the Parliament's opinion then the legislation is adopted and is signed by both the Presidents of the Parliament and the Council and becomes EU law.

Second, if the Council proposes amendments to the opinion of the Parliament then it must do so by adopting a common position. In most instances the Council adopts a common position by qualified majority voting.[10] However, as seen in the case study at the end of this chapter, the Council goes through a number of stages when adopting a common position on the Parliament's amendments. The legislation with the amendments is then sent back to the Parliament via the Commission. If the Parliament rejects the amendments by absolute majority the legislative proposal fails. If it takes no action within three months or alternatively approves the amendments, then the legislation is deemed to have been adopted in accordance with the wording of the Council.

Third, if the Parliament passes by majority further amendments to the Council's amended legislation, then the legislation is returned to the Commission for an opinion on whether the Parliament's amendments should be accepted. If the Commission's view is that the Parliament's amendments should be accepted and the Council agrees, then it can adopt the legislation by qualified majority. If the Commission's view is that the Parliament's amendments should not be accepted then the Council can only adopt the legislation by acting unanimously.

The fourth course is where the Council still cannot approve the amendments made by the Parliament. In that case a conciliation committee of both the Council and the Parliament is convened to seek agreement on a joint text. For the proposed joint text to become law it must be adopted by a majority of the Parliament and by a qualified majority of the Council. If this does not occur then the legislation fails.

The case study below outlines the process involved in enacting the mediation directive.[11] It will be seen that there is much preparatory work preceding a Commission proposal and that there can be a long lead time between the idea for legislation and it actually coming into effect.

[10] Qualified majority voting under the Lisbon Treaty will require 55% of the member states to approve the legislation, accounting for 65% of the EU's population. If these majorities are not achieved, then at least four states must be involved in the blocking action. Otherwise the relevant majorities will have been deemed to have been achieved. This latter provision is to protect smaller states from having two or three of the larger states only having the ability to block legislation because of their large populations.

[11] Directive 2008/52/EC [2008] OJ L136/3.

There are a limited number of special procedures that apply under various treaty articles (as amended by the Lisbon process).[12] The special procedures involve the Council and the Parliament working together in ways different to that specified by the ordinary legislative procedure. The Lisbon Treaty attempts to confine these special procedures to a minimum. They apply in situations including the following:

- The Council can adopt a legislative proposal by unanimous vote after seeking the consent of the Parliament (e.g. measures to combat discrimination).
- The Council can adopt a legislative proposal by unanimous vote after consulting with the Parliament (e.g. measures concerning social security, identity cards and passports; judicial cooperation in civil matters).
- The Council can adopt a legislative proposal by qualified majority after obtaining the consent of the Parliament. There is only one article that deals with this (measures to implement the use of the EU's own resources).
- The Council can adopt a legislative proposal by qualified majority after consulting with the Parliament. There are only three articles that provide for this (measures to facilitate diplomatic protection, specific programs implementing the research framework, outermost region initiatives).

The Parliament has the right to pass some legislation on its own initiative after consulting or obtaining the consent of either the Council or the Commission or both. This only applies to the statute for the members of the Parliament; the provision concerning the Parliament exercising its right of enquiry; and the statute for the European Ombudsman.

While most regulations are made by the Parliament and the Council acting together in one of the above ways, the Commission may sometimes enact regulations on its own. Most frequently this arises if a piece of legislation enacted by the Council and the Parliament under one of the procedures described above has delegated power to the Commission to enact implementing regulations. Examples include the power of the Commission to promulgate regulations relating to the customs tariff and block

[12] For the full list of treaty articles where special legislative processes apply, see European Parliament, Committee on Constitutional Affairs, *Report on the Treaty of Lisbon*, 20 January 2008, <http://www.europarl.europa.eu/sides/getDoc.do?type=REPORT&reference=A6-2008-0013&language=EN>.

exemption regulations from EU competition laws. These will be referred to in greater detail in Chapters 4 and 6 respectively.

## DIRECTIVES

Directives are most common in areas of legislation in which both the EU and the individual member states share competence to enact laws. Directives differ from regulations in that they rarely have direct effect because they require each member state to implement them by enacting laws at the nation state level. Thus, they are only binding on citizens and firms when implemented by each individual member state. Frequently the manner and form in which the directive is implemented by each member state is left up to that member state but each member state must implement it in such a way that the aim of the directive is achieved.

The reasons for allowing member states to choose the manner and form of implementation are that directives seek to harmonise laws across member states rather than impose an overriding unifying law. It is often the case that member states already have significant and longstanding laws in place in the area where directives seek to achieve harmonisation. Company law is a good example here, as is commercial law. Most states had company and commercial laws in place long before the EU came into existence. Directives in these areas are often implemented by individual member states incorporating the provisions required by the directive into their existing company or commercial laws.

Most directives provide a fairly lengthy time frame by which member states must bring their legislation into line with the directive. An example here is the recent directive on mediation which gives states until 2011 to implement it.

## DECISIONS

Decisions are made by the Commission where it is empowered to do so by the treaties, regulations or directives. Examples include decisions to recover state aid from a member state that has given assistance to firms that go beyond what is permitted under the regulations for state aid, and decisions to require a member state to remove measures that impede freedom to establish a business presence in its state by firms from other member states. These are discussed in more detail in Chapter 8. Decisions have direct effect in that they are binding on those to whom they are addressed and legal action may be taken to enforce them.

## OPINIONS, RECOMMENDATIONS AND GUIDELINES

Frequently the Commission will issue guidelines or opinions to provide detailed advice as to how it will exercise its powers in supervising the implementation of various pieces of legislation. Opinions, recommendations and guidelines are not law as such but are used by the ECJ and by national courts as a guide to interpreting laws. Important guidelines issued by the Commission for the purposes of this book include the guidelines on the block exemption for agreements involving vertical restraints and the guidelines on state aid. These are discussed in Chapters 6 and 8 respectively.

### Case study

**The process involved in making a directive – the mediation directive**

The idea for a mediation directive originated with the European Council in 1999 when it called for alternative extra-judicial proceedings to be made available by the member states to improve access to justice in the EC. The Commission presented a green paper in 2002 that set out the existing situation regarding alternative dispute resolution mechanisms in Europe along with recommendations for legislation at the EU level. Widespread consultations with the member states and other interested parties followed. The consultations supported improving alternative dispute resolution procedures.

The result was that the Commission developed a proposal for a mediation directive in 2004. In its explanatory memorandum, the Commission noted that mediation held considerable potential for improving access to justice but that the outcomes of mediation proceedings should be able to be enforced if it is be effective. The Commission also drew attention to the need to ensure that the quality of mediation was of a high standard in all member states. The Commission was of the view that Article 65 of the EC Treaty that includes civil procedure rules provided sufficient competence for legislation at the EU level. Article 65 provides for the use of the co-decision procedure. The Commission considered that harmonised standards throughout the EU in relation to mediation would improve the functioning of the internal market. It was of the view that such harmonisation could not be adequately dealt with at the member state level and that the proposed directive did not go beyond what was reasonably necessary to bring about this harmonisation. Accordingly the directive complied with the principles of subsidiarity and proportionality.

The proposed directive was transmitted to the Council and the Parliament at the end of 2004 and an opinion was sought from the Economic and Social Committee. Following some discussion at the Council, it took some time for the proposed directive to reach the top of the European Parliament's agenda. At the first reading of the proposed directive by the European Parliament, a number of amendments were proposed, including one that related to the extent to which voluntary agreements between parties to mediate should be enforceable and one that court-directed mediation should be covered in the directive.

The directive with amendments was then sent to the Council. The relevant Ministers who comprised the Council were the Ministers of Justice and Home Affairs for the various states. The Council did not accept all of the amendments of the European Parliament and in particular was concerned about the range of voluntary agreements to mediate that would exist if the Parliament's amendments were accepted as they stood. Accordingly, the Council's final common position required that the directive could only apply to mediation agreements where the relevant law of the applicable state permitted that the matter could be the subject of mediation. The Council was also concerned about the Commission's original proposal that the directive should extend to all disputes between citizens rather than only those disputes with a cross-border element. The Council and the Parliament were of the view that the relevant legislative power required a cross-border element to justify legislation at the EU level. Consequently, the Council confined the application of the directive to cross-border disputes, although it defined these as widely as possible to take the Commission's views into account.

The Council referred its common position back to the Commission which accepted the Council's arguments and forwarded the directive as amended by the Council to the Parliament. The Parliament accepted the directive as amended. It was finally signed into law on 21 May 2008.

The following flow chart shows the various steps which took place from the time of the Commission's original proposal. It shows that creating law at the EU level can be a lengthy matter. From the time of the original idea in 1999, it took more than eight years to finally have a directive on the matter. In addition, member states are given until 2011 to implement it.

*Figure 1.1 Flow chart of decision-making process for the mediation directive*
*Source: Adapted from European Commission, PreLex, 'Monitoring of the decision making process between institutions', <http://ec.europa.eu/prelex/detail_dossier_real.cfm?CL=en&DosId=191867>.*

# 2 Contracts for the sale of goods to an EU buyer

## INTRODUCTION

THERE ARE SEVERAL key matters that need to be agreed upon by a buyer and a seller in an international sale of goods transaction. It will be seen that each of the issues discussed below will frequently involve obligations on the part of both parties. The important areas for agreement could be listed as follows:

- the identity of the parties
- the description of the goods
- time and place for delivery of the goods
- transport arrangements for the goods
- inspection of the goods by the buyer
- the price and how the price is to be paid
- the passing of title in the goods from seller to buyer
- the respective obligations of the parties if unforeseen events make performance impossible
- the law that will apply to the contract
- the type of dispute resolution mechanism that will be used.

Firms that have been engaged in international business transactions for many years will most likely have developed a standard form of international contract of sale that is forwarded to a potential buyer. The terms and conditions are likely to contain much more than the basic terms and conditions listed above. For example, there may be detailed provisions to provide for delay in delivery, such as requiring the seller to pay damages for each day delivery of the goods is delayed. In addition, there might be a provision that the buyer will pay interest for every day in which they are late with payment after the due date if payment is made after the goods are received.

Frequently, terms and conditions will be developed in line with what is standard in the industry of the seller. This is particularly important for the sale of goods to a European buyer given the industry standards that goods sold on the EU market must meet. The buyer might then accept the terms of the offer or suggest some amendments whereupon the parties will have to negotiate and arrive at an agreed set of terms. In either case, most experienced international businesspersons will say that it is as well to have the final set of terms and conditions signed by both parties to prevent confusion later about what exactly has been agreed.

On the other hand, many smaller firms and those new to export might overlook the matter of a written and signed contract entirely and simply agree on the fundamentals of what is being sold, when it is to be delivered, the price and when it will be paid.

This chapter seeks to outline what might be considered key areas that should be agreed, the obligations of each party in relation to them and an explanation of why they are important. Some of the areas of agreement are discussed in much more detail in the following chapters on transport, customs, payment, and dispute resolution. Where this is the case, the reader will be referred to the appropriate later chapter.

## THE IDENTITY OF THE PARTIES

The bulk of international sale of goods transactions occur between companies or corporations because, in most countries, the company or corporation has become the dominant form of business organisation. The primary reason for this is that the company provides limited liability for its owners or shareholders. This means that the shareholders only have liability to the extent of the value of their shareholdings for the company's business transactions. The company has to meet all obligations validly entered into by the company from company assets. Likewise, profits made from company activities belong to the company until distributed to the shareholders of the company. This principle of the corporation as an entity separate and distinct from its owners has been almost universally accepted in company laws across the world. Where differences tend to have crept in is in the area of balancing the interests of shareholders of the company against those of outsiders who may have suffered as a result of dealing with the company rather than with its owners as individuals. Frequently, the means of addressing this issue is to impose personal liability on directors and managers if they have breached what the law regards as their duties as company officers. It is in this area of striking a balance between the interests of owner/managers and outsiders that company laws have undergone most development and perhaps most divergence in recent decades.

In international sales transactions it is important for both buyer and seller to know that the person they are dealing with is empowered to act on behalf of the company. Most countries have laws requiring companies to disclose who is authorised to represent the company. The EU is no exception and as long ago as 1968 required companies to disclose this information and set down procedures as to how this was to be made available to the public pursuant to the disclosure directive.[1] This directive is discussed in more detail in Chapter 8. Its importance in this context is that firms from outside of the EU can be confident that they are able to check whether the person signing a contract on the company's behalf is actually authorised to do so.

## DESCRIPTION OF THE GOODS

Most export contracts will describe the goods being sold in some detail. In cases where specifications of the goods are involved and lengthy, this will be accomplished by annexing the detailed description of the goods in a schedule to the contract. This is a common occurrence in the case of contracts with EU buyers because, for many classes of goods, there are detailed EU-wide standards that the goods must meet to be sold in the EU and, in the interests of certainty, a buyer might insist that they be included in the contract of sale.

The description of the goods has important legal implications for both buyer and seller if it is found that the goods supplied do not conform to that description. The precise implications will depend on what law it is that governs the contract between them. In the case of sales to buyers in most EU countries, the relevant law will be the Convention on the International Sale of Goods of 1980 (CISG).[2] This convention arose out of negotiations between countries to formulate a standard international sale of goods law so that sellers and buyers would face the same sets of legal requirements regardless of the countries from which the goods were being exported or the country where the buyer was located. The CISG has been widely adopted, with some 72 countries around the world having adopted it as their own law for the international sale of goods.

[1] Directive 68/151/EEC [1968] OJ L065/8.

[2] United Nations Convention on Contracts for the International Sale of Goods, 11 April 1980.

All member countries of the EU have adopted the CISG, other than the UK, Ireland, Malta and Portugal. Three of these countries have a British legal tradition and while there are differences between it and the CISG, those differences are not great for the most part. The CISG will apply if the parties specify it to be the law of the contract. It will also apply if the parties both have their place of business in different signatory states.[3] It might also apply even if only one of the parties is from a signatory state if the law of the contract chosen by the parties is that of a signatory state.[4]

The CISG does not apply to a range of transactions that are considered not to be sales of goods. These include sales of shares, sales of services, consumer sales and sales of ships and aircraft.[5] It will also not apply if the parties specifically exclude it as the governing law of their international sales transaction. It also does not apply to international sales transactions if both parties are from the Scandinavian states because these states had an international sales law that predated the CISG that they wished to continue to apply to transactions between parties in Scandinavia.

The CISG sets out the exporter's obligations to provide goods in conformity with the contract in Article 35. This article requires the seller to provide goods that are of the quantity, quality and description as agreed in the contract and to package the goods appropriately. It goes further and states that goods will not conform to the description if they are not fit for the purpose for which such goods are ordinarily used or for any specific purpose made known by the buyer to the seller. They will also not conform if they do not meet the qualities of a sample of such goods or if they are not packaged in a manner usual for such goods or, if no manner is usual, then in a manner to adequately protect and preserve the goods. The seller can only escape liability for non-conformity if the buyer knew or could not have been unaware of the non-conformity at the time of delivery.[6]

Failure to provide goods that conform to the contract description provides the purchaser with a range of legal remedies, including avoidance of the contract for non-conformity that amounts to a fundamental breach of the contract;[7] a right to demand substitute goods if the non-conformity amounts to a fundamental breach;[8] or a requirement for repair of the

[3] CISG, Article 1(1)(a).
[4] CISG, Article 1(1)(b).
[5] CISG, Articles 2 and 3.
[6] CISG, Article 35(3).
[7] CISG, Article 49(1)(a).
[8] CISG, Article 46.

goods[9] or a reduction in price[10] for lesser breaches. Damages are also available in addition to these remedies.[11]

Despite the seemingly clear language of Article 35, there are numerous cases based on this article.[12] A cursory examination of the cases shows that at least half have been decided by European courts and considerably more than half have involved firms from EU member countries as parties. A detailed discussion of the issues raised in the cases is beyond the scope of this book. However, the cases raise two particularly important issues that an exporter of goods to an EU buyer needs to consider. These are the standards that the goods must meet in order to satisfy the fitness for purpose test in Article 35, and secondly the packaging requirements for the goods. As will be noted in Chapter 4, the EU has specific standards for many classes of goods in order for them to be able to be sold in the EU marketplace. There are also very specific labelling requirements for most goods.

The case law suggests that goods will be fit for the purpose for which goods are ordinarily used even if the goods do not meet the standards in the buyer's country but do satisfy standards in the seller's country.[13] However, this will only be the case where the buyer has not made the seller aware of the required standards or if there are special circumstances through which the seller should have become aware of those standards. Special circumstances might include the seller having some presence or representative in the buyer's country or if there has been a longstanding relationship between the seller and the buyer. For these reasons it is likely that buyers from the EU will be quite specific in their contracts about the standards that the goods must meet.

The case law suggests that goods will not meet packaging requirements if the packaging does not comply with the labelling requirements of the country of the buyer and the seller knew that the goods were to be sold there.[14] Thus exporters to the EU run the risk of having no recourse under the CISG if their goods do not meet either EU labelling requirements or

[9] CISG, Article 46(3).

[10] CISG, Articles 50 and 51.

[11] CISG, Article 45(1)(b).

[12] See the discussion of the cases on Article 35 in UNCITRAL Digest of Case Law on the United Nations Convention on the International Sale of Goods ('UNCITRAL Digest'), <http://www.cisg.law.pace.edu/cisg/text/digest-art-35.html>.

[13] *New Zealand Mussels Case* [1996] 3 *European Current Law: Monthly Digest* (Euro CL) No. 84 [72-3].

[14] *Caiato Roger v Société Française de Factoring,* Case 48992, Cour d'Appel de Grenoble, Chambre Commercial, 13 September 1995.

the labelling requirements of the EU country where the goods are to be sold.

## TIME AND PLACE FOR DELIVERY

It is usual for international sale of goods contracts to provide for both a time and place for delivery. As will be seen below, the time and place fixed by the contract for delivery have important legal consequences for both buyer and seller.

Article 33 of the CISG provides that the seller must deliver on the date fixed for delivery or, if none, then within a reasonable time. The buyer is also obligated to accept delivery at the time and place nominated.[15] Failure to deliver on time by the seller will amount to a fundamental breach entitling avoidance of the contract if delivery on time is expressed to be fundamental to the contract. Failure by the buyer to accept delivery may also constitute a fundamental breach.[16] The CISG permits a buyer to give additional time to the seller for delivery and, if they do so, not to pursue any remedy for breach of contract during that period.[17] However, the CISG allows the seller to cure any defects in delivery if the goods are delivered before the delivery date and this does not cause any unreasonable inconvenience or expense to the buyer.[18]

The place where the seller has to deliver the goods is often covered by the parties' selection of what is known as an 'incoterm'. A standard set of incoterms was first developed by the International Chamber of Commerce (ICC) in 1936 to promote certainty with regard to the obligations of each party to an international sales transaction regarding delivery of goods. It has been revised regularly to keep abreast of changes in international trade practice. There are currently 13 ICC Incoterms divided into 'E', 'F', 'C' and 'D' terms. The place where the seller has to deliver the goods will depend on which incoterm is chosen.

The following table shows the obligations that the incoterms impose on the exporter regarding delivery of the goods. The table shows not only who is responsible for which stages of the transport but also, most importantly, when risk in the goods passes from the exporter to the buyer and which party bears the transport costs and costs of customs clearance. Risk passes at the point of delivery.

[15] CISG, Article 53.
[16] CISG, Article 64.
[17] CISG, Article 47.
[18] CISG, Article 37.

The table reflects the division of costs and responsibilities from the point of view of the exporter. These costs and responsibilities are least for the 'E' terms and increase for the 'F', 'C' and 'D' terms respectively. However, it is readily apparent that transport costs and obligations not mentioned as being the responsibility of the exporter are the responsibility of the buyer. For example, it is noted that only certain of the incoterms require the exporter to take out insurance after the point at which transfer of risk has occurred. Other than in those cases, it is the exporter who bears the risk up until the point of delivery and the buyer bears it from that point on. Consequently each party should arrange insurance to cover themselves to accord with the point of transfer of risk.

Freight to Europe and transport within Europe can consume a sizeable proportion of the exporter's potential profits if they do not take these costs into account when negotiating with a buyer as to the appropriate incoterm and the pricing of their goods. For example, if an exporter agrees to the term 'Delivered Duty Paid' they will face significant transport costs. On the other hand, if they negotiate an 'Exworks' delivery term then the buyer will face those costs. It is for these reasons that it is more usual when exporting to Europe for buyers and sellers to negotiate one of the intermediate terms – either an F or a C term. As indicated above, there is a range of F and C terms to cater for either port to port shipment or multimodal transport. Exporters need to ensure that they use the most appropriate term of the type of transport arrangement to be used. However, it needs to be added that Europe is a very competitive market and in order to secure a customer it may be necessary for an exporter to agree to assume most of the transport costs and obligations.

## TRANSPORT ARRANGEMENTS FOR THE GOODS

While the incoterm chosen by the parties will determine who has to arrange transport, many standard form contracts also require the parties to nominate a carrier. This helps resolve any uncertainty about the matter and allows the party responsible for transport to make use of longstanding arrangements that they may have with a particular carrier. Chapter 3 discusses transport of goods and the various international legal conventions that apply in the case of sea, air, road, rail and inland waterway carriage. In cases where a seller has agreed to deliver the goods door-to-door using 'Delivered Duty Paid' incoterms, transport to a buyer in Europe may involve a combination of types of carriage. In these situations, it is quite

*Table 2.1 Place of delivery, passing of risk and transport costs under the ICC Incoterms*

| Incoterm | Passing of risk and delivery | Transport costs borne by exporter |
|---|---|---|
| Exworks (EXW) | When the goods are placed at the disposal of the buyer at the place named by the exporter | |
| Free Carrier (named place) (FCA) | When the goods are delivered to the place named by the buyer (usually the carrier's place of business) | Transport to the place of the carrier as nominated by the buyer; customs clearance for export |
| Free Alongside Ship (named port of shipment) (FAS) | When the goods are placed alongside the ship at the port nominated by the buyer | Transport to the port of shipment and up to point of the goods being alongside ship; customs clearance for export |
| Free on Board (named port of shipment) (FoB) | When the goods cross the ship's rail at the port nominated by the buyer | Transport to the port; customs clearance for export; port and loading charges |
| Carriage Paid To (named place of destination) (CPT) | When the goods are delivered to the carrier arranged by the seller to take the goods to the named place of destination | Transport to the port of export; customs clearance for export; port and loading charges; freight; unloading and transport in country of destination (only if included in contract of carriage); customs clearance for import (only if included in contract of carriage) |
| Carriage and Insurance Paid To (named place of destination) (CIP) | When the goods are delivered to the carrier arranged by the seller to take the goods to the named place of destination | Transport to the port of export; port and loading charges; freight; insurance; customs clearance for export; unloading and transport in country of destination (only if included in contract of carriag); customs clearance for import (only if included in contract of carriage) |
| Cost and Freight (named port of destination) (CFR) | When the goods cross the ship's rail at the port of shipment arranged by the seller | Transport to the port of export; port and loading charges; freight; and unloading at port of import (if agreed); customs clearance for export |

| Incoterm | Passing of risk and delivery | Transport costs borne by exporter |
|---|---|---|
| Cost Insurance and Freight (named port of destination) (CIF) | When the goods cross the ship's rail at the port of shipment arranged by the seller | Transport to the port of export; port and loading charges; freight; insurance; customs clearance for export; unloading and transport in country of destination (only if included in contract of carriage); customs clearance for import (only if included in contract of carriage) |
| Delivered Ex Ship (named port of destination) (DES) | When the goods arrive on board the vessel at the port of destination ready for unloading | Transport to the port of export; customs clearance for export; port and loading charges; freight; insurance |
| Delivered Ex Quay (named port of destination) (DEQ) | When the goods are placed on the wharf in the buyer's country | Transport to the port of export; customs clearance for export; port and loading charges; freight; insurance; unloading at the port of import |
| Delivered Duty Unpaid (named place of destination) (DDU) | When the goods arrive at the named place of destination not unloaded | Transport to the port of export; customs clearance for export; port and loading charges; freight; insurance; unloading at the port of import; freight to the named place of destination |
| Delivered Duty Paid (named place of destination) (DDP) | When the goods arrive at the named place of destination not unloaded | Transport to the port of export; customs clearance for export; port and loading charges; freight; insurance; unloading at the port of import; freight to the named place of destination; customs clearance for import; import duty |
| Delivered at Frontier (named place) | When the goods are placed at the disposal of the buyer at the named place on the arriving transport at the frontier not unloaded | All transport and customs costs to the named inland border |

common for a seller to contract out the entire freight arrangements to one of the major freight forwarding companies which will arrange all of the transport.

## INSPECTION OF THE GOODS

It is usual to include provisions in international sale of goods contracts to nominate the arrangements for inspection of the goods. This needs to be framed with the relevant inspection obligations contained in the CISG in mind. However, the parties can override these provisions by making some other agreement concerning inspection. If so, it needs to take into account what remedies the parties will have if there is a failure to inspect the goods. Many standard contracts provide when and where the goods are to be inspected but do not override the remedies for failure to inspect contained in the CISG. For that reason, the following discusses the remedies that the CISG provides if the contract does not deal with the matter.

The CISG provides that where goods have been transported to a buyer, the buyer is required to inspect the goods upon arrival at the place of destination.[19] If a seller has redirected the goods in accordance with their rights under the various transport conventions discussed in Chapter 3, then the appropriate place for inspection will be the arrival of the goods at the redirected destination. If non-conformity is discovered then the buyer must give notice of it to the seller. If the buyer does not give notice of non-conformity then they may lose any rights to claim against the seller for this.[20] Exporters of goods to the EU therefore need to know what rights a buyer may have against them as well as what a buyer must do to exercise those rights.

Article 38(1) of the CISG requires the buyer to conduct an examination of the goods within as short a period as is practicable in all the circumstances. Two issues have dominated decisions on the interpretation of this provision.[21] The first concerns the time within which the buyer must inspect the goods. The second is the type of examination that must be carried out.

The decided cases give little clear guidance as to the time frame within which an inspection should be carried out. Some have been quite specific as to the time frame within which the examination should occur and equally

19 CISG, Article 38(2).

20 CISG, Article 39(1).

21 See the discussion of the cases on Article 38 in UNCITRAL Digest, <http://www.cisg.law.pace.edu/cisg/text/digest-art-38.html>.

specific about how long after arrival is considered to have been too long for an inspection to take place. Others have adopted a more flexible standard as to when an examination should take place. Considerations as to what is an appropriate time frame have included the type of goods, the efforts needed for an examination, whether there has been a pre-shipment inspection or even whether there have been defects in prior deliveries. Further problems have arisen regarding defects that are not discoverable for some time until after the delivery has taken place. Here some courts have suggested that the buyer should be constantly monitoring the goods so as to identify any latent defects. Other cases suggest that it is only when such defects become apparent that the buyer should then become alert to possible problems and then undertake a through examination.[22]

The second issue concerns the type of examination that should occur. While the cases tend to suggest that the examination should be in accordance with what is reasonable in the circumstances, this has still left considerable room for argument about the significance of such matters as the type of goods, the method of packaging, the circumstances of the buyer, the costs required to carry out the examination, and the need for spot checking or sampling in determining the 'reasonableness' of the examination.

Article 39 requires the buyer to give notice of non-conformity. There is no requirement as to the form of the notice but it must be given to the seller. Even a verbal notice may be sufficient as long as it has been shown by the buyer to have been communicated to the appropriate person in the seller's organisation. The notice must be specific as to the extent and nature of the defect and the goods to which it applies to enable the seller to take action to check the information.[23] The notice must also be given within a reasonable time. There are a large number of decisions about what amounts to a reasonable time, leading to the conclusion that much depends on the circumstances of every particular case. In any event the maximum period for giving notice is set at two years unless the seller has given a guarantee to the buyer that extends beyond this period.[24]

The considerable diversity within reported decisions about the time for examination of the goods, the type of examination required, and the time for and content of notice that must be given if the examination reveals any non-conformity leads one to the view that exporters wanting more certainty regarding potential claims by customers would do well to insert

22 Ibid.

23 See the discussion of the cases on Article 39 in UNCITRAL Digest, <http://www.cisg.law.pace.edu/cisg/text/digest-art-39.html>.

24 CISG, Article 39(2).

more specific provisions into their international sales agreements relating to these matters. Article 6 of the CISG allows parties to derogate from the provision of the convention and accordingly does not preclude more specific requirements regarding inspection and notice.

## PRICE AND METHOD OF PAYMENT

The price for the goods and the method by which that price will be paid are essential for any contract for the international sale of goods. While Article 55 of the CISG provides that the validity of the contract will not be affected if the price is not stated but there is a means of ascertaining the price, common sense suggests that to avoid any confusion the price should be stated along with the currency in which the price is to be paid.

Chapter 5 outlines the four major ways in which the buyer pays the seller in an international sales contract. In order of least to most risk for the exporter these are payment in advance, payment by letter of credit, payment against documents and payment on open account. The procedures involved in each of these methods of payment along with strategies to minimise the risk associated with each are discussed in greater detail in Chapter 5.

The failure of the buyer to pay in accordance with the agreed method and at the agreed time will amount to a fundamental breach of contract for which the seller is entitled to avoid the contract and sue for damages.[25]

## RETENTION OF TITLE IN THE GOODS BY THE SELLER UNTIL PAID

In order to cater for the possibility that the buyer either rejects the goods or does not pay, it is common practice to see a clause in international sale of goods contracts that states that title in the goods does not pass from the seller to the buyer until the seller is paid. In addition, if the buyer should become bankrupt the retention of title clause has the effect that the seller can recover the goods rather than having to take their place in the queue of other creditors. However, it needs to be noted that where the goods have been on-sold by the buyer to a purchaser without notice of the seller's right to title, then the seller may be placed in a position of contesting the rights to the goods with that buyer. In some legal systems the court may come to the conclusion that the rights of a buyer without notice supersede those of the seller.

[25] CISG, Article 64.

## RESPECTIVE OBLIGATIONS OF THE PARTIES IF UNFORESEEN EVENTS MAKE PERFORMANCE IMPOSSIBLE

The CISG provides that if an impediment arises beyond one of the parties' control that prevents their performance of the contract then the party is excused from performance during the period for which the impediment exists. The party must give notice of the impediment to the other party and must then resume performance once the impediment has passed.[26] If the failure to perform is due to an impediment that prevents a third party (e.g. a transport operator) from performing obligations on which the performance of the main contract depends, then the party seeking to rely on the impediment preventing the third party from performing must show that it was beyond the control of the third party.

Many international sales contracts prefer to be more specific about both the list of circumstances that are to be regarded as an impediment to performance and the rights of the parties should one of those events arise. This is because one or both of the parties will inevitably lose out as a result of the impediment. For example, if extreme weather conditions delay the delivery of goods to be exported, the buyer has customers waiting for those goods and the seller is relying on payment after their arrival, then both parties will suffer losses. However, it is readily apparent that the range of circumstances that might impede performance as well as the position of the parties at the time such circumstances arise is infinitely variable. Thus, no matter how carefully such a clause is drafted, it may well do no more to resolve the situation than the generally worded provision of the CISG.

## THE LAW THAT WILL APPLY TO THE CONTRACT

As noted above, the CISG will automatically govern international contracts for the sale of goods if the parties to the contract have their place of business in different states, both states are signatories to the convention and the subject matter of the contract is 'goods' as defined in the CISG. If the CISG applies, it will be the body of law that a court uses in filling in gaps that the parties might have left in determining their precise obligations, whether parties have complied with those obligations, and the remedies available to the party not in default.

[26] CISG, Article 79.

However, it is advisable to specifically state that the CISG will apply if that is the parties' intention. The reasoning here is that not all states are signatories to the convention and not all states are bound by all of its provisions. This is because the convention allows states to opt out of certain parts of it. Thus for certainty it is best to state that the CISG will be the governing law of the contract.

The CISG allows parties the freedom to contract out of its provisions by specifying that certain provisions of the convention will not apply to their agreement or by excluding the CISG completely and having some other law govern their entire contract.

If the parties fail to choose which law governs the contract, then in the event that a dispute arises, a court must decide what law it should use to determine the substantive rights of the parties. Each country has developed its own set of criteria (conflict of law rules) that a court must use to decide the governing law of the contract in the absence of a choice between the parties. A common approach is to use the law that has the closest connection with the contract. Inserting a choice of law clause in the agreement can avoid the substantial cost and delay associated with later argument over which law a court should use to determine the parties' rights and obligations under the agreement.

## THE TYPE OF DISPUTE RESOLUTION MECHANISM THAT WILL BE USED

Chapter 9 discusses the three major methods for the resolution of disputes in international business transactions along with the advantages and disadvantages of using each in a transaction with a party from one of the member states of the EU. The three main dispute resolution methods discussed are litigation, arbitration and mediation. If the parties do not choose a method for the resolution of disputes that may arise, then they must either agree at the time of the dispute to use a particular method of dispute resolution or alternatively take court action. As will be seen in Chapter 9, there are significant disadvantages in simply relying on litigation for the resolution of international business disputes. Accordingly to avoid these difficulties it is best to choose the method of dispute resolution at the time that the contract is entered even though, at that time, the parties might be reluctant to even consider that a dispute might arise between them.

# 3 Transport of goods to an EU buyer

## INTRODUCTION

TRANSPORT OF GOODS to a customer in an EU country will typically involve a road or rail leg in the country of the exporter; a sea or air leg to deliver the goods to a port or airport in the EU; and then either road, rail or inland waterway transport, or some combination of these, to deliver the goods to the customer's place of business. Each of these legs of transport is likely to be covered by a different legal regime. The reason for this is that over the years different international conventions have been entered into for sea transport, air transport, road transport, rail transport and transport by inland waterway. This means that the extent of liability of the carrier for loss or damage to the goods often depends on the leg of the journey where the loss or damage occurred and the relevant international convention applicable to that leg as well as the terms and conditions of carriage set out in the transport document issued by the carrier.

This chapter begins with an introduction to transport arrangements for goods to and within the EU to provide readers with some understanding of the significance of each form of transport as well as some insight into how each form of transport is likely to develop in coming years. The chapter then reviews the major international conventions governing sea transport, air transport, road transport and rail transport within the EU. The emphasis in this chapter is on the international legs of the transport chain. The law governing the road or rail portion of the transport within the exporter's country will vary depending on the country in which the exporter is located and the relevant domestic transport law for internal transport.

## EU TRANSPORT SYSTEMS

Sea transport is the main method by which goods reach the EU market, with 90% of goods by volume exported to and from EU countries arriving by ship.[1] Statistics published by the European Sea Port Organization show that 42% of sea cargo consists of liquid bulk (predominantly fuels), 25% consists of dry bulk (minerals, grains and so on), 15% of container cargo and 11% of roll-on roll-off cargo (e.g. cars).[2]

The more established ports of continental Europe and the Mediterranean are the main ports of entry for goods destined for the EU market. The following table shows the ranking of the top 15 ports in terms of gross weight of goods handled and the top 20 ports in terms of volume of container cargo handled. It can be seen that the older ports of Rotterdam, Antwerp, Hamburg, Le Havre, Bremen, Genoa, London and Marseilles figure prominently in both sets of rankings. However, the table also suggests that some ports may be more specialised in terms of handling container-type cargo. For example, the Spanish ports of Barcelona and Valencia are in the top 10 ports for container cargo but do not even figure in the rankings for gross weight of goods handled. The same applies to Felixstowe and Southampton in the UK.

The arrival of goods at their European port of destination is not the end of the transport chain. Goods must then be transported to the customer. The predominant and fastest-growing form of inland transport within the EU is road transport. Road freight accounts for 44% of freight movement within the EU. Over the 10-year period of 1995–2004, road freight increased by 35% in the EU – the fastest-growing of all means of internal transport.[3] Road transport is expected to grow by a further 55% between 2006 and 2020.[4] Further, 85% of all goods carried by road within the EU (by weight) travel less than 150 kilometres. Only 1–2% travel distances over 1000 kilometres.[5] It therefore seems likely that most exports to the

[1] European Commission, Directorate-General for Energy and Transport, *Keep Europe Moving: Sustainable Mobility for Our Continent*, Office for Official Publications of the European Communities, Luxembourg, 2006, p. 11.

[2] European Seaports Organization, Yearly Figures, 2004, <http://www.espo.be/downloads/archive/178cc6b7-b559-4d94-ae4e-01533a554e98.pdf>, p. 43.

[3] European Commission, Directorate-General for Energy and Transport, *Keep Europe Moving*, op. cit., p. 34.

[4] Ibid., p. 35.

[5] Proceedings of 'Mid Term Review of the White Paper on European Transport Policy', a conference held in Brussels, 1 December 2005, p. 6, available from <http://ec.europa.eu/transport/strategies/2001_white_paper_en.htm>.

*Table 3.1 Ranking of EU ports by gross weight of goods handled and by volume of container cargo handled*

| Ranking | Gross weight of goods handled | Container cargo |
|---|---|---|
| 1 | Rotterdam (Netherlands) | Rotterdam (Netherlands) |
| 2 | Antwerp (Belgium) | Hamburg (Germany) |
| 3 | Hamburg (Germany) | Antwerp (Brussels) |
| 4 | Marseilles (France) | Bremen (Germany) |
| 5 | Bergen (Norway) | Gioia Tairo (Italy) |
| 6 | Le Havre (France) | Felixstowe (UK) |
| 7 | Grimsby and Immingham (UK) | Le Havre (France) |
| 8 | Genoa (Italy) | Valencia (Spain) |
| 9 | Tees and Harlepool (UK) | Barcelona (Spain) |
| 10 | London (UK) | Piraeus (Greece) |
| 11 | Algeciras (Spain) | Genoa (Italy) |
| 12 | Amsterdam (Netherlands) | Southampton (UK) |
| 13 | Trieste (Italy) | Las Palma (Spain) |
| 14 | Dunkerque (France) | Algeciras (Spain) |
| 15 | BremenBremerhaven (Germany) | London (UK) |
| 16 | | Marseilles (France) |
| 17 | | La Spezia (Italy) |
| 18 | | Goteborg (Sweden) |
| 19 | | Medway (UK) |
| 20 | | Liverpool (UK) |

Source: European Seaports Organization, Yearly Figures, 2004, <http://www.espo.be/downloads/archive/178cc6b7-b559–4d94-ae4e-01533a554e98.pdf>, pp. 40–1.

EU will be directed to the port closest to their final destination and accordingly may not need to cross country boundaries during the final transport phase. This is of significance for the legal liability of carriers, as will be pointed out below.

Because of congestion and growing concerns about the effects of vehicle pollution on global warming, the European Commission has been attempting for some years to diversify the means of internal transport. There has been a considerable degree of success with promoting short sea shipping through ideas such as the motorways of the sea project which aims to promote major sea routes in the Baltic, east and west Mediterranean and the Spain to North West Europe route. Short sea shipping accounted for 39% of EU internal transport in 2004, showing a 31% growth rate over the 1995–2004 decade.[6] Short sea shipping is predicted to overtake road transport as the main means of internal transport by 2014.[7] However, bottlenecks continue because of the varying efficiency of European ports and the necessity to comply with internationally mandated procedures each time a ship travels from one port within Europe to another. Attempts are now being made to simplify the procedural difficulties for shipping between European ports. There are also plans to further increase the use of inland waterways for freight transport. In 2004, only 3% of freight was carried in this manner and this is not projected to increase over the 2000–2020 period.[8]

Rail is less significant in terms of internal freight movement. It comprises only 10% of internal freight movements and showed a growth rate of only 15% over the 1995–2004 decade.[9] There are major projects underway to attempt to coordinate European railways so that more goods can be transported by this means. However the task of upgrading facilities and coordinating railways is not an easy one. At present there is an attempt to promote certain rail corridors within Europe to make the rail transport of goods more efficient. However, bottlenecks arise because of the lack of interoperability between different national systems. For example, the length and weight of freight trains that tracks can accommodate vary between countries. It is difficult to resolve these and other problems when there is weak coordination of infrastructure between different national rail authorities. For this reason a new European Railway Agency was established in 2004 to make recommendations to the Commission on improving interoperability. That this is a long-term task is recognised by the projections that rail freight will only grow by 13% between 2006 and 2020 and its actual contribution as a percentage of overall movement of goods within the EU will fall from around 11% in 2000 to around 8% by 2020.[10]

As noted above, freight arriving in European ports arrives either in bulk, in containers or as roll-on roll-off freight. The following discussion highlights the key legal issues that arise for these various classes of freight. It assumes that it is the exporter who is responsible for the transport

6 European Commission, Directorate-General for Energy and Transport, *Keep Europe Moving*, op. cit., p. 34.
7 Ibid., p. 35.
8 Ibid., pp. 34–5.
9 Ibid., p. 34.
10 Ibid., pp. 34–5.

arrangement. However, it needs to be borne in mind that the incoterm used by the parties determines which of them makes the transport arrangements as well as splitting the cost and risk associated with the transport between them.

Exporters shipping bulk freight (grains, fuel, minerals) tend to do so by making direct arrangements with the shipping company. They may also make separate arrangements with rail or road carriers to have the goods delivered to the port for loading assuming that they do not have their own transport system. The contractual arrangements with the shipping company can be either to use one of the ships of the shipping company or alternatively to charter a vessel for the transport of the goods. If the goods are shipped by one of the major shipping companies using their ships, then the shipping company will issue the exporter with an ocean bill of lading that sets out the terms and conditions of shipment. In the case of charter operations there will also be a contract of charter. The bill of lading for charter operations frequently is very short and simply incorporates the conditions of the charter contract. The bill of lading is issued subject to the law of the place of shipment. Since most countries have adopted what is known as the Hague-Visby Rules[11] into their law, then the bill of lading must be consistent with these rules.[12] The bill of lading and the Hague-Visby Rules are discussed in more detail below.

Exporters who use container shipping have a range of transport options. If the exporter is large and owns its own land transport then it will likely make arrangements directly with the shipping company and deliver the goods to the shipping company's container terminal. As with the shipment of bulk items the shipping company will issue the exporter with a bill of lading.

[11] The Hague-Visby Rules – The Bill of Lading Convention 1924 (Hague Rules) as amended by the Brussels Protocol 1968.

[12] Most EU member countries have adopted the Hague-Visby Rules. However, some of the landlocked EU countries (Czech Republic, Slovakia, Hungary, Austria and Romania) have adopted the more recent Hamburg Rules (Hamburg Rules – United Nations Convention on the Carriage of Goods by Sea, 1978) that tend to be more onerous on shipping companies. Most of the EU's major trading partners have also adopted the Hague-Visby Rules. The major exceptions are the USA which continues to use the Hague Rules, the earlier version of the Hague-Visby Rules, and China which has adopted its own rules that are a combination of the Hague-Visby and Hamburg Rules. Some countries have also made their own amendments to the Hague-Visby Rules. Australia, for example, has made an amendment to impose liability for delay on carrying companies in very limited circumstances.

However, with carrying companies becoming more globalised and diversified in terms of the type of transport that they can arrange, increasing numbers of exporters are choosing the door-to-door option for container shipping, with costs and risks being split between exporter and importer depending on the incoterm that has been chosen. Global firms such as TNT, DHL, UPS and FEDEX are increasing their position of dominance in the international transport of goods. These and other international carriers own their own ships, aircraft, and road transport vehicles. If an exporter utilises the services of one of these types of companies then it is likely that the carrying company will collect the container from the exporter's premises, transport it to the port, have it loaded onto the ship, unloaded at the port of destination and then transport it through to the customer's place of business.

While the major international carriers who own their own forms of transport are coming to dominate international carriage of goods, there are other options for the exporter when arranging door-to-door transport. First, the exporter might engage a shipping company as principal carrier and that company will subcontract out the land carriage portion to another company. Second, the exporter might engage a non-vessel owning carrier that will subcontract out the shipping portion but may own its own land transport. Third, the exporter might engage a freight forwarder that will assume primary responsibility for all parts of the carriage but will subcontract out each of the stages of the journey to different carriers.

Thus, there is frequently just one contract of carriage that the exporter enters into to cover all stages of the journey. The document that is issued to the exporter is most commonly called a combined transport bill of lading, or a forwarder's bill of lading if issued by a freight forwarder. However, the extent of liability of the carrier for loss or damage to the goods will depend on which leg of the journey the loss or damage occurred. This is because each leg of the journey will be subject to a separate legal regime. The transport from the exporter's premises to the port will be governed by the relevant laws in the country of the exporter concerning the land transport of goods; the sea portion will be most likely governed by the Hague-Visby Rules and the land portion in the country of destination will be governed by the land transport laws in that country. Additional complications arise in the case of shipments that arrive at a port in one country in Europe but are then transported by road or by rail to another country in Europe. In this situation, the carrier's liability will be determined by the law governing the land portion of the transport in Europe.

## Case study

### Transport of goods to the EU using a freight forwarder

A major international freight forwarding company, a.hartrodt was founded in 1887 in Hamburg, Germany. It has now grown to 170 offices worldwide, with partnerships in more than 80 countries. Its business encompasses the entire range of transport- and logistics-related services, including sea and air freight, door-to-door service, supply chain management, customs clearances and transport insurance. It makes use of the latest developments in e-commerce to manage shipments and enable customers to track their shipments.

The company has provided the following information and advice to those wishing to use their services for a shipment of containerised goods for a door-to-door shipment to a destination within the EU. The process begins with a customer contacting the company for a quotation. If accepted, the customer will then be required to provide details of the shipment on a forwarding instruction, including the consignor, consignee, description of the goods, weight, the relevant incoterms and payment conditions. Many exporters to the EU use the most appropriate 'C' incoterm because this tends to save both the seller and the buyer costs. The company's office in the seller's country is often able to obtain for the seller the best rates for transport within and from the country while the company's office in the buyer's country is in the best position to obtain the best rates for transport within the county of destination.

The company will then make a booking with a suitable shipping line and arrange for a container to be delivered to the customer. Most shipping lines have their own containers. Larger exporters can use their own containers but these must have been certified as acceptable by the relevant shipping line and have the relevant ISO[13] plates on them. Not only does this provide assurance to the shipping line that neither the container nor its contents are going to damage other cargo, but it facilitates the sale of the container in the overseas country once it has been unpacked. This is often a cheaper option rather than bearing the cost of sending it home empty. In most locations the company uses independent contractors to collect the container from the shipping line's depot and

[13] ISO, or International Organization for Standardization, is the international organisation that sets standards for many industrial products. Manufacturers whose products meet the standards are able to make this known to potential producers, thereby facilitating sales.

deliver it to the customer. Most customers request that the container be delivered with a truck that has a side lifter attachment to enable the container to be lowered to the ground. The company recommends that once delivered, and during the packing process, containers are stored in a secure area at the customer's place of business. It is not uncommon for partly packed containers to 'disappear' from the customer's premises if not adequately secured.

The customer needs to give at least two days notice to the company to arrange for collection of the container to allow for delivery to the port. Prior to collection of the container, the company will have made arrangements for the customer to obtain an export declaration number required by Australian Customs for the export of the goods from Australia and also will have sent a pre-receival advice to the port authorities to notify them of the container's impending arrival.[14] The company advises that customers need to take care with the accuracy of their statements regarding the weight of the container because domestic transport regulations specify maximum weights which can be transported by various types of truck. There may also be a problem with loading of the container on the ship if the container is overweight.

Once the container arrives at the port area, it will be loaded onto the ship. However, customers need to be aware that it is common practice in the shipping industry for shipping lines to overbook. This means that it is possible that a customer's container might not make the first voyage out of the port by the shipping line. Customers need to be aware of this possibility when entering into contracts with overseas buyers. If time is to be of the essence, customers should advise the company accordingly and guaranteed shipment on a set day can occur if a higher rate of freight is paid.

Once the goods are shipped, the company receives its own bill of lading from the shipping line. It, in turn, issues a forwarder's bill of lading to the customer to enable the customer to either transmit it to the overseas buyer via the banking system or directly depending on the means of payment used. The bill of lading issued by the company to the customer is known as a forwarder's bill of lading or express bill of lading that is issued for the transport of the goods from the customer's premises through to the premises of the buyer in a door-to-door shipment. The company will have received its own separate transport documents from the various carriers that it subcontracts. This will include the land carrier

[14] Australian procedure is used as an example here but customs authorities of all exporting countries are likely to have similar procedures for clearing of goods for export.

in the country of export, the sea carrier and the land or other transport carrier in the country of the buyer.

In a door-to-door transaction, the company will arrange with its overseas office in the country of the port of entry of the ship to handle the clearance of the goods through customs authorities in the EU. The company advises that customs clearance is best done at the port of entry even if the final destination is in a different EU country to the port of entry. Thus, if the container arrives in Rotterdam in the Netherlands, clearance should occur there even if the final destination is in Germany. The overseas office of the company will arrange for the transport of the goods from the port of entry to the final destination and obtain their own transport document (consignment note, delivery docket). The overseas office will use the most convenient means of internal EU transport bearing in mind the port at which the goods arrive and the time frame within which the goods are required. While inland waterway is often the most economic, it is not always available. In addition, time constraints generally mean that road transport is used. Rail tends to be more expensive and time consuming than road.

After arrival of the goods and unpacking, the container will need to be returned by the buyer to the nearest depot of the shipping line as advised by the shipping line.

Having outlined some of the general characteristics of transport systems to and within the EU, we now turn to the relevant legal regimes. The following discussion deals with each of the major international conventions that govern international sea transport, international air transport and then transport of goods by road, rail and inland waterway within the EU.

## INTERNATIONAL CONVENTIONS GOVERNING SEA TRANSPORT OF GOODS TO THE EU

The bill of lading is the standard document evidencing a contract for the sea carriage of goods. An examination of standard form bills of lading reveals that many of their provisions either reflect or expand upon the provisions in the Hague-Visby Rules. The following discussion therefore draws attention to some of the more important provisions of the Hague-Visby Rules and notes how those provisions are expanded in standard form bills of lading.

The Hague-Visby Rules apply to any carriage of goods by sea. Most ocean bills of lading specifically state that they are issued pursuant to the

Hague-Visby Rules (or Hague or Hamburg Rules for those countries where the Hague-Visby Rules do not apply). Combined transport and forwarder's bills of lading frequently state that the Hague-Visby Rules apply to that part of the carriage that occurs by sea.

Goods do not include live animals or cargo that is stated as being carried 'on deck'. Standard ocean and combined transport bills of lading reflect this with a term stating that cargo that the shipper expressly agrees to be carried on deck is the risk of the shipper. However, where the carrier (and not the shipper) decides to carry the cargo above deck, the carriage will still be subject to the provisions of the Hague-Visby Rules. Most standard bills of lading contain a term that gives the carrier the right to carry cargo on deck or below deck as it wishes.

Article 3 of the Hague-Visby Rules sets out the primary responsibilities of the carrier. They are to make the ship seaworthy, properly man staff and equip the ship, and make all parts of the ship fit and safe for the carriage of the goods. This article also requires the carrier to issue the shipper with a bill of lading that allows the goods to be identified as belonging to the shipper and that shows the number of packages or containers, their weight and the condition that they were in at the time of receipt. The bill of lading is prima facie evidence of the receipt by the carrier of the goods and their conditions at the time of receipt. In the hands of a third-party consignee, the bill of lading becomes conclusive evidence of the carrier's receipt of the goods as described in the bill. On the other hand, the rules provide that the shipper guarantees the accuracy of the information provided to the carrier about the goods. This is particularly important in the case of container shipments because carriers cannot be expected to open every container to check the accuracy of the information that the shipper has provided about what is contained in it. Article 3 concludes by requiring the person who is entitled to delivery of the goods in the country of arrival to immediately give notice in writing to the carrier about any loss or damage to the goods. If the loss or damage is not immediately apparent, the recipient has three days to give the notice.[15]

The standard bills of lading expand upon many of the provisions of Article 3. It is common to find provisions that the shipper not only guarantees the accuracy of the information provided to the carrier but also agrees to indemnify the carrier for any loss the carrier suffers a result of the

[15] It should be noted that the standard International Federation of Freight Forwarders bill of lading sometimes used by freight forwarders extends the period of notice from three to six days.

goods being misdescribed. This is often supplemented by a provision containing detailed obligations on the shipper to comply with all regulations related to carriage of dangerous goods. A clause is often inserted to allow the carrier the right to inspect the contents of containers. Further, not only is the shipper to be responsible for packing the container, but it has to satisfy itself that the container is suitable for the carriage of the type of goods and has no right to expect that refrigerated containers will be capable of freezing down cargo to the required temperature for transport. Some bills of lading also require advice by the shipper if containers fall within the category of 'heavy lift containers' so that appropriate arrangements can be made by the carrier for loading.

Most bills of lading not only repeat the time limit for notification of claims but also expressly limit the time for bringing any action against the carrier and also where that action can be brought.

Article 4 of the Hague-Visby Rules is perhaps the most important in terms of limiting the liability of the carrier. It states that the carrier will not be liable for any loss or damage other than that caused by the failure of the carrier to make the ship seaworthy in accordance with its obligations in Article 3. Article 4(2) goes much further and sets out a list of events for which a carrier will not be held responsible. These include loss or damage due to fire, perils of the sea, act of God, act of war, quarantine restrictions, act or omission of the shipper or their agent, strikes, riots and civil disturbances, insufficiency of packaging, and latent defects in the goods not discoverable by due diligence or any other cause that is not the actual fault of the carrier. Article 4(4) permits the carrier to make any deviation to attempt to save life or property or any other reasonable deviation. If the carrier is liable, Article 4(5) limits the carrier's liabilities to 666.67 units of account[16] per package or 2 units of account per kilogram, whichever is the higher. However, the carrier will not be entitled to the limitation as to amount of liability if the damage is proved to result from the carrier's intentional or reckless acts. The carrier and the shipper have the option of agreeing to a higher amount of liability.

Some standard bills of lading repeat the events set out in the Hague-Visby Rules. Others simply rely on what is contained in the Hague-Visby Rules by stating that the bill of lading is issued subject to those rules. It is quite common for bills of lading to repeat and expand upon the rights

[16] One unit of account is the amount of the shipper's currency that is equivalent to 1 SDR. SDR (Special Drawing Rights) is the means used by the International Monetary Fund to give a standard value to each of the world's different currencies. For example, as at the end of February 2009, 1 SDR was equivalent to 2.3 Australian dollars and 1.16 euros.

of the carrier to take any actions that they deem necessary in relation to the goods in the event that a hindrance to their performance of the carriage arises. Bills of lading also state that the carrier can take any route or make any deviation to the route for the carriage of the goods. In terms of liability as to amount, some bills of lading specifically state that the carrier will not be liable for any consequential loss arising from the loss or damage to the goods. Others such as the standard FIATA bill of lading[17] limits consequential loss to twice the amount otherwise provided for by the Hague-Visby Rules. Some also make provisions as to how goods are to be valued for the purposes of assessing loss, particularly in circumstances where a higher amount of potential liability has been agreed between the carrier and the shipper.

Article 4 bis of the rules provides for the carrier's exemption from liability to extend to the carrier's servants and agents unless the act of the servant or agent causing the damage was either intentional or reckless. Despite these relatively clear provisions, most bills of lading contain a clause along essentially the same lines as Article 4 bis. It is appropriate in this context to note that when carriers contract as principals with the shipper to arrange the various legs of transport, the carrier itself is primarily liable. In the case of the standard FIATA bill of lading, the forwarder is liable to the shipper as principal and must recover any loss from the carrier concerned. However, some combined transport bills of lading issued by non-vessel owning carriers expressly provide that the carrier only acts as agent for the shipper in respect of arranging the carriage of the goods. In this case the shipper would have to pursue the carrier responsible for the leg of transport where the damage occurred. Because it is often difficult for a shipper to establish this, such bills of lading often contain a provision that states that if it cannot be determined where the damage occurred, then it is presumed to have occurred during the sea transport leg of the journey.

Other provisions of the Hague-Visby Rules that need to be mentioned include a right of a carrier to surrender their rights or immunities under the rules if so agreed with a shipper and provided that this is specifically provided for in the bill of lading. Given the bargaining power of carriers vis-a-vis shippers, this provision would seem to have little practical application for the vast majority of exporters. Further, in the case of shipments that are not 'ordinary commercial shipments made in the ordinary

[17] The FIATA bill of lading was developed by the International Association of Freight Forwarders ('FIATA' in French) and is the recommended form for a house bill of lading that freight forwarders issue to shippers.

course of trade', the rules permit carriers to enter into any agreement that they wish concerning liability for carriage of the goods. Again, because of the exclusion of ordinary commercial shipments, this provision is not of significant practical application for most exporters. As noted earlier, the Hague-Visby Rules are not applicable to charter party agreements. However, if bills of lading are issued pursuant to charter party agreements, then the Hague-Visby Rules will apply.

The foregoing discussion has emphasised the point that bills of lading tend to reflect and expand upon the provisions of the Hague-Visby Rules. However, standard bills of lading also contain some additional matters. These additional matters relate primarily to freight charges. They are not precluded by the rules and have some significant practical application for shippers. For example, it is common for bills of lading to refer to the carrier's tariff rates and require payment in accordance with these. Freight is expressed to be earned when the goods are received by the carrying company. Further, bills of lading contain a provision giving carriers a lien over the goods if freight is not paid. A provision is also often included to allow the carrier to store goods at the shipper's expense if the person responsible for accepting delivery does not collect the goods upon arrival.

## INTERNATIONAL CONVENTIONS GOVERNING AIR TRANSPORT OF GOODS TO THE EU

While the overwhelming method for transport of goods to EU countries from outside countries is by sea, air freight plays an important role in transporting high-value items, and parts and equipment required in a very short time frame. The regulatory regime for international air transport has undergone a significant change since 1999. Prior to that time, there was a confusing array of international conventions that could have governed the international transport of goods by air. These included the Warsaw Convention of 1929, the amended Warsaw Convention, the Guadalajara Convention of 1961 and the Montreal Protocol No. 4 of 1976. The confusion resulted largely from the adoption of a lowest common denominator approach. For example, if the sender of the goods was from a country that had adopted the Warsaw Convention and the receiver of the goods was in a country that had acceded to the amended Warsaw Convention, then the governing international regime would be the original Warsaw Convention.

The Montreal Convention of 1999[18] has been a major step forward in reducing the confusion. This convention superseded all of the other conventions for those countries that have acceded to it. All member states of the EU adopted this convention in 2001. Most of its major trading partners, including the USA, Japan, Korea, China and Australia, have also acceded to it. As at the time of writing some 83 countries worldwide have ratified it and brought it into effect. However, as with the previous regime, a lowest common denominator approach remains and accordingly air transport between countries that have not acceded to the Montreal Convention and the EU will be governed by the relevant convention adopted by that other country. Because most of the EU's trading partners have adopted the Montreal Convention, this discussion of the regulatory regime for international air transport will confine itself to a review of some of the more significant provisions of the Montreal Convention as it relates to the transport of goods.

As noted, the convention applies to the air transport of goods between two member states regardless of whether there is a stop in a non-member state. It also applies where the air transport is carried out by successive carriers if the parties have agreed that it is a single operation.[19] The primary document of carriage is the air waybill, although a provision exists to allow consignors and carriers to agree on some other form of document to evidence the contract for the carriage of the goods.[20] The requirements of the air waybill are set out in Articles 5 and 7 of the Montreal Convention. The convention conforms with the practice of most other conventions relating to the international carriage of goods in that it imposes obligations on the consignor for the accuracy of the information contained in the document of carriage[21] and to provide any necessary documents to meet customs requirements.[22] The consignor has the right to give instructions regarding the disposal of the consignment[23] and, if no instructions are received to the contrary, the named consignee has the right to require the goods to be delivered to it.[24]

Article 11 contains important provisions regarding the evidentiary value of statements in the air waybill. The effect of Article 11 appears to be that statements relating to the weight, dimensions, packing and number of

[18] Convention for the Unification of Certain Rules for International Carriage by Air, Montreal, 28 May 1999.

[19] Montreal Convention, Article 1.

[20] Montreal Convention, Article 4(2).

[21] Montreal Convention, Article 10.

[22] Montreal Convention, Article 16.

[23] Montreal Convention, Article 12.

[24] Montreal Convention, Article 13.

packages are prima facie evidence of the facts as stated. However, more specific statements relating to the quantity, volume and condition of the cargo will not be evidence as against the carrier unless these matters have been checked by the carrier in the presence of the consignor and this is stated in the air waybill. Statements as to the *apparent* condition of the cargo in the air waybill will be evidence of such apparent condition. This is a significant matter because of the limited number of defences that the carrier has in the case of loss or damage to the goods or delay in their delivery.

Article 18 of the Montreal Convention provides that the carrier is liable for any loss or damage to the goods during the carriage by air. The period of carriage by air includes not only the actual time that the goods are in the aircraft but is extended to cover any period during which the carrier is in charge of the goods. However, it only includes any land transport outside of an airport if that land transport was for the purpose of 'loading, delivery or transshipment of the goods'.[25] The carrier is exempted from liability for loss or damage if it was due to inherent defects, insufficient packaging, acts of war or an act of a public authority relating to the entry or exit of the goods in the country of departure or arrival as the case may be. The carrier is also liable for damages for delay unless it can prove that it took 'all measures that could reasonably be required to avoid the delay or that it was impossible for it to take such measures'.[26]

Unless the carrier caused the loss or damage intentionally or recklessly, the limit of liability is set out in the convention at 17 SDRs per kilogram.[27] Complaints about loss or damage to the goods must be made in writing forthwith after discovery of the damage but in any event within 14 days after receipt of the cargo.[28] Any action against the carrier must be brought within two years.[29]

## INTERNATIONAL CONVENTIONS GOVERNING ROAD TRANSPORT OF GOODS WITHIN THE EU

The Hague-Visby Rules or applicable air transport convention apply to the portion of the carriage that occurs by sea or air in getting the goods to the relevant EU country. Other international conventions will apply in

[25] Montreal Convention, Article 18(4).
[26] Montreal Convention, Article 19.
[27] Montreal Convention, Article 22(3).
[28] Montreal Convention, Article 31.
[29] Montreal Convention, Article 35.

determining liability of the carrier for the land portion of the transport. In the case of export to European countries, three other conventions require discussion. These are the 'CMR Convention'[30] for international road transport, the 'CIM Rules'[31] for rail transport and the 'CMNI Convention'[32] for transport by inland waterway.

The CMR Convention was originally agreed to by a number of European countries in 1956 to facilitate trade in goods between members of the fledgling European Economic Community. At present there are 47 countries that have ratified the convention including all EU member states having land boundaries with other EU member states. Other than in the very limited range of circumstances set out in its Article 1, the CMR Convention applies to all carriage of goods by road when the place of taking over the goods and the place of delivery are in two different states of which at least one is a member of the convention.

Exporters who have agreed to deliver goods to a customer in an EU country different to the country in which the port of arrival is located will frequently utilise the services of a freight forwarder or non-vessel owing carrier to handle all aspects of the carriage. The freight forwarder or non-vessel owning carrier will likely subcontract out the EU road portion of the carriage to one of the main road transport companies operating throughout the EU, unless one of the major global companies are used who own their own land transport within the EU. The CMR Convention will govern the contract between the forwarder and the road transport company.

The primary document evidencing the contract for the road transport of the goods is the consignment note. Article 6 of the CMR Convention sets out the matters that a consignment note must contain. A standard format for the consignment note has been devised by the International Road Transport Union and is revised from time to time.[33] These are similar to the particulars required to be set out in a bill of lading. Consignment notes are issued in triplicate. One is provided to the sender or the sender's agent who arranges for the goods to be loaded onto the road transport, one to the consignee on delivery of the goods and a further copy is retained

[30] Convention on the Contract for the International Carriage of Goods by Road ('CMR' in French), Geneva, 19 May 1956, as amended by Protocol to the CMR, Geneva, 5 July 1978.

[31] The Uniform Rules Concerning the Contract of International Carriage of Goods by Rail ('CIM' in French) are contained in Appendix B to the Convention Concerning International Carriage of Goods by Rail ('COTIF' in French), Bern, 9 May 1980.

[32] Budapest Convention on the Contract for the Carriage of Goods by Inland Waterway ('CMNI' in French), Budapest, 3 October 2000.

[33] The standard consignment note can be found at <http://www.iru.org/index/en_media_press_pr/code.900/lang.en>.

by the road carrier. The sender of the goods bears responsibility for the accuracy of all information contained in the consignment note and will be liable for any loss or damage that the road carrier sustains if the information provided is inaccurate[34] or for defective packaging of the goods unless the carrier is aware of this and notes it at the time of taking over the goods.[35] On the other hand, the road carrier is responsible for checking the apparent condition of the goods and, if in packages, the number and their identifying marks. The road carrier must specify in the consignment note any reservation that the carrier has in relation to the condition of the goods[36] and if this is not done then the goods shall be presumed to be in good condition when handed over.[37]

There are a number of provisions that provide for problems that the carrier may have with delivery of the goods to the consignee. If it becomes impossible for the carrier to deliver the goods the carrier must ask the sender of the goods for instructions.[38] The sender has the right to ask the carrier to stop the goods in transit, change the place of delivery or deliver to a person other than the named consignee.[39] If the consignee refuses to accept the goods then the sender may dispose of them.[40] Because an exporter or a freight forwarder acting on their behalf will want to ensure that they follow the various procedures for breach of contract as set out in the United Nations Convention on Contracts for the International Sale of Goods (CISG), it may be necessary to store the goods. However, even if a consignee has refused the goods they can still require delivery to them provided that the carrier has received no instructions from the sender.[41] Thus the sender bears considerable responsibility in keeping the carrier advised of any changed arrangements. The CMR Convention provides that the carriage is concluded once the carrier unloads the goods and places them for the account of the person entitled to dispose of them.[42] This may be the consignee or other person nominated by the sender if the sender has elected to change the consignee. However, the carrier is also given the right to sell the goods if no instructions can be obtained from the sender in time

34 CMR Convention, Article 7.
35 CMR Convention, Article 10.
36 CMR Convention, Article 8.
37 CMR Convention, Article 9.
38 CMR Convention, Article 14.
39 CMR Convention, Article 12.
40 CMR Convention, Article 15.
41 CMR Convention, Article 15.
42 CMR Convention, Article 16.

and they are perishable or other circumstances require such immediate action.[43]

The CMR Convention provides that the carrier is liable for loss or damage to the goods as well as for delay in delivery other than where this was caused by the claimant.[44] While this is not made specific in the convention, it envisages that the claimant would ordinarily be the consignee or other person entitled to delivery. The liability of the carrier extends to actions of the carrier's servants and agents and any other person who the carrier makes use of for the carriage of the goods.[45] There is a list of special circumstances in which the carrier will not be liable for loss or damage. These include defective packaging, handling, loading or stowage by the sender, the inherent nature of the goods rendering them susceptible to deterioration or insufficiency and inadequacy of identification markings on the goods.[46] However, the burden of proving that the loss, damage or delay was due to one of these circumstances rests with the carrier.[47] Delay in delivery occurs if the carrier does not deliver within the stated time or, where no time frame has been agreed, is outside of the time it would be reasonable to allow a carrier to deliver the goods.

If the goods are lost or damaged then the amount of the carrier's liability is limited to the value of the goods (as defined in Article 23) but in no case shall the liability exceed 8.33 units of account per kilogram.[48] If a claim is made against the carrier for damages due to a delay in delivery, the carrier's liability is limited to the cost of the carriage.[49] As in the case of the Hague-Visby Rules, carriers and senders are entitled to agree on a higher value of the goods but in that case the rules specifically state that the carrier can impose a surcharge.[50] If a higher value is agreed then it will be that value that determines compensation for loss or damage. The convention contains provisions regarding apportionment of liability if there are two or more successive carriers.[51]

Unless a consignee advises the carrier immediately upon delivery of the goods of apparent loss or damage, then the goods will be deemed to

[43] CMR Convention, Article 16.
[44] CMR Convention, Article 17.
[45] CMR Convention, Article 3.
[46] CMR Convention, Article 17.
[47] CMR Convention, Article 18.
[48] Units of account are defined in terms of SDRs as is the case under the Hague-Visby Rules.
[49] CMR Convention, Article 23(5).
[50] CMR Convention, Article 24.
[51] CMR Convention, Articles 34–40.

have been delivered in the condition as set out in the consignment note.[52] Where the loss or damage is not apparent the consignee must advise the carrier within seven days in writing.[53] There is a one-year time limit for the bringing of any court action.[54]

## INTERNATIONAL CONVENTIONS GOVERNING RAIL TRANSPORT OF GOODS WITHIN THE EU

While carriage of goods by rail accounts for a much lesser proportion of the internal carriage of goods within the EU, transport planning authorities hope to increase the use of rail over the coming years. The establishment of the European Railway Agency in 2004 is evidence of a move in this direction. The original Convention on International Carriage of Goods by Rail ('COTIF' in French) was also amended and modernised in 1999 in an attempt to achieve greater uniformity with other conventions related to international transport – most particularly the CMR Convention discussed above. The Uniform Rules for the International Carriage of Goods by Rail ('CIM Rules') are set out in Appendix B to the COTIF Convention. Almost all EU member states brought the newer convention and rules into force as from 1 July 2006.

Although the CIM Rules are intended to follow the CMR Convention as closely as possible, there remain some significant differences due in part to the physical differences between the two modes of transport and also possibly due to a desire to make the CIM Rules slightly more favourable to the sender of goods. This could be due to the desire on the part of EU transport authorities to promote rail transport. The following deals with the major areas where the CIM Rules diverge from the CMR Convention. They do so in four main areas. First, there are different provisions concerning the examination of the goods and the consequences that follow from that. Second, there are differences in relation to modifying the contract of carriage. Third, the amount and extent of liability of carriers is both more flexible and more generous to senders of goods than under the CMR Convention. Finally, the manner in which claims are made also differs from the convention.

The CIM Rules apply to all international rail carriage of goods where the taking over of the goods occurs in a member state and the delivery

[52] CMR Convention, Article 30.
[53] CMR Convention, Article 30.
[54] CMR Convention, Article 32.

of the goods also occurs in a member state.[55] However, in addition, the rules can apply if either the place of taking over the goods or the place of delivery of the goods is in a member state and the parties agree that the rules should apply. Further, if there is a single contract for the transport of the goods and if road or inland waterway transport is used internally in a member state to supplement the main international carriage of goods by rail, the rules will also apply. The CIM Rules will also apply to all sea and transport carriage by inland waterway if the sea or inland waterway transport supplements the main carriage by rail and if it occurs on routes that are listed by the member states.[56]

As is the case with the CMR Rules, the main document of carriage is the consignment note. There are provisions for an electronic consignment note to be issued. The information to be contained in the consignment note is similar to that required for road carriage and the responsibilities of the sender for the accuracy of the information and packaging of the goods is also similar to the provisions in the CMR Convention.

The first major area of difference between the CIM Rules and the CMR Convention concerns the examination of the goods. The carrier has the right to examine the goods at any time to ensure that they are in accordance with what has been set out in the consignment note. However, because goods are often loaded by the sender of the goods, the rules give the sender the right at their expense to require the carrier to examine the goods to verify that they are as stated in the consignment note.[57] If the carrier has loaded the goods then the consignment note is evidence of their condition as shown on the consignment note, or if no indication is shown as to their condition then the consignment note is evidence of their apparently good condition when taken over.[58] If the consignor has loaded the goods then the consignment note will only be evidence of the sound condition of the goods if this is stated on it. If there is no notation of the soundness of the goods and the consignor has loaded the goods, then the consignment note will not be evidence of the apparently sound condition of the goods unless the carrier has examined them and made a notation of the findings on the note.[59] The responsibility for loading the goods has to be agreed between the parties, but in the absence of agreement the carrier is to have responsibility for loading and unloading. However, for full wagon

55 CIM Rules, Article 1(1).
56 CIM Rules, Article 1(4).
57 CIM Rules, Article 11(3).
58 CIM Rules, Article 12(2).
59 CIM Rules, Article 12(3).

loads (presumably including containers) the responsibility rests with the consignor and unloading with the consignee.

The second main area of difference to the CMR Rules is the rights as between consignor and consignee to modify the contract of carriage. While the consignor has the right to request the carrier to discontinue carriage of the goods, delay their delivery, or to deliver to a different person or place, the consignee is also given rights to modify the contract of carriage from the time when the consignment note is drawn up unless the consignor indicates otherwise in the consignment note. The explanatory memorandum regarding the new rules introduced by the 1999 modernisation suggests that this may lead to a 'race' between the consignor and the consignee to make amendments. For that reason and because of the possible difficulties that could arise in relation to the contact of sale between an exporter and a buyer, it would seem to be desirable for consignors to insert a provision that the consignee cannot request modifications.

The third area of major difference between the two sets of rules relates to the extent and amount of liability. The amount of liability of the carrier for loss or damage is limited to 17 units of account per kilogram unless the parties have agreed to a higher value. This limitation as to amount will also not apply if the loss or damage was due to the wilful or reckless actions of the carrier. There are also provisions concerning the extent of liability for wastage for goods which are, by their nature, subject to this when in transit.[60] The method for valuing the goods to determine the exact amount of loss is almost identical to that provided in the CMR Convention. The CIM Rules contain quite specific provisions regarding damage caused by delay. The rules specify that the consignor and the carrier shall agree to the transit period. If this has not been agreed and in the absence of some specified exceptional circumstances, the maximum carriage time is 24 hours for the each 400 kilometres of carriage.[61] The time can be extended by the carrier if rail transport is combined with road, sea or inland waterway transport or if there is a change in gauge of the rail tracks. These maximum time periods tend to suggest that rail carriage of goods may well be a slower option than road transport. This is no doubt one of the issues that the European Railway Agency will be addressing in order to increase the competitiveness of rail. If the carrier is liable for delay, the amount of liability is limited to four times the charge for the carriage.[62]

60 CIM Rules, Article 31.
61 CIM Rules, Article 16.
62 CIM Rules, Article 33.

The final major area of difference concerns the manner in which claims are made and who is entitled to make a claim against the carrier. As is the case with the CMR Rules, the carrier is also responsible for the actions of their servants and agents.[63] The rules are much more specific than the CMR Rules as to who is entitled to make a claim against the carrier. The CIM Rules have the effect that in the case of loss or damage the person entitled to bring an action is the person who has possession of the consignment note. Thus the consignor is only entitled to make a claim against the carrier until the consignee has taken possession of the consignment note, accepted the goods or modified the contract of carriage as described above.[64] In order to make a claim for partial loss or damage to the goods, the person entitled must request the carrier to draw up a report without delay setting out the nature of the loss or damage, the condition of the goods and the extent of loss or damage and can refuse to accept delivery until the examination to establish loss or damage has been carried out.[65] If the person entitled to delivery disputes the report, they have the right to call in an independent expert.[66] The report must be requested by the person entitled to make a claim either immediately upon discovery of the loss or damage if such is apparent or, if not apparent, within seven days of accepting the goods. A claim must be made in writing and will not be able to be made unless the person bringing it produces the consignment note and has had the report referred to above carried out. In the case of damages for delay the person entitled needs to assert their rights within 60 days. The time limit for bringing a court action is one year.

## INTERNATIONAL CONVENTIONS GOVERNING TRANSPORT OF GOODS WITHIN THE EU BY INLAND WATERWAY

There is a further convention that needs to be mentioned in connection with internal transport of goods within the EU. This is the Budapest Convention on the Carriage of Goods by Inland Waterway (CMNI) of 2000. The CMNI Convention applies to all inland water transport where the place of loading of the goods and place of delivery of the goods is in two different states and at least one is a party to the convention. It also applies to any contract for the carriage of goods that includes a portion of sea shipment

[63] CIM Rules, Article 40.
[64] CIM Rules, Article 44(1).
[65] CIM Rules, Article 17(4).
[66] CIM Rules, Article 42.

of goods provided that the portion of sea shipment is less than the portion of inland water transport and provided that a maritime bill of lading has not been issued in relation to the voyage.[67] At the time of writing the European signatories to the CMNI Convention include the Netherlands, Luxembourg, Germany, Czech Republic, Switzerland, Bulgaria and Romania. These countries contain the major cross-border inland shipping routes through central Europe. Notable absences from the list of signatory countries are France and Belgium.

The CMNI Convention has much in common with both the CIM Rules and CMR Convention. Accordingly there is a considerable degree of uniformity introduced between the three conventions concerning the requirement of the carrier to deliver the goods within the time period stated;[68] the obligations of the sender concerning dangerous goods;[69] the matters of which they need to advise the carrier;[70] what must be included in the transport document;[71] the requirement on the part of the carrier to note on the transport document any reservations concerning the condition of the goods;[72] and the rights of the holder of the transport document to instruct the carrier regarding disposal of the goods until the consignee has the consignment note.[73]

There are a number of features specific to the CMNI Convention requiring special mention here. First, the convention states that unless it is otherwise agreed, the taking over and delivery of the goods shall take place on board the vessel. This means that the person responsible for arranging this means of transport has to arrange for the cost and risks of loading and unloading the goods.[74] Second, the transport document that is to be issued may either be a consignment note or a bill of lading. A bill of lading will only be issued if this was agreed before the goods were loaded. Where a bill of lading is issued then 'it alone shall determine the relations between the carrier and the consignee'[75] but the 'conditions of the contract shall continue to govern the relations between the carrier and the consignor'.[76] Third, if the goods being transported are in a container

67 CMNI Convention, Article 1.
68 CMNI Convention, Article 5.
69 CMNI Convention, Articles 7–9.
70 CMNI Convention, Article 6.
71 CMNI Convention, Article 11.
72 CMNI Convention, Article 12.
73 CMNI Convention, Articles 14 and 15.
74 CMNI Convention, Article 3(2).
75 CMNI Convention, Article 11(4).
76 CMNI Convention, Article 11(4).

and if the container has not been damaged nor the seals broken by the carrier or their agents, then there is a presumption that any damage to the goods did not occur during that part of the carriage.[77] Fourth, if there is loss, damage or delay the carrier is presumed to be liable unless it can show it took all the precautions of a diligent carrier.[78] However, there is a list of special exoneration from liability including loss caused by acts of the shipper, nature of the goods, defective packaging, and inadequacy of markings on the goods or salvage operations. The maximum amount of liability of the carrier is specified at the same rate as in the Hague-Visby Rules – 666 units of account per package or two units of account per kilogram[79] but with the important change that where a container is lost, that amount will be replaced by 1500 units of account for the container alone and 25 000 units of account for its contents. Liability for delay only is limited to the amount of the freight. The convention also provides for time limits for giving notice and bringing actions.[80]

It has been noted earlier that if a freight forwarder is engaged to handle all of the transport arrangements from the exporter's premises to the importer, then it will usually be the case that the freight forwarder will engage the various subcontractors, be they short sea carriers, road transport companies, rail companies or inland waterway transporters. Thus, under most multimodal transport documents, the freight forwarder will be responsible for compensating the party responsible for engaging the forwarder and the forwarder will then have to pursue the carrier that damaged the goods. The foregoing discussion reveals a number of implications for both forwarders and those engaging them. First, the forwarder will only compensate the party engaging them to the extent to which the subcontractor is liable under the relevant legal regime applying to that portion of the carriage of the goods. As has been seen, both the circumstances where the carrier is liable and the extent of their liability are slightly different under each of the conventions discussed above. Second, forwarders themselves may have considerable difficulty in determining the leg of the transport where any loss or damage occurred. They need to be aware of the implications of the place of taking over the goods for each leg and the place of delivery as well as the obligations for notifying any loss or damage. It has also been noted above that, in some contracts of carriage, there is a condition that the carrier only contracts as agent for the person arranging the carriage.

[77] CMNI Convention, Article 12(3).

[78] CMNI Convention, Article 16.

[79] CMNI Convention, Article 20.

[80] CMNI Convention, Articles 23–24.

This means that the person entering into the contract with the carrier will themselves have to determine where the damage occurred and then pursue that carrier to the extent of liability possible under the relevant convention.

The complexities of dealing with different carriers and legal regimes for each portion of the carriage of goods have resulted in attempts to negotiate an overarching international convention on carriage by multimodal transport. It is understandable that EU authorities would be supportive of such efforts because a standard international convention might facilitate the attempts to shift the burden of internal transport within the EU away from road transport and towards other means such as rail and inland waterway. On the other hand, the logistical as well as legal difficulties of door-to-door transport tend to work very much in favour of utilising just two means of transport – sea and road. Further, attempts to shift a greater percentage of inland transport away from road towards rail and inland waterway may be being hindered because of the growing global interconnectedness of sea and road companies as opposed to integration between sea and the other means of transport. In addition, studies have shown that the percentage of loss or damage is very small in relation to overall quantities of goods transported. One study showed that more than 75% of shippers suffered losses of less than 0.1% of cargo in intra-EU transport and less than 5% of shippers had losses of more than 1%.[81] Further, a position paper by the European organisation representing freight forwarders argued that a single liability regime to cover all forms of EU transport may not only create confusion because of its lack of universality but would also likely lead to an increase in insurance costs because of the greater limits of liability that a new convention might impose.[82] For all of these reasons then, there is little support for a new international multimodal convention for transport of goods and it seems that for the foreseeable future, exporters and importers will have to live with multiple liability regimes.

81 See European Commission, *The Economic Impact of Carrier Liability on Intermodal Freight Transport*, Executive Summary of a study by IM Technologies Limited, 22 January 2001, London, <http://ec.europa.eu/transport/ontermodality/highlights/doc/executive-summary.doc>, which reported survey results that showed more than 80% of US shippers sending to the EU reported a loss of less than 0.1%.

82 CLECAT, position paper presented to the Joint ECMT/UMECE Working Party/Group on Intermodal Transport and Logistics, 5 September 2006, Brussels, <http://www.unece.org/trans/wp24/wp24-inf-docs/documents/id06-06e.pdf>.

## INSURANCE

Obligations to insure the goods during transport are determined by the incoterms. For most of the incoterms, the seller needs to arrange insurance up to the point of transfer of risk and the buyer thereafter. Only where the seller has accepted insurance obligations beyond the point of transfer of risk (such as with the CIF and CIP incoterms) need the seller insure beyond the point of risk transfer. Many exporters take out what is known as open cover insurance policies to cover their insurance obligations for export transactions over a set period of time.

Most insurance policies for the international transport of goods use standard terms known as the Institute Cargo Clauses.[83] There are three common versions of the Institute Cargo Clauses. These are Institute Cargo Clauses A or 'all risks', Institute Cargo Clauses B and Institute Cargo Clauses C. Institute Cargo Clauses C provide the least amount of cover. The A clauses provide the most cover and the B clauses are an intermediate position. All three versions exclude a number of events from insurance cover. A brief summary of the risks covered by each category follows before listing the exclusions that apply to all three.

Institute Cargo Clauses A cover all risks other than the excluded risks. Institute Cargo Clauses B only covers loss or damage due to the following specified causes. These are loss or damage due to fire or explosion; stranding or overturning of the vessel or land transport; collisions; discharge at a port due to distress; general average sacrifice; washing overboard; entry of sea, lake or river water into the ship or a container; loss of goods overboard; and loss or damage due to being dropped while loading onto or off the vessel or craft. Institute Cargo Clauses C cover the same risks as B clauses other than loss or damage due to entry of sea, lake or river water; loss of goods overboard; and damage while loading or unloading.

All three categories exclude loss or damage arising from a wide range of events. These are circumstances attributable to the wilful misconduct of the assured; ordinary leakage, ordinary loss of weight, volume or ordinary wear and tear; insufficient packaging; inherent vice of the goods; delay; insolvency or financial default of the owners or masters of the vessel; deliberate damage by the wrongful act of any person; loss or damage from weapons of war including nuclear weapons; unseaworthiness or unfitness of the vessel when this was known by the insured; war, civil unrest or hostile

[83] Although the use of the Institute Cargo Clauses is widespread, there are other standard sets of clauses that insurers may use. These include the UNCTAD model clauses on marine hull and cargo insurance.

acts by a belligerent power; capture or seizure or detainment of the vessel other than through piracy; strikes, riots or civil commotions; and acts of terrorism. If additional cover is required for some of these risks then it can be taken out. For example, there are standard Institute Cargo Clauses that cover war and also strikes. The cover for these additional items will require the addition of these clauses to the insurance contract with the insurer and will result in additional premiums being payable.

It should be noted that the foregoing may not be the only exclusions from cover. Some standard insurance policies may also exclude certain classes of goods from cover, such as bulk carriage of commodities, livestock, precious metals or computer equipment. For shipments of these classes of goods, variations to standard terms will be required. There is a range of Institute Cargo Clauses that the parties can agree to for particular classes of goods such as the Institute Frozen Food Clauses and the Institute Frozen Meat Clauses. It is also reasonably common to exclude carriage from and to countries where there is high risk. Again, special cover needs to be arranged in these cases.

Institute Cargo Clauses A are the most common level of cover taken out by the party (seller or buyer) who bears the risk of loss or damage to the goods. The reason is that the party bearing the risk of loss or damage wishes to cover themselves for the maximum range of risks. However, it needs to be noted that the two incoterms that require a seller to take out insurance (CIP and CIF) only specify that it needs to be on minimum terms – in other words, Institute Cargo Clauses 'C'. Thus buyers who agree to these two incoterms may wish to have a provision in their contract of sale that requires a higher level of cover. This is because even though the seller has to take out the insurance, it is the buyer who bears the risk of loss or damage under these two incoterms.

# 4 Customs law and procedure within the EU

## INTRODUCTION

AN EXPORT OF GOODS to a country within the EU will involve both a clearance of the goods for export from the country of the seller and a clearance of the goods for entry into the EU either where the goods arrive or in the country of the buyer. The incoterm chosen by the parties will determine the responsibilities for export and import clearance.

Other than in the case of the incoterm 'Exworks', it is the responsibility of the exporter to arrange export clearance in their own country following the procedure that their particular country adopts for this. Due to ongoing work by the World Customs Organization (WCO), export clearance systems are increasingly being harmonised so that firms with export operations in a number of countries are not confronted with entirely different procedures for the export of goods. Nonetheless, this work continues and variations are found from country to country.

Other than in the case of the incoterm 'Delivered Duty Paid', and sometimes 'Carriage Paid to' and 'Carriage and Insurance Paid to',[1] the responsibility for clearance of the goods for import rests with the buyer. Thus in many export transactions a seller will not need to have detailed working knowledge of the procedures for customs clearance in the importing country. However, a general knowledge of the procedures within the EU is very useful for exporters. The EU is a very competitive marketplace and to gain an advantage over their competitors exporters may find that to sell to customers within the EU it is necessary to agree to terms that require import clearance. In addition, exporters need to be familiar with

[1] See Table 2.1 in Chapter 2.

some of the obstacles that their customers may face in meeting EU regulatory requirements for imports and, in particular, some of the requirements that the production of the goods for export to the EU must meet. This chapter therefore provides an outline of some of the basic procedures and regulatory issues that arise when importing into the EU.

The very nature of a customs union is that once goods enter one country that is a member of the union, then goods should be free to move within the entire union area with little restriction. In the case of the EU this principle is referred to as freedom of movement and the program that is in place to bring this about is referred to as the 'single market'. Attaining the single market not only for freedom of movement of goods, but also persons and capital, is a work in progress particularly as the EU continues to expand. Prior to accession to the EU, each country had its own import regulations. However, upon accession to the EU countries must agree to a common procedure and common rates of duty for imported goods. Subject to some exceptions that will be dealt with later, once goods enter one EU member country then they are free to move to any other member country with no requirement for customs clearance.

## EU CUSTOMS ENTRY PROCEDURE

The following flow chart sets out a list of steps that an exporter should take if the relevant incoterm requires them to arrange clearance of the goods into an EU member country. The customs entry document and duty rates have been standardised on an EU-wide basis and, accordingly, regardless of the country to which the goods are being exported, the basic customs entry document will be the same. Likewise, the steps that must be taken for entry of goods to the EU will conform to the basic pattern presented in the flow chart. However, there may be some slight variations of this procedure depending on the EU member country and the type of goods. This is discussed in more detail below. The procedure for the UK has been used as an example here to illustrate the requirements for customs clearance that will be found throughout the EU.[2]

Other than for those exporters who have a permanent business presence within the EU, the first step taken by many exporters is to appoint a customs agent to deal with all of the necessary paperwork and ensure that all relevant EU regulations for import of the particular class of goods have

[2] A detailed explanation of the procedure can be found in HM Revenue & Customs, *Guide to Importing and Exporting: Breaking Down the Barriers*, January 2009, available from <http://customs.hmrc.gov.uk/index.htm>.

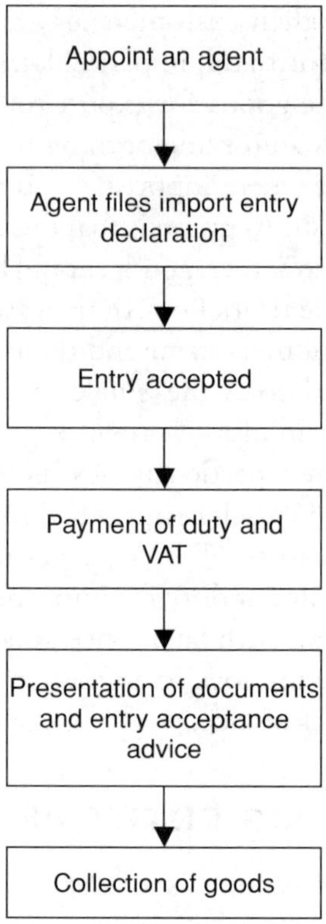


*Figure 4.1 Flow chart of import procedure (UK)*

been complied with. Even those exporters who have a permanent presence may still find it less expensive to hire a customs agent to handle import matters rather than bear the significant administrative costs of hiring staff who have the broad range of knowledge needed for this task. In the UK, all importers are required to have a unique 12-digit number (a Traders Unique Reference Number or TURN) in order to import into the UK. The TURN will be the trader's VAT registration number plus a three digit suffix. An exporter who wants to clear goods for EU entry but does not have a permanent EU presence or a customs agent must apply for what is known as a 'pseudo turn' for the particular transaction. This is time consuming and expensive and hence appointing an agent is the better option. In addition, agents will know the detailed requirements for various classes of goods, including duty rates and the necessity for obtaining any special licence or quota and what is needed to comply with both EU-wide and particular country standards and technical requirements. While exporters are authorised to appoint agents to lodge customs entries on their behalf, it needs to be pointed out that the agent will make the declaration on behalf of the exporter. The exporter is therefore responsible for the accuracy of the information and should check declarations made on their behalf.

The second step in the flow chart above is for the agent to file the import entry declaration. As noted, this document is standardised for all EU countries and is referred to as the 'Single Administrative Document', or 'C88'. An extensive amount of information is required to complete the C88.[3] Some of the requirements are reasonably straightforward items, including the details of the exporter, importer, lodging agent, port of arrival, country or origin, description of the goods and invoice number. However, some items require further discussion here. They are the customs procedure code, the commodity code and the value of the goods.

The customs procedure code (CPC) is determined by the use to which the imported goods will be put. Most exports will be intended for use within the EU and therefore attract the relevant CPC. However, if goods are intended to be re-exported or some exemption or reduction of duty is applicable, a separate CPC will apply. The various circumstances in which goods might be exported or attract reduced duty are discussed in a later section.

The commodity code is the specific tariff code that applies to the goods being imported. This code is uniform to all EU member countries and, in addition, is largely standardised internationally through the work of the WCO. The commodity code determines the appropriate rate of duty applicable to that class of good and, accordingly, having the correct commodity code is significant. The European Commission publishes the common customs tariff and regularly updates this. The entire list of commodity codes is reproduced in each country's customs legislation. In the case of the UK the 16 600 commodity codes are contained in Volume 2 of the 'Integrated Tariff of the United Kingdom'.[4]

The third issue requiring comment is that of valuation. Value of goods imported will ordinarily be their transaction value calculated in accordance with the CIF (cost, insurance and freight) price regardless of whether buyer or seller actually pays the freight and insurance. If transaction value is not appropriate then there is a defined hierarchy of other valuation methods that must be used to determine the value of the goods. This hierarchy of valuation methods is enshrined in the WTO agreements and is therefore

[3] A useful website that goes through a step-by-step procedure for the completion of the 54 boxes on the C88 is <http://www.ukimports.org/C88.html>.

[4] At <http://www.uk-customs-tariff.com/Login.aspx?ReturnUrl=%2fDefault.aspx>.

binding upon all member countries including all EU countries. Detailed discussion of each of the valuation methods can be found in the various valuation publications available for purchase from the WCO.[5]

UK customs has two other procedures that might assist regular exporters. First, if the agent obtains authorisation, they may be able to lodge a simplified version of the C88 and gain accelerated release of the goods. The agent is then able to lodge the full details after release of the goods within a specified time frame set out by customs. Second, exporters who regularly supply the same customer may be able to have their customer lodge what is known as a 'general valuation statement', which sets out the value of the goods that are supplied. This statement will remain valid for three years as long as the details supplied do not change. This system may help exporters who are regularly supplying distributors. These two simplified procedures are available to importers in the UK. There may be individual country variations on these procedures for other EU member countries.

The third step in the flow chart above is that the agent will receive an acceptance of the entry. In almost all cases this acceptance will be transmitted electronically to the agent because all agents will use the electronic system for import entries. In the UK this system as known as the Customs Handling of Import and Export Freight (CHIEF) system.

The fourth step is for the agent to pay the duty calculated in accordance with the rate of duty applicable to the particular goods in question and any value-added tax (VAT) that is payable. As noted, this is determined from the commodity code. Most agents adopt what is known as a deferred payments system. This allows the agent to pay the import duty monthly rather than upon the release of the goods. In order for the agent to defer payment on an exporter's behalf, it is necessary to provide the customs authority with financial security from a bank or other financial institution up to a certain amount and an authority to deduct funds. That amount cannot be exceeded for any given month.

The next step is the presentation of the import documents to customs at the port of arrival of the goods to collect the goods. In the case of multimodal transport, it is useful to use a firm that not only handles the transport but also has authorisation to deal with customs matters.

The earlier discussion of transport of goods within the EU noted that most goods are cleared through customs at the EU port of arrival either by an agent of the exporter or an agent of the buyer. However, the possibility

[5] See WCO bookshop website, <http://publications.wcoomd.org/index.php?language=en>.

exists to defer clearance through customs until the goods reach the customs point closest to the buyer's location. This system is known as 'community transit'. In the case of goods being exported to the EU from a third country, the system allows the exporter or their agent to allow goods to move within the community subject to final clearance at the port of destination.

A brief summary of the procedure is as follows. The person requesting permission for the transit of goods normally lodges electronically a form T1 with the customs authority in the country where the port of arrival of the goods from overseas is situated. The customs authority in this country then provides the person lodging the form with a Transit Accompanying Document, which must accompany the goods. The goods usually must remain sealed within their containers at all times during transit. The person lodging the form also has to provide a guarantee for payment of the duties should something go wrong and the goods go missing. The customs authority in the EU country where the goods first land transmit the information lodged by the person requesting a transit authority to the customs authority within the country of the buyer. Once the customs authority in the country of the buyer has cleared the goods, it authorises the release of the guarantee that has been provided by the person requesting the transit authority. For regular traders or their agents a simplified form of transit authority can be obtained. Detailed information regarding transit procedures can be found on Europa, the European Commission's website.[6]

The T1 procedure is the most common form of transit procedure for exporters outside of the EU whose goods arrive at a port in a country different to the final port of destination. However, other arrangements for transit of goods from countries close to the EU also exist. The Transit International Routier Convention ('TIR Convention') signed by some 55 countries allows goods from some North African and Asian countries to move through internal EU borders without the need for customs clearances until the goods arrive at the customs point in the country of destination.[7]

There is also a special procedure for goods that are imported into the EU on a temporary basis. This might occur, for example, if goods are intended for a trade show and are to be taken out of the EU by the exhibitor immediately after the trade show or if samples of goods are sent to the EU to show to prospective buyers. Two possibilities exist here. The first is that an authorised agent within the EU can request what is known as a 'temporary importation relief from duty'. Customs will then authorise the

[6] The Transit Manual is available at <http://ec.europa.eu/taxation_customs/customs/procedural_aspects/transit/common_community/transit_manual_en.pdf>.

[7] Details of these procedures can also be found in the Transit Manual.

movement of the goods within the EU without payment of duty provided that a suitable security deposit is paid or guarantee given. The guarantee or deposit will be released provided the goods leave the EU within the required time frame. The second alternative is to use the worldwide ATA Carnet system. Essentially this allows an exporter attending a trade show, for example, to obtain a voucher for the movement of goods within the EU provided that the person requesting the Carnet pays a suitable security deposit. There are also schemes for suspension of import duty on goods that are being imported into the EU to be incorporated into exports.[8] Many countries outside of the EU also have such schemes so that their exports are not at a competitive disadvantage because of the duty imposed on imported components.[9]

## EU-WIDE RESTRICTIONS ON THE ENTRY OF GOODS

This section deals with the common EU-wide restrictions that an exporter is likely to confront regardless of the EU member country where the goods arrive. It does so by first examining restrictions on agricultural goods and then restrictions on manufactured goods. The next section deals with additional restrictions that may exist at the individual country level.

## AGRICULTURAL PRODUCTS

Many categories of both raw and processed agricultural goods will have a tariff applied to them when entering the EU. As noted earlier, the specific tariff rate for any product can be found in the common customs tariff. In addition, the EU imposes above-quota tariffs on a large range of goods.

The tariff quota system is a WTO-authorised system that allows countries to charge a set rate of duty on goods up to a certain quantity of those goods and then to impose a much higher rate of duty for imports of those goods in excess of the specified quantity. Exporters need to check the commodity code in the tariff schedule to ascertain if a tariff quota applies to the goods they are intending to export. If so, the importer will need to make a request for a share of the quota. This is usually done as part of the import entry documentation and administered by the customs authority in the country of import. However, because quotas are EU-wide

[8] See <http://ec.europa.eu/taxation_customs/customs/customs_duties/tariff_aspects/suspensions/index_en.htm>.

[9] For further details of temporary relief from duty or claiming back duty paid in the UK see the section on transit systems in HM Revenue & Customs' *Guide to Importing and Exporting*, op. cit.

and a share is available in any EU member country, the European Commission monitors the allocation of quotas of each good on an EU-wide basis. Quotas may apply either generally to worldwide imports of the particular good for which the quota exists or alternatively may apply for those countries that have a preferential agreement with the EU for a quota of goods at a preferential rate (see below for further discussion of preferential arrangements).

In both of these cases, quotas are allocated on a first-come first-served basis. Once the quota is used up, then any imports of those goods will be charged the higher rate of duty. Importers can check how much of a given quota remains for any particular good by referring to a website that exists for this purpose.[10] However, even if an importer ascertains that a share of the quota is still available, there is no guarantee that at the time the import documentation is lodged it will still be available and, accordingly, there is the possibility of payment of the higher rate of duty. When the quota is almost exhausted a system is in place to designate the quota allocation as critical. If this is the case then importers may need to lodge a security deposit to cover the additional duty if they fail to make the quota.

Imports of some agricultural goods are also subject to a licensing requirement. In 2008, the list of these was reduced significantly from some 500 products down to 65.[11] Previously, the licensing system was a means of enforcing quotas but, with the move to numerical quotas (first-come first-served), licensing has been removed for all but the most sensitive agricultural products and some products which are imported under preferential arrangements where the numerical quota system cannot be used. Sensitive products that still require a licence include most cereals, sugar, olives, garlic, apples and bananas.[12]

Most imported agricultural goods will need to have been certified by competent authorities in the exporter's country as meeting the relevant EU food safety standard. This will often require exporting countries to have satisfactory measures in place to monitor food production to ensure that it is in conformity with these standards.[13] The EU publishes a list of countries that are permitted to export food of animal and plant origin to it. In a work of this length it is impossible to list all of the numerous

[10] See <http://ec.europa.eu/taxation_customs/common/about/welcome/index_en.htm>.

[11] See 'Commission Takes Latest Step in CAP Simplification Process', Press Release, IP/08/922, 12 June 2008.

[12] See Commission Regulation (EC) No. 514/2008 [2008] OJ L150/7.

[13] See European Commission, Health and Consumer Protection Directorate-General, *Guidance Document on Certain Key Questions Related to Import Requirements and the New Rules on Food Hygiene and on Official Food Controls*, 5 January 2006, <http://ec.europa.eu/food/international/trade/interpretation_imports.pdf>.

regulations and directives that apply to the import of food to the EU. There are detailed requirements for product labelling and packaging for various classes of goods, provisions relating to veterinary checks and food hygiene, directives on animal nutrition, health and welfare that need to be complied with by producers in exporting countries as well as details of the type of checks required for plant products. A useful source of information is the food safety section of the Europa website.[14] The EU has put in place a European Food Safety Authority that has the overriding function of ensuring that member countries utilise the most up-to-date scientific information for determining food safety as well as a rapid alert system to advise member countries of contaminated food. It needs to be noted that because of the rigorous standards that must exist in the producing country, EU buyers wanting to import from some food producing countries will simply not be able to get a licence. The detailed procedures applying to beef imports into the EU from Australia are set out in the case study below to illustrate just how detailed the requirements can be for a single product.

## Case study

### Exporting beef to the EU – regulatory considerations

To ensure food safety and quality standards the EU has a 'farm to fork' policy for the monitoring of every step of the food production and distribution chain.[15] The requirements imposed on beef producers and processors, exporters and EU importers and retailers demonstrate how EU regulation works in relation to this single product. The following describes how EU regulatory requirements affect each step of the production chain in Australia and the final import and distribution for the product in the EU.

Australian beef producers aiming to access the EU market must go through an accreditation process (the European Union Cattle Accreditation Scheme) with the Australian Quarantine and Inspection Service (AQIS).[16] The key issue for accreditation is that cattle destined for the

[14] At <http://ec.europa.eu/scaplus/leg/en/s80000.htm>.

[15] See European Commission, Health and Consumer Protection Directorate-General, 'EU Import Conditions for Fresh Meat and Meat Products', <http://ec.europa.eu/food/international/trade/im_cond_meat_en.pdf>.

[16] Australian Government, Australian Quarantine and Inspection Service, 'European Union Cattle Accreditation Scheme: Questions Answered', last reviewed 5 October 2007, <http://www.daff.gov.au/aqis/export/meat/elmer-3/eucas/questions-answered>.

EU market must be free of hormone growth promotants (HGPs). Accordingly, beef producers must have no HGP cattle on their property at any time; they must only buy stock from other accredited producers; they must only buy and sell through accredited sale yards; and all cattle that are destined for the EU market must be identified by special tail tags at all times. In addition, all stock must be registered with the National Livestock Identification Scheme to ensure that they are able to be traced from birth. Sale yards themselves are also subject to strict requirements in that they must keep EU-identified stock separate from all other stock that are sold in the sale yards. Beef producers can be audited at any time and sale yards are audited annually to ensure that these requirements are being implemented. Audits are usually carried out by AQIS.

Each time cattle are sold the owner must complete an EU Vendor Declaration that requires the Property Identification Code number (PIC) of the vendor; details of the cattle being sold; their destination; how long the cattle have been owned by the vendor; whether the cattle have been raised in accordance with an independently audited QA program; whether the cattle have been treated with any chemicals or been fed on by-product stock feeds (that might contain HGPs or chemicals) within a certain time frame; and whether the cattle are still within a withholding period following treatment with any veterinary drug or chemical. The aim of the declaration places the onus on the vendor to verify that the cattle will not contain any chemical residues or HGPs.

The EU approves individual countries as being eligible to export to it based upon their ability to demonstrate the following: they have a system in place for ensuring that abattoirs and export establishments meet EU health and hygiene standards; there are adequate monitoring systems in place to ensure any chemical residues in the meat do not breach EU standards; the country has in place suitable measures for the control of livestock disease including BSE (mad cow disease); and establishments meet the required conditions for the humane slaughter of animals.[17] Each country seeking accreditation must have a competent veterinary authority which has power to monitor all parts of the production chain. The Food and Veterinary Office of the EU will undertake a mission to any country wishing to be accredited to assure themselves that the country meets the requirements mentioned. In Australia, AQIS is the competent authority and is responsible for designating abattoirs and export

[17] See European Commission, Health and Consumer Protection Directorate-General, 'EU Import Conditions for Fresh Meat and Meat Products', op. cit.

establishments as 'approved establishments' in accordance with EU standards and, after a submission is made by AQIS, to the EU authorities on behalf of the plant seeking approval. Only approved establishments can export beef to the EU. AQIS is responsible for monitoring approved establishments to ensure that they continue to comply with EU standards, as well as providing a veterinary inspection service for meat that is to be exported.

Although beef is a fully harmonised product and, therefore, standards are the same throughout the EU regardless of the country of import, beef importers must still abide by set requirements. Importers must ensure that beef imports arrive through a designated border inspection post within the EU and that prior to the arrival of the consignment authorities are notified and import documentation is accompanied by the relevant veterinary and other certifications. Beef from Australia must be accompanied by the standard AQIS health certificates. An AQIS inspector must be present for the loading of each container and an AQIS seal is placed on the outside of the container. Despite harmonisation at the EU level, there may still be some additional documentary and testing requirements depending on the EU country that the beef is being sent to. Border inspection posts will carry out documentary checks, identity checks and physical checks as necessary.[18] The importer is also responsible for ensuring that the beef comes from an approved country and an approved establishment.

Importers must also apply for a share of the quota. Australia has a quota of 7500 tons for high-quality beef and up to that limit beef will attract an import duty rate of 20%. Beyond that limit, high quality beef will attract a duty rate of 12.5% plus between €141.4 and €304.1 per 100 kilograms depending on the cut of beef. This will raise the overall duty rate well beyond the 20% level that applies to in-quota beef. When imported beef is sold it must meet EU labelling requirements. The basic requirements are as follows. Each carton of beef must have the E in the oval E label showing that it is eligible for the EU. In addition, there must be two AQIS EU tamper evident seals on each carton for security purposes. If the seals are broken the carton will not be accepted. The standard Ausmeat labelling that applies to cartons of Australian beef is also included. In addition, individual EU countries might have their own specific labelling requirements such as dual language on the label.

[18] See European Commission, Health and Consumer Protection Directorate, *Guidance Document on Certain Key Questions Related to Import Requirements and the New Rules on Food Hygiene and on Official Food Controls*, op. cit.

## MANUFACTURED GOODS

The EU also has numerous standards in place at the EU level in relation to many categories of manufactured goods to ensure that products conform to certain quality standards and to ensure that they are safe for consumers. In order to ensure that goods conform to quality and safety requirements throughout the EU, directives are issued that either set out standards for particular goods or refer to specific industry standards for them. Becoming familiar with these standards is a task for the specialist. For example, there are over 100 directives in place that relate to the construction and functioning of motor vehicles.[19] This highlights the need for an exporter to be aware of EU standards for the particular good to reduce the risk of it simply not being able to be sold in the EU market.

Because of the logistical problems that would arise in testing all goods to ascertain whether they meet the relevant standards, the EU has instituted what is known as the 'CE marking' system (or *Conformité Europiénne*) that applies to many manufactured goods.[20] A listing of the categories of goods which are eligible for CE marking can be found on the various websites of organisations that specialise in providing CE marking advice to exporters.[21] As harmonisation proceeds at the EU level, the range of goods eligible for CE marking has increased. If a particular product is required to have a CE mark, then the manufacturer must demonstrate that the product has complied with the relevant requirements that are contained in the directives that relate to the product. The directives will frequently only set out what the attributes of the product should be. In order for a product to satisfy those attributes, the manufacturer needs to consult the detailed standards for the product set by the relevant industry standards bodies to see what must be done technically in the manufacture of the product to ensure that it measures up to the attributes set out in the directive. Once the manufacturer has complied with all of the relevant requirements and has the necessary evidence to prove this, then the manufacturer can issue what is known as an 'EC Declaration of Compliance' and then apply the CE mark to the goods. If the CE mark has been applied to goods and they are subsequently found not to comply with the requirements of the relevant directives, then those goods can be withdrawn from sale within the entire EU market. The Commission currently has a legislative

19 See <http://www.europarl.europa.eu/facts/4_7_4_en.htm>.

20 A useful guide for Australian exporters can be found at <http://www.innovation.gov.au/Section/Industry/Pages/CEmarkingofAustralianproductsforexporttotheEuropeanUnion.aspx>.

21 See for example <http://www.ce-marking.org>.

proposal to increase market surveillance procedures to detect unsafe and non-compliant goods.[22]

The directives and standards applicable to some classes of goods will require the manufacturer to have their product tested or the process of manufacture certified by an independent body as meeting the requirements. Many countries have in place what are known as mutual recognition agreements (MRAs) to allow the testing and certification procedures to be carried out in the country of export. However, the MRAs will only apply to certain classes of goods. In Australia, for example, the MRA applies to automotive products, electrical safety, electromagnetic capabilities, telecommunications equipment, machinery safety, medical devices, pharmaceuticals and pressure equipment.[23] If the MRA does not apply to the manufactured good intended for export and CE marking is required, then the exporter will have to have a relevant European body carry out the procedures.

## Case study

### An example of CE marking – recreational craft

A recreational craft manufacturer that wants to sell its product in the EU must have a CE mark attached to each boat. This is because the standards that recreational craft must meet have been harmonised on an EU-wide basis by virtue of Directive 94/25/EC[24] as amended by Directive 2003/44/EC.[25] The process for obtaining the CE mark is complex. Each part of the boat must be manufactured in accordance with the relevant standard for that component of the boat. For example, there are detailed standards in place for hull construction, stability and buoyancy assessment and categorisation, electrical systems, steering mechanisms, fire protection and inboard diesel engines.[26] There are some 60 standards in all. Not all are applicable to every type of boat.

22 See 'New Internal Market Package for Goods', <http://ec.europa.eu/enterprise/regulation/internal_market_package/index_en.htm>.

23 See European Community–Australia Mutual Recognition Agreement, <http://www.innovation.gov.au/Section/Industry/Pages/EuropeanCommunityAustraliaMutualRecognitionAgreementFrequentlyAskedQuestions.aspx>.

24 [1994] OJ L164/15.

25 [2003] OJ L214/18.

26 European Commission, 'Commission Communication in the Framework of the Implementation of the Directive 94/25/EC of the European Parliament and of the Council on the Approximation of the Laws, Regulations and Administrative Procedures of the Member States Relating to Recreational Craft' No. 2008/C 109/05 [2008] OJ C109/8.

Construction of the craft in accordance with the relevant standards needs to be verified before the product can be marketed in the EU. The relevant regulatory authorities within EU member states designate certain organisations (mostly consultants) who can verify compliance with the standards.[27] These organisations are called 'notified bodies'. To meet the requirements of the verification body the craft manufacturer must first of all present to the verifying authority all of the technical documentation relating to the product. This technical documentation includes the following:[28]

- a general description of the type of product
- conceptual design and manufacturing drawings, and schemes of components, sub-assemblies and circuits etc.
- descriptions and explanations necessary for the understanding of the drawings
- a list of the standards that applied in the manufacture of the product
- results of design calculations made and examinations carried out
- test reports or calculations regarding stability and buoyancy of the vessel
- exhaust emission test reports
- sound emission test reports.

The verifying body uses this technical information when assessing whether the product meets the requirements of the directive. There are a number of matters upon which a verifying body must satisfy itself.[29] First of all, the manufacturer will provide the verifying body with a sample of the product and the verifying body ensures that the sample complies with the technical documentation provided, including all standards. It does so by carrying out whatever examinations and tests are necessary. The product is then given what is known as a 'type examination certificate' to the manufacturer. This certificate contains the details of the manufacturer, conclusions of the examination, conditions for its validity and the necessary data for identification of the approved type. The manufacturer must keep the type certificate as well as the technical specifications for a period of at least 10 years. There must also be a person in the EU who is responsible for placing the product on

27 A list of notified bodies can be found at <http://ec.europa.eu/enterprise/sectors/maritime/files/regulatory/notified_bodies_94_25_080410_en.pdf>.

28 See *Application Guide to the Amended Recreational Craft Directive*, 20 February 2008, <http://ec.europa.eu/enterprise/maritime/maritime_regulatory/doc/cc_guide_cons20feb2008.pdf>.

29 This summary has been prepared from the *Application Guide to the Amended Recreational Craft Directive*.

the EU market. They must also have the technical specifications for the product.

In order to ensure that every craft is eligible to have the CE mark applied, it is necessary to have procedures in place to ensure that each product will be the same as the sample for which the type certificate has been issued. First, the manufacturer is required to satisfy the verifying body that they have in place a suitable quality control system for the production, inspection and testing of the product; final product testing is in place; and the system is fully documented. The verifying body audits the quality control system before approving it and monitors it afterwards. Second, the verifying body either examines every product to ensure its compliance with the type or more commonly checks that random samples of the products comply with type.

Provided that the verifying body is satisfied, the manufacturer themselves is then entitled to fill in a declaration of conformity of recreational craft with the design, construction and noise emission requirements of Directive 94/25/EC as amended. It is noted that it is the manufacturer who takes sole responsibility for the accuracy of the Declaration of Compliance. The declaration requires the manufacturer to list all of the applicable standards that have been used in its manufacture. Products that are subsequently found to have had the CE mark applied when the product does not need the requirements of the directive can be withdrawn from sale in the EU.

Exporters of manufactured goods to an EU member country may also be confronted with tariff quotas for some products. As with agricultural products, exporters need to check the tariff schedule to ascertain if a quota applies and, if so, the importer will need to make application for a share of the quota. Some manufactured goods might also be subject to licensing requirements (e.g. chemicals, ozone depleting substances, radio equipment) either on an EU-wide basis if the legislation relating to that particular item has been harmonised or, if not, then at the individual country level. Again, specialist advice from an import agent can be obtained to clarify if particular goods are subject to licensing.

## INDIVIDUAL COUNTRY RESTRICTIONS ON THE IMPORT OF GOODS

It may seem baffling to the outside observer that individual countries can impose restrictions on goods given that the EU is meant to be a single market. The outside exporter would tend to assume that once a good meets the standards for entry into one EU member country then it should be able to be freely marketed in all other member states. If the EU has set standards at the EU level (known as harmonisation) then there are very limited circumstances for individual countries to set different standards. Article 95 of the EC Treaty has the effect that once standards are set at the EU level, then individual countries can only maintain existing contrary standards provided that they justify these and cannot impose their own new standards without going through a rigorous process. Thus if the class of goods that an exporter is exporting to a particular EU country is subject to harmonised EU standards, the exporter can be more confident that those goods will have free movement within the EU and not be subject to additional barriers at the individual country level.

However, the harmonisation process of quality and safety standards at the EU level is a work in progress. The European Commission notes that around one quarter of all goods traded internally within the EU are not subject to harmonised rules.[30] If there are no EU-wide directives applicable to the particular agricultural product or manufactured good being exported, then the exporter will need to ensure that the good meets the quality and safety standards of the EU country in which it is intended to be sold. Once it meets those standards then the well-recognised principle of mutual recognition in the EU will mean that the product is most likely to be able to be sold in all member states. The mutual recognition principle means that if a product can be sold in one EU member state and meets the standards applicable in that state for the product, other member states must recognise those standards and not impose additional standards.

The mutual recognition principle has been given added impetus by Regulations 764/2008 and 765/2008,[31] which seek to eliminate technical barriers to trade between member states by establishing product contact points in each member state and conformity assessment bodies. If a product has been approved by a conformity assessment body after obtaining the relevant standards from the product contact point, then other member states cannot impose additional requirements on that product for it to be marketed in their own particular state. However, this regulation applies primarily to technical standards, and while it goes a considerable distance in stopping additional barriers being imposed by member states in relation to technical matters, it does not eliminate all possibilities of states imposing

30 See 'New Internal Market Package for Goods', <http://ec.europa.eu/enterprise/regulation/internal_market_package/index_en.htm>.

31 Regulation (EC) No. 764/2008 [2008] OJ L218/21; Regulation (EC) No. 765/2008 [2008] OJ L218/30.

other barriers, as will be seen in the discussion below. The explanation of why this is the case is complicated but needs to be understood by those intending to export to the EU. The explanation deals first with quantitative barriers that individual countries seek to impose and then with pecuniary barriers such as taxes and charges that they might seek to levy on imports.

## QUANTITATIVE AND OTHER TECHNICAL BARRIERS TO IMPORTS OF GOODS FROM OTHER EU MEMBER STATES

Because of the principle of freedom of movement of goods that underlies many provisions of subsequent versions of the EC Treaty and the ongoing work of the Commission to bring about a 'single market', member countries of the EU are limited in imposing restrictions on the entry of goods into their own particular country once those goods have legally entered another member country, even if there is no harmonisation at the EU level. Article 28 sets out the general rule that member countries cannot impose 'quantitative restrictions or measures having equivalent effect' on goods coming from another member state. Despite this general rule, Article 30 of the treaty does allow some restrictions but only for the purpose of public morality, public policy, public security, protecting health and life of humans, plants and animals, protection of cultural property, and protection of industrial and commercial property.

Article 28 seems to have a plain meaning on first reading. However, a problem arises from the wording 'or measures having equivalent effect' and what exactly these words are meant to cover. In 1970 the EC promulgated a directive[32] that divided such measures into two categories – measures that apply only to imports from other EU member states as opposed to locally produced goods (distinctly applicable measures) and measures that apply to both imports from other EU member states and locally produced goods (indistinctly applicable measures).

The European Court of Justice (ECJ) has had an easier time identifying distinctly applicable measures that amount to quantitative restrictions on imports. Examples of such measures include phytosanitary inspections on imported apples when locally produced apples did not require any similar inspection,[33] a requirement by the Irish government for importers to buy

[32] Directive 70/50/EEC [1970] OJ Spec Ed 17.

[33] *Rewe-Zentralfinanz v Landwirtshaftskammer* [1975] ECR 843.

a percentage of their oil supplies from Ireland's sole oil refinery,[34] and a German ban on the advertising of foreign medicinal products.[35]

However, the same cannot be said for indistinctly applicable measures. The famous *Cassis de Dijon* case[36] was one of the first illustrations of this. In that case, Germany refused to allow French *cassis* (blackcurrants) to be used for the production of a particular alcoholic beverage because Germany had a mandatory requirement for 25% alcohol content for the beverage and French cassis did not have the characteristics to allow this to occur. The Commission challenged the German exclusion of French cassis imports on the grounds that it infringed what was, at the time, the predecessor of Article 28. In a famous ruling the ECJ said that if the measures were necessary so that mandatory requirements could be met, then 'reason' suggests that the state should be able to impose them. However, the mandatory measures must clearly be necessary and there should be no other means of achieving the same end. In this case, the ECJ said that labelling could have been used to indicate the differences in alcoholic content and it was not therefore necessary to exclude the French cassis.

More recent examples of measures which have been held to amount to indistinctly applicable measures that amount to quantitative restrictions include an English requirement that certain products had to show the place of origin,[37] and an Irish requirement that water pipes sold to a public authority had to meet the Irish standard for those pipes.[38] In both cases the measures applied to both locally produced goods and goods imported from other EU member states. However, in the first case, showing the place of origin (predominantly France) was held to be a measure that would discriminate against imports because consumers would be more likely to choose the product that originated in England. In the second case, there were international standards equal to the Irish standards and therefore requiring all products to meet the Irish standard resulted in a favouring of local products and therefore discriminated against imports.

One area that has produced considerable debate concerns the difference between measures that relate to the intrinsic nature, packaging or labelling of the product on the one hand and pure selling arrangements for the product on the other. In *Keck*,[39] the court held that national measures

[34] *Campus Oil ltd v Minister for Oil and Energy* [1984] ECR 2727.

[35] *Lucien Ortscheit GmbH v Eurim-pharm GmbH Case* [1994] ECR I-5243.

[36] *Rewe-Zentralfinanz v Bundesmonopolverwaltung fur Branntwein* [1979] ECR 649.

[37] *Commission v UK* [1985] ECR 1202.

[38] *Commission v Ireland* [1988] ECR 4929.

[39] *Keck and Mithouard* [1993] ECR I-6097.

that relate purely to selling arrangements (such as advertising) and that affect domestic and imported goods equally would not offend Article 28. However, the courts apply this rule strictly. For example, it was held that a ban on alcohol advertising in Sweden offended Article 28 because the effect of the ban was that consumers would be more likely to buy what they already knew (Swedish brands of alcohol) rather than imports. Accordingly, the ban did not have the same effect on both locally produced goods and imports.[40] Likewise, a German ban on the sale of pharmaceutical products by mail order or over the internet was held to be in breach of Article 28 because the ban would affect foreign pharmaceutical sellers more than German pharmacies even though the ban applied to both equally.[41]

Thus while states still technically have open to them the possibility of imposing additional barriers to imports from other member states, the ECJ looks carefully to determine if there is any protectionist effect at all and, if so, will strike the regulation down as offending Article 28. As noted above, Regulations 764/2008 and 765/2008 should make the courts' job easier in relation to technical barriers. However, as seen in the case examples above, not all barriers relate to product standards and technical specifications so the jurisprudence on Article 28 is likely to continue to grow.

Article 30 of the EC Treaty provides a range of circumstances where countries can impose restrictions on imports. It allows member states to regulate imports on the grounds of public morality, public policy, public security, protecting health and life of humans, plants and animals, protection of cultural property and protection of industrial and commercial property. Regulations 764/2008 and 765/2008 continue to allow these grounds for restricting the entry of goods. However, these provisions are construed narrowly by the ECJ in the interests of upholding the principles of freedom of movement of goods, mutual recognition of standards throughout the community and the promotion of the single market. Nonetheless, some measures have been found to have been justified under Article 30 even though they were found to be quantitative restrictions under Article 28. Thus the ban on the advertising of foreign drugs in Germany was permitted under Article 30 because those drugs were not authorised in Germany and therefore could pose a health risk.[42] It was noted in this case that in the absence of harmonising legislation at the EU level, countries were free to impose their own health requirements. Similarly, the requirement of the

[40] *Konsumentombudsmannen (KO) v Gourmet International Products AB (GIP)* [2001] ECR I-1795.

[41] *Deutscher Apothekerverband Case C-322/01* – not reported – judgement delivered 11 December 2003.

[42] *Lucien Ortscheit GmbH v Eurim-pharm GmbH Case* [1994] ECR I-5243.

Irish government for a certain percentage of oil to be purchased locally was held to be justified under Article 30 because Ireland needed to maintain its only oil refinery for national security purposes.[43] In addition, the ban on mail-order pharmaceuticals was held to be justified in relation to prescription drugs (but not non-prescription drugs) because of a potential adverse affect on the health of German citizens, even though it was an indistinctly applicable measure that restricted imports. Examples of cases where the court has refused to allow justification under Article 30 include a ban by England on imported turkeys because of an alleged threat of Newcastle disease. In this case the court found the risk to public health was small and the ban related more to the loss of market share by English turkey farmers.[44] A French prohibition on the import of milk substitutes was also struck down because milk substitutes were not considered to be a risk to public health.[45]

Finally, rather than set standards that will apply throughout the EU in relation to a particular matter, the Commission has, on occasion, only set minimum standards. This may be because it has been impossible to achieve agreement for the one universal standard and all that has been possible is agreement on a minimum standard. In those cases, individual member countries may set standards higher than the minimum. However, if the measure introducing the 'minimum standard' has specifically provided that there is to be no impediment to market access as a result of the setting of a minimum standard, then countries can only apply higher standards to products within their own market and not to products coming from another EU member. If the directive introducing the 'minimum standard' does not specifically mention market access, then countries may set higher standards even in relation to goods coming from other member countries. This, however, needs to be justified in accordance with the Article 30 exceptions mentioned above.

## PECUNIARY BARRIERS

Movement of goods from one EU country to another might be deterred because of taxes and charges that the importing country levies on those goods. Because of the potential for such taxes and charges to be an impediment to the freedom of movement of goods, there are a number of provisions in the EU Treaty that control the ability of states to levy them.

43 *Campus Oil ltd v Minister for Oil and Energy* [1984] ECR 2727.

44 *Commission v UK* [1982] ECR 2793.

45 *Commission v France* [1988] ECR 793.

Article 25 prevents any country from levying customs duties or charges having equivalent effect on imported products. Accordingly, a Belgian levy on imported diamonds to fund social security benefits for workers in the diamond industry contravened the then equivalent of Article 25.[46] Even a service provided to the importer may amount to a charge having equivalent effect to a customs duty. Thus, a levy by Belgian customs authorities on goods that were temporarily in storage waiting for customs clearance was a charge having equivalent effect to a customs duty.[47] However, if the charge is for an inspection that a member state is required to undertake under community law in the general interest of the community (such as a veterinary check), then it will not offend Article 25, provided that the charge does not exceed the actual costs of the inspection and the charge promotes the free movement of goods by, for example, imposing uniform inspection procedures that are less costly than if individual countries could conduct whatever inspections they liked.[48] Even in the case where charges are levied on both domestically produced goods and imports of similar goods, the charge will offend Article 25 if it applies to imports if different criteria are used to impose the charge on imports.[49]

Article 90 of the treaty provides that no state can tax products of any other state at a greater rate than the taxes that apply to their domestically produced products. It has two limbs. Article 90(1) applies if the imported product is similar to the domestically produced product. Thus, where smaller breweries from outside Germany were not able to avail themselves of the lower rate of beer tax applicable to domestic German brewers, the German tax was held to be in breach of Article 90(1) and discriminatory.[50] Article 90(2) applies where the products are not similar but where the lower tax on the domestically produced product has the effect of discriminating against the imported product. A lower tax on domestically produced beer in the UK accompanied by a much higher tax on wine was held to be discriminatory. The significant difference in tax rates between the two products had the effect of protecting domestic beer producers from foreign wine imports. The UK produced very little wine and the price difference meant UK consumers were led to prefer beer.[51] A similar result applied

[46] *Sociaal Fonds voor de Diamantarbeiders v SA Ch Brachfeld & Sons* [1969] ECR 211.

[47] *Commission v Belgium* [1983] ECR 1649.

[48] *Commission v Germany* [1988] ECR 5427.

[49] *Marimex v Italian Finance Administration Case* [1972] ECR 1309.

[50] *Bobie Getrankvertrieb v Hauptzollamt Aachen-Nord* [1976] ECR 1079.

[51] *Commission v UK* [1983] ECR 2263.

where bananas were taxed at a much higher rate in Italy than other fruit that was produced domestically.[52]

The possibility of states having their own special restrictions on intra-EU movement in the case of some categories of goods reinforces the earlier suggestion that it is necessary for exporters to obtain advice from a knowledgeable customs agent to advise on the requirements for any particular category of good.

## ANTI-DUMPING, COUNTERVAILING AND SAFEGUARD MEASURES

All member states of the EU are also members of the WTO and accordingly are bound by the WTO agreements on the imposition of anti-dumping duties, countervailing duties and safeguard measures. The agreements set out the rules and procedures for the application of these different forms of duty and are common to all WTO members. The EC Treaty gives authority to EU institutions to impose these duties at a community-wide level. The body that has responsibility for these matters at the EU level is the Directorate-General for Trade.

Anti-dumping duties can be imposed on imports originating from a country outside of the EU when the export price of those imported goods is less than the normal selling price of those goods in the country of export. Countervailing measures are imposed on goods where the production of those goods has attracted a WTO illegal subsidy from the government in the country of export of those goods. Safeguard measures are temporary measures imposed where a surge of imports of particular goods threatens that industry within the EU.

The EU releases a report each year that provides significant detail not only about the numbers and types of measures that have been taken during the year but also very useful summaries of the individual cases. The 2006 report notes that as at the end of that year, the EU had in force 134 anti-dumping measures, 12 anti-subsidy measures and only one safeguard measure. Because of the predominance of anti-dumping measures, the following discussion emphasises the process that the EU adopts in an anti-dumping investigation, illustrating the various stages by reference to actual cases. It should be noted that many of the steps involved in an anti-dumping investigation also apply in the case of the other two types of

[52] *Commission v Italy* [1987] ECR 4157.

measures. Additional detail on anti-subsidy and safeguard measures can be found on the Europa website.[53]

The first step in an anti-dumping investigation is that producers who represent a significant portion of the production of the type of goods within the EU (usually 25% of the production within the EU) must file a complaint with the Commission about the dumping of competing goods from a third country. An advisory committee consisting of a representative of the Commission and a representative of each member state makes preliminary findings as to whether the complaint contains sufficient evidence to warrant proceedings being taken to impose anti-dumping duties. If so, the Commission then sets about an investigation to determine two matters. The first of these is whether actual dumping has occurred and the second is whether the dumping has resulted in an injury to domestic producers. The investigation is conducted for the time period not less than the six-month period prior to the initiation of proceedings. During the investigation the Commission can request member states to supply information, interview and request information from relevant parties, and even conduct investigations in the country of export provided that the government of the country agrees.

During the period 2002–2006, 122 investigations were carried out involving imports from 30 countries.[54] The major countries from which the alleged dumped products originated were China (36 investigations), Russia (nine investigations), India (eight investigations), Taiwan and Malaysia (seven each), and Korea (six investigations). The major sectors involved were chemical and related industries (32 investigations), iron and steel (22 investigations), and electronics (17 investigations). The observation may be made that these are industries where European firms are finding it difficult to withstand the winds of global competition and are keen to ensure that such competition is fair.

One of the outcomes of an investigation is that no anti-dumping duties will be imposed. This can occur not only because the Commission finds that there is no dumping or injury as a result but also because it is considered not in the interests of the community to impose duties. Of the 36 investigations initiated in 2006, 18 resulted in no anti-dumping duties being imposed.[55] Four of the cases where no duties were imposed concerned

53 At <http://ec.europa.eu/trade/issues/respectrules/anti_subsidy/index_en.htm>.

54 European Commission, *25th Annual Report from the Commission to the European Parliament on the Community's Anti-dumping, Anti-subsidy and Safeguard Activities 2006*, 21 October 2007, Brussels, <http://trade.ec.europa.eu/doclib/docs/2007/august/tradoc_135643.pdf>, p. 23.

55 Ibid., p. 35.

the import of cathode ray tubes for colour TV sets from China, South Korea, Malaysia and Thailand. Although the investigation found that the dumping margins were between 0–20% for the Chinese imports, 10.5–14.5% for the Malaysian imports, 0–15% of the South Korean imports and 41–47% for the Thai imports, no duties were imposed because the decline in the EU industry was primarily due to falling demand for cathode ray tubes with the advent of plasma and flat screen televisions.[56] Thus the injury was not primarily due to the dumping. A further seven cases related to the import of DVDs from China, Taiwan and Hong Kong, and CDs from China, Hong Kong and Malaysia. In these cases, the investigation found that the local producers had a very small share of the EU market (only around 1–2%) and that the benefits of cheap imports for consumers, importers, retailers and distributors outweighed the benefits to producers of protection against anti-dumping.[57]

On the other hand, an investigation may result in anti-dumping duties being imposed. This can occur in two stages. The Commission may impose provisional duties if a provisional determination has been made that there is dumping and injury. Provisional duties must be imposed within nine months of the commencement of the investigation and last for no more than six months during which time a decision is made as to whether to impose definitive anti-dumping duties. Subject to the rights of review (see below), these will last for five years and may be extended.

In 2006, anti-dumping duties were imposed on chamois leather from China; footwear with leather uppers from China and Vietnam; lever arch mechanisms from China; plastic sacks and bags from China and Thailand; refrigerators from Korea; salmon from Norway; seamless steel pipes from Croatia, Romania, Russia and Ukraine; and tartaric acid from China.[58] Of these the footwear case has been described as the most significant.[59] Several hundred thousand people are employed in footwear related industries in the EU. Conversely, many EU companies have moved offshore to places like China and Vietnam to produce goods more cheaply to benefit European consumers. Hence this case involved a careful balancing of interests between consumers, importers and offshore producers on the one hand, and workers and domestic footwear producers on the other. The investigation commenced in July 2005 and provisional duties were imposed in April 2006. The final investigation found that there had been

56 Ibid., p. 40.
57 Ibid., p. 39.
58 Ibid., p. 26.
59 Ibid., pp. 31–5.

some 40 000 job losses in footwear industries in the EU in the past two years and that a further 200 000 were at stake. An investigation of a number of producers found that the dumped goods were the major factor causing injury to domestic producers and, further, that consumers would be little affected by the imposition of duties. Accordingly, despite some adverse impacts on importers, anti-dumping duties in the order of 9–16% were imposed on imports from China and 10% on imports from Vietnam.

An interesting side issue in the case concerned the request by several Chinese producers for what is known as 'market economy status'. Dumping duties are ordinarily calculated on the difference between the export price and the normal domestic price, but in the case of non-market economies it is difficult to determine the normal price because of the significant role of the state in determining market prices, not so much directly, but through various measures that are given to assist industry, including tax holidays, subsidised finance and land at below market prices. The investigation found that all of these measures prevented the footwear producers from being entitled to market economy status, and accordingly the normal price had to be calculated by reference to production costs.

## PREFERENTIAL ARRANGEMENTS

The EU has in place a number of preferential agreements that allow goods to be imported at lower rates of duty than those listed in the standard customs tariff. They tend to fall into three groups. First, there are bilateral agreements with some countries that allow preferential access for specific goods. Second, there are bilateral free trade agreements between the EU and some countries that tend to give preferential access to a wide class of goods at nil or low duty rates. Third, there are a series of multilateral agreements that the EU has either entered into or is currently negotiating that allow for preferential access of goods between EU member countries and the other countries that are a part of the multilateral trade agreement. The following discussion deals with each of these categories in turn.

The EU has bilateral agreements in place with the vast majority of countries around the world. However, many of the agreements are quite general in nature, such as the many trade development and cooperation agreements with developing countries. However, when it comes to preferential access for specific goods from specific countries, the bilateral agreements that the EU has in place tend to have a fairly narrow coverage. The Europa website has a section that provides a detailed analysis of individual agreements by country and by region.[60] In relation to specific goods, this source shows that there are agreements in place to allow preferential access for wine from Canada, Australia and South Africa; textiles from Brazil and the Ukraine; sugar from India; and an agreement that relates to quantities of steel that can be imported from the Ukraine. In addition, the EU has in place mutual recognition agreements relating to standards and quality of nominated products. Mutual recognition agreements were discussed earlier and the EU has these in place with Canada, Australia, Japan and New Zealand. There are also special customs cooperation agreements with Canada, India and Korea to achieve mutually compatible customs systems to allow easier access for goods and also to prevent fraud.

The second category of agreements is free trade agreements with individual countries. Currently the EU has in place comprehensive preferential agreements with Switzerland, Turkey, Chile and Mexico. There are over 100 separate agreements with Switzerland that cover relations between it and the EU and include much more than trade cooperation. They extend back to the 1950s when European cooperation began with the formation of the European Coal and Steel Community. The composite effect of the agreements effectively gives Switzerland de facto EU membership in relation to commercial matters while allowing the country to retain significant independence from the EU's institutional and political structure. The agreement with Turkey takes the form of a customs union and covers free trade in industrial goods but not in agriculture (other than processed agricultural products). The free trade agreements with Mexico and Chile are of much more recent origin – Mexico from 2000 and Chile from 2003. Both are compressive trade agreements that extend preferential access for industrial goods and some agricultural products as well as including trade facilitation arrangements such as mutual recognition agreements for standards in industrial products and phytosanitary agreements for standards in agricultural products. In line with current international trends in relation to free trade agreements, the Chile and Mexico agreements deal with not only preferential access for goods but with a series of trade related issues including investment facilitation, intellectual property protection, customs cooperation, government procurement and technical standards for goods.

60 See <http://ec.europa.eu/trade/issues/bilateral/countries/index_en.htm> and <http://ec.europa.eu/trade/issues/bilateral/regions/index_en.htm>. In addition, an annotated summary of the EU's bilateral and multilateral agreements can be found on the treaties database on the Europa website, at <http://ec.europa.eu/world/agreements/default.home.do>.

In addition to bilateral free trade agreements already in place, the EU is currently negotiating with Russia and Canada. Canada currently has several preferential agreements with the EU but recent negotiations for a trade and investment enhancement agreement cover much broader issues – similar to those covered in the Mexico and Chile free trade agreements. It is noteworthy that both Canada and Mexico are members of the North American Free Trade Agreement (NAFTA) and the aim of negotiation of free trade agreements between these two countries with the EU seems to be to give European firms some of the advantages that the NAFTA agreement gives to US firms in those markets. The EU is also negotiating a Common Economic Space agreement with Russia that tackles similar issues to the EU's existing free trade agreements.

There are several multilateral agreements between the EU and groups of countries. Perhaps the most far reaching of these is the European Economic Area agreement with Norway, Iceland and Liechtenstein. This agreement was entered into in 1992 and creates a single market between the EU and these countries for trade in all goods other than agricultural products and fish. Thus exporters of industrial products to the EU from third countries effectively have access not only to all EU member countries but also free movement of goods to Norway, Iceland and Liechtenstein subject to the exceptions that were noted earlier in relation to general restrictions on movement of goods within the EU.

The second major multilateral arrangement that the EU has in place is the Generalized System of Preferences (GSP) that exists within the WTO system. This allows developing countries preferential rates of duty for many categories of goods exported to industrialised countries. A full list of goods that have preferential access under the GSP can be found in the Common Customs Tariff of the EU. There are 178 countries that have such access. There are procedural requirements that need to be met for exporters from developing countries in order to take advantage of the preferential rates of duty that exist. The major requirement is a GSP Form A that is essentially a certificate of origin signed by the relevant authority in the exporting country to show that the goods were manufactured or produced in the exporting country. There are detailed rules in relation to the origin of goods that authorities need to follow when issuing these certificates. The importer in the EU then has to produce this certificate to obtain the preferential duty rate. Not all goods in a particular category might be eligible for the preferential rate because, for some goods, the preferential rate only applies to a set quota of goods. Once the quota is exhausted then the normal rate of duty applies. The system that the EU has in place for allowing exporters to assess the extent to which a quota has been filled was described earlier.

In addition, the EU has set up special relationships with several groups of developing countries. The oldest of these dates from the 1970s with the African, Caribbean and Pacific (ACP) countries whereby preferences were given by the EU to exporters from those countries. The EU is currently updating this general arrangement with specific economic partnership agreements with sub-regional groupings of the original ACP member states. The Balkan states also have access to the EU for all exports other than agriculture without customs duties or limits on quantities.

The EU is in the process of negotiating two major multilateral free trade agreements. The first of these is with the Mediterranean countries including Tunisia, Turkey, Israel, Morocco, Jordan, Egypt, Algeria, Lebanon, Syria and the Palestinian Authority. The aim of the European–Mediterranean Free Trade Area is to achieve duty-free access in industrial products between the EU and the Mediterranean countries as well as between Mediterranean countries themselves and to achieve gradual liberalisation of trade in agricultural goods.

The second major agreement under negotiation is between the EU and the Mercosur countries of Latin America.[61] At present negotiations have been put on hold pending the outcome of the Doha trade agenda. Should the Doha round of global trade negotiations not proceed, the EU and Mercosur may move forward to an agreement. If this proves to be the case it may make negotiation of the mooted Free Trade Agreement of the Americas that much more difficult for the USA. The USA first proposed a free trade agreement of the Americas in the late 1990s but progress in negotiations has been slow and, in recent years, there has been a trend towards bilateral agreements between the USA and other countries. Chile is currently the only South American country to have a comprehensive free trade agreement in place with the USA.

However, the EU is also exploring free trade agreements with other regional groupings of countries. The process of entering into free trade agreements is underway with the South Caucasus (Armenia, Azerbaijan and Georgia), the Gulf States (Bahrain, Kuwait, Oman, Qatar, Saudi Arabia and United Arab Emirates) and the ASEAN countries (Indonesia, Malaysia, Myanmar, Vietnam, Singapore, the Philippines, Thailand, Brunei, Cambodia and Laos).

[61] Full members of Mercosur are Brazil, Argentina, Venezuela, Paraguay and Uruguay. Chile, Peru, Ecuador and Bolivia are associate members.

A key procedural matter for exporters seeking preferential access under agreements between their countries and the EU is the need to obtain certificates of origin for the goods. These accompany other export documents such as the transport document, commercial invoice and insurance certificate when those documents are transmitted to the buyer either directly or through the banking system. There are no standard globalised rules for determining when goods can be said to 'originate' in the country of export. Thus, each of the EU preferential agreements might contain slightly different rules and exporters need to check the relevant rule and agreements to ensure procedural matters are met.

# 5 Payment and risk management in international sales

THERE ARE FOUR main methods by which an exporter can be paid for goods in an international sales transaction. In order of least to most risk for the exporter these are: pre-payment; payment by letters of credit; payment against documents; and payment on open account. A discussion of each of these methods of payments follows together with some observations regarding the way in which exporters can minimise risk of non-payment in each case.

## PRE-PAYMENT

Pre-payment occurs when the exporter is paid for the goods before they leave the exporter's place of business. Pre-payment usually occurs electronically with the purchaser arranging with their bank to transfer the funds to the account specified by the exporter in the contract of sale. While most exporters would prefer this means of payment, it is difficult to get a buyer to agree unless there is a long-established relationship between the parties and a sufficient degree of trust to allow any problems with conformity of the goods or their transport to be resolved in an amicable fashion.

## LETTERS OF CREDIT

Payment by letter of credit is perhaps the most frequently used method of payment in international trade. A 2001–2002 survey of UK exporters revealed the extent of use of letters of credit for export transactions between

UK exporters and buyers in third countries.[1] For importers in Asia, Africa and the Middle East, letters of credit represented around 50% of all payment types. For importers from Latin America, letters of credit were used 27% of the time, while in Australia and New Zealand letters of credit only accounted for 17% of payments. Letters of credit were much less frequently used by importers from other EU countries and North America. In those cases, letters of credit were only used for around 10% of transactions. A probable explanation for this is that as trading relationships become more established and risk is less of a factor, exporters tend to rely less on letters of credit and more on open account terms. However, it seems likely that when using open account terms they will protect against non-payment by using credit risk insurance. Premium rates for more developed countries that exhibit less political risk will also be lower and may be cheaper than using letters of credit.

The process of payment by letter of credit commences with the exporter and the buyer agreeing in their contract of sale that this is to be the means of payment for the goods. An important part of the contract of sale is the list of documents that need to be presented in order to obtain payment under the letter of credit. These will usually include the transport document, the commercial invoice, the packing list, a certificate of origin and the insurance certificate. As will be seen, early agreement on these matters is essential to avoid exporters having problems when presenting documents to the relevant bank in exchange for payment. Once these matters have been agreed, the buyer approaches its bank to issue a letter of credit in favour of the exporter. The buyer's bank will usually require the buyer to have sufficient funds in its account before they will agree to do this. The buyer's bank transmits the letter of credit electronically to a bank in the exporter's country that will advise the exporter of the opening of the credit. This bank is known as the 'advising bank'. Upon shipment of the goods the exporter is able to present the documents required by the letter of credit to a bank in the exporter's country named in the letter of credit as the bank to which documents should be presented for payment. The documents are usually accompanied by a bill of exchange drawn by the exporter and addressed to the buyer or buyer's bank requiring them to pay. Provided the documents are in order, the bank will pay the exporter and transmit the documents to the issuing bank. The buyer receives the documents from

[1] SITPRO, *Report on the Use of Export Letters of Credit 2001–2002*, 11 April 2003, <http://www.sitpro.org.uk/reports/lettcredr/lettcredr.pdf>.

*Figure 5.1 Flow chart for simple letter of credit procedure*

the issuing bank to enable them to collect the goods. The paying bank receives reimbursement from the buyer's bank.

Banks have standard procedures for the issue of letters of credit and since most have agreed to submit themselves to the standard rules contained in the Uniform Customs and Practices for Documentary Credits,[2] letters of credit have become reasonably uniform throughout the world. These rules, the current version of which is the 'UCP 600', require letters of credit to contain certain particulars including the following:

- the name of the applicant for the letter of credit (the buyer)
- the name of the issuing bank (buyer's bank)
- the beneficiary of the letter of credit (the exporter)

[2] ICC Uniform Customs and Practice for Documentary Credits, *UCP 600*, ICC Publication No. 600, 2007 edn.

- the advising bank
- the bank where the documents are to be presented (the bank with which it is available)
- an expiry date for presentation
- the date by which goods must be shipped
- the port of shipment
- the name and signature of the carrier on the transport document
- the date of issue of the letter of credit
- the amount for which the letter of credit is issued (usually the contact price)
- whether the drafts drawn under the letter of credit are payable at sight or by deferred payment, acceptance or negotiation
- the documents required to be presented with the draft to allow the letter of credit in exchange for payment – usually include the transport document, the commercial invoice, insurance certificate, packing list and certificate or origin
- whether the letter of credit is confirmed by the exporter's bank (see below).

The UCP 600 has the effect that all letters of credit are, by definition, irrevocable. In the past, letters of credit could be either revocable or irrevocable. A revocable letter of credit meant that the bank issuing it could revoke it at any time prior to payment under it. This devalued the letter of credit as a means of payment and, accordingly, the UCP 600 requires letters of credit to be irrevocable.

A letter of credit might not only be enforceable against the bank issuing it but may also be enforceable against a bank in the exporter's country that has agreed to confirm it. Having a confirmed letter of credit therefore minimises any risk for the exporter of the issuing bank not honouring it. It should be noted that if a letter of credit is not confirmed then the bank that actually pays the exporter will do so on a 'with recourse' basis. This means that if they are unable to recover the funds from the issuing bank they can call on the exporter to reimburse them.

There are a number of variations on the standard letter of credit as described above. A special type of letter of credit can be used to allow an exporter to draw funds under it earlier than shipment of the goods to finance production of the goods (red clause credit). A letter of credit can be issued to allow for repeated drawings up to a certain amount to allow the same letter of credit to be used for a number of shipments (a revolving credit). This saves the exporter and the importer having to arrange a separate letter of credit for each shipment where there is to be a number of shipments over a set period. Letters of credit can also be transferable. A transferable letter of credit is used when the exporter has to purchase the goods from a manufacturer or supplier before sending them to an overseas customer. The exporter arranges for the letter of credit to be transferred in favour of the supplier so that the supplier can collect their price for the goods under the transferred letter of credit. The exporter then obtains the documents from the supplier and substitutes their invoice for that of the buyer. The invoice that the exporter presents to their bank will be for the contract price with the buyer. This will be for a higher amount than the supplier invoice allowing the exporter to derive a profit on the transaction. These are three of the common variations on letters of credit.

While letters of credit are regarded as a secure means of obtaining payment in international trade transactions, there are two major categories of risk with their use. First, there is the risk that the issuing bank will refuse to reimburse the negotiating bank, leading to that bank requiring the exporter to repay the funds. To guard against this risk, many exporters will consult their own banks in an attempt to establish the reliability of the bank issuing the letter of credit before finally agreeing to this means of payment. Further, credit insurance may be taken out to protect against failure of the issuing bank to pay. If the issuing bank or political circumstances in the importer's country is regarded as posing a risk, exporters might request that the letter of credit be confirmed. However, confirmation may be costly; one estimate suggests that the cost of confirmation may vary between 2 and 8% of the value of the amount for which the letter of credit has been issued.[3]

The second category of risk lies with the exporter and the attention to detail that letters of credit require. The UK-based SITPRO survey referred to earlier reported that despite letters of credit having been widely used in international trade transactions for the past 150 years, banks continue to reject almost half at the first attempt of presentation because of insufficient attention to detail by the exporter. While the survey deals only with UK exporters, it seems likely that its findings might be generally applicable to exporters in many countries. This survey questioned three banks as to the most common reasons why letters of credit were not honoured on the first attempt at presentation. The following table sets out the most common reasons why negotiating banks refuse to pay on letters of credit along with who bears the responsibility for the errors.

[3] SITPRO, op. cit., p. 11.

*Table 5.1 Top 10 discrepancies leading to rejection of letters of credit*

| Discrepancy | Reason | Responsibility |
|---|---|---|
| Inconsistent data | Different information between the different documents | Exporter |
| Absence of documents | Documents required by the letter of credit are missing | Exporter |
| Other | Other documentation reasons not specifically noted | Exporter; any third party, e.g. carrier |
| Late presentation | Documents presented later than 21 days after the shipment or after the number of days stipulated in the letter of credit | Exporter |
| Carrier not named and signing capacity | Name of the carrier on the transport document is missing or not signed by the carrier | The transport provider |
| Incorrect data | Information on the set of documents is not in conformity with the letter of credit | Exporter |
| Letter of credit expired | Documents presented after the letter of credit have expired | Exporter |
| Incorrect goods description | Goods description on the documents differs from that on the letter of credit | Exporter |
| Incorrect or absence of endorsement | Bill of lading, insurance certificate or bill of exchange is not endorsed by the exporter or other party | Exporter or insurance company |
| Late shipment | Goods shipped after the last date given for shipment | Exporter or carrier |

Source: SITPRO, *Report on the Use of Export Letters of Credit 2001–2002*, 11 April 2003, <http://www.sitpro.org.uk/reports/lettcredr/lettcredr.pdf>, p.13.

Most of the risks set out in Table 5.1 can be prevented by sound training in letters of credit procedure and careful negotiation with buyers about what the letter of credit is to contain before it is issued by the buyer's bank. There are now many export service companies that provide computerised export documentation programs that assist in ensuring that all export documents are consistent and comply with what is required by the letter of credit. The

UCP 600 allows for submission of documents to banks electronically. It remains to be seen whether this leads to more or fewer discrepancies.

If the buyer and the banks involved do not agree to allow the exporter to correct discrepancies or accept documents that do not strictly comply with the letter of credit, the exporter may be faced with attempting to secure payment in some other way that will incur more costs. However, it needs to be noted that the UCP 600 contains strict procedures that banks must follow if the letter of credit is not to be honoured. These include giving notice of its dishonour within a reasonable time.

Failure of the exporter to obtain payment under the letter of credit does not absolve the buyer from the obligation to pay.[4] It simply means the exporter has to bear the additional expense of arranging payment by some other means. This can also be problematic because confusion has arisen in a number of cases[5] where discrepant documents were forwarded by negotiating banks to issuing banks 'on a collection basis'. The question that arose was whether this meant that the letter of credit was no longer relied on as the means of payment and that payment was to be made on a documentary collection basis, or whether the letter of credit was still active and the documents were simply forwarded to the issuing bank to see if the applicant would accept them with discrepancies. The difference is significant because if the letter of credit remained active then the issuing bank may have maintained some liability to pay. However, if the means of payment had been converted into a documentary collection, the bank was simply obliged to hand the documents to the applicant in exchange for payment. If the applicant failed to pay, the exporter was usually left only with recourse against the buyer.

The best protection against the risks posed by letters of credit is to ensure that the documentary and other requirements of the letter of credit are complied with precisely. In addition, exporters' banks will often offer a service that allows exporters to gain some appreciation of the creditworthiness of the issuing bank.

## PAYMENT AGAINST DOCUMENTS (DOCUMENTARY COLLECTION)

If payment against documents is the agreed means of payment in an international transaction, the parties must first agree on what documents

4 See *Samsung American Investment v Yugoslav-Korean Consulting and Trading Co. Inc.* [1998] 670 NYS 2d 466, and the discussion in K. Fung, *Leading Court Cases on Letters of Credit*, ICC Publishing, Paris, 2004, p. 20.

5 See *Harlow and Jones v American Express Bank* [1990] 2 Lloyd's Rep 343 and the discussion in Fung, ibid., at pp. 99–108.

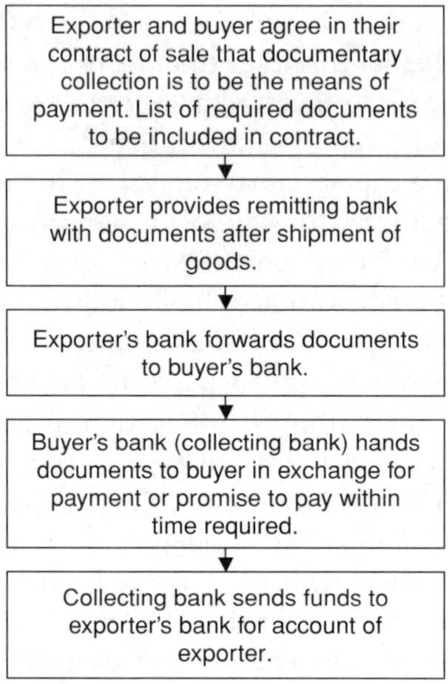


*Figure 5.2 Flow chart for documentary collection procedure*

are necessary to be produced to the buyer to require them to pay. As with letters of credit, the documents are usually agreed in the contract of sale between the exporter and the buyer. Because the transmission of documents and funds occurs through the banking system, it is also necessary for the parties to agree on the identity of the relevant banks.

The procedure for obtaining payment begins with the exporter shipping the goods and then forwarding the agreed documents to the agreed bank in the exporter's country. That bank (the remitting bank) then transits the documents to the buyer's bank (the collecting bank) along with a collection order and a bill of exchange (draft) drawn by the exporter requiring the buyer to pay. The draft will require the buyer either to pay in exchange for the documents (documents against payment) or within a certain period of receiving the documents – usually 30, 60 or 90 days (documents against acceptance). The buyer's bank then transmits the funds received from the buyer through the banking system to the exporter.

This form of payment differs from letters of credit in that the bank in the buyer's country is only obligated to examine the documents to ensure that they conform with what is set out in the collection order before handing them over to the buyer. There is no obligation on the bank itself to pay but merely to transit the payment through to the exporter's bank. This obligation is set out in the Uniform Rules for Collections[6] developed by the ICC and accepted by most banks as the basis upon which they will agree to assist parties to engage in this mechanism of payment in international transactions.

An interesting web-based survey conducted in 2005 leads to the tentative conclusion that many exporters do not favour this means of payment.[7] Given a choice of four means of payment – letters of credit, advance payment, payment against documents and other means – only 6% of over 1 500 respondents preferred payment against documents. By way of contrast, 47% preferred payment by letters of credit and a further 30% preferred advance payment. No analysis is provided of the results but a reading of the comments of those responding suggests that many were not aware of the payments against documents procedure as a means of payment in international transactions. Of those who were, many considered letters of credit to be a safer option.

There are several risks to the exporter if this method of payment is used. First, the process gives the buyer the opportunity to reject documents and hence not make payment because of some minor discrepancy. The Uniform Rules for Collections provide that neither the remitting nor the collecting bank has any obligation to verify the content or the authenticity of the documents. Thus the exporter is left in an uncertain position as to whether an unscrupulous buyer might find some minor discrepancy and refuse to pay. A second risk for the exporter is that in a documents against acceptance transaction, the exporter has to wait until the relevant 30, 60 or 90 days have elapsed before the buyer has to pay. If the buyer defaults, the exporter is then confronted with the expense of legal proceedings to recover the purchase price. A third risk for the exporter is that this means of payment is not appropriate for air transport of goods given the time that it takes for documents to be transmitted through the banking system. Since the buyer needs the documents to collect the goods from the relevant transport operator and clear them through customs, the documents need to arrive before the goods. This may not occur in the case of air transport.

If payments against documents is to be the method of payment, then to minimise risks the exporter needs to ensure that all documents are in order so that buyers have little room to validly reject them. Further, exporters may wish to consider credit insurance as a means of protecting against non-payment. Credit insurance is discussed in more detail below.

6 ICC Uniform Rules for Collections, *URC 522*, ICC Publication No. 522, 1995 edn.

7 See <http://resources.alibaba.com/topic/100/What_is_your_preferred_payment_method_.htm>.

## OPEN ACCOUNT

In open account transactions the buyer pays for the goods after they have arrived. Sometimes this occurs within 30, 60 or 90 days after the buyer themselves has had the opportunity to resell the goods. For that reason open account payments are common in distribution relationships. These are discussed in detail in the next chapter. However, as noted earlier, open account transactions are very common where there appears to be little credit risk. This helps to explain the very high percentage of transactions conduced within the EU and between EU and North American buyers on this basis.

There are considerable risks involved for the exporter in an open account transaction. The buyer might simply refuse to pay on the alleged basis that the goods do not meet the contract requirements. Alternatively, the goods may be rejected by customs. In either case, the exporter will then be faced with extensive legal costs in attempting to recover the money. Two common options for minimising the risk are either to take out credit risk insurance or to engage the services of a factor to collect the debt on their behalf. Each of these strategies is discussed below.

## CREDIT INSURANCE

There are a number of globally based companies that specialise in providing credit risk insurance to exporters as well as a number of national agencies that provide such a service for firms located in their countries. Credit risk insurance is available not only for open account transactions but also to cover risks involved if other payment methods are adopted such as payments against documents or even letters of credit. Frequently the global risk insurers will offer other services to their clients including credit risk assessment and debt collection.

When considering credit risk insurance, exporters need to be aware of a number of issues. These include what is covered by the policy, what is excluded, the obligations of the insured (the exporter) and the obligations of the insurance company. As with all insurance contracts it is absolutely necessary to read the fine print at the time of entering into the contract. Also, as with other types of insurance it is common practice for there to be an 'excess'. Only losses above the excess will be able to be claimed. Credit insurance companies have a variety of ways of calculating an excess and this can be negotiated at the time of taking out the policy. It is also common practice to set maximum limits for any one buyer and a maximum limit for all claims within a given time period. Because of the specific nature of credit risk insurance, it is also common to find limitations on the maximum terms of credit that can be extended to a buyer and maximum time limits for which the payment period can be extended before a claim is made.

## Case study

### Credit risk insurance

Atradius is a leading credit insurer with total revenues of around €1.8 billion and a 31% share of the world credit insurance market. It insures against non-payment and provides a comprehensive range of risk transfer, financing and trade receivables management services. With 4000 staff and more than 160 offices in 40 countries, Atradius has access to credit information on 52 million companies worldwide and makes more than 22 000 credit limit decisions daily. It is 'A' rated by Standard & Poor's and 'A2' by Moody's. Atradius has provided the following information in response to issues put by the author.

*The benefits that taking out credit risk insurance with Atradius can have for exporters dealing with EU firms and the matters that an exporter needs to consider before doing so*

Growing an international client base is an exciting and potentially lucrative opportunity but with that increased growth comes increased risk: transporting and delivering goods, currency fluctuations, language barriers, different business regulations, political and economic instability, dealing with unknown customers and debt defaults are some of the issues that face exporters.

There are a number of measures exporters can take in order to mitigate potential risk when dealing with EU and international customers.

The first step in risk mitigation is to get to know the target market and customers. Exporters can access general information on political, legal and regulatory conditions and gain introductions to potential business partners from local government agencies. They can also speak to their insuring agent or broker to seek advice on entering particular markets.

For a more detailed overview of a market or potential buyers, business intelligence experts with on-the-ground resources such as credit insurance companies can provide more specific information on the high-level economic drivers in each market, as well as gathering intelligence on individual buyers and their credit history. In many cases, these agencies can visit potential customers to add personal knowledge and interaction to publicly available data if an exporter cannot visit the potential buyer.

In addition to information gathering before selling, exporters need to protect both their goods while in transit and their cash flow to ensure they are paid and paid in reasonable time. Companies supplying goods overseas may choose cargo or marine insurance that covers potential damage or loss of goods while in transit. However, this does not insure companies against loss of business if a client chooses another supplier due to any damage or loss incurred in transit.

Credit insurance, or trade insurance, insures a business against customer insolvency and payment default. Businesses may choose to protect themselves for insolvency of the buyer and non-payment or payment default for both domestic and export trade. Research shows that overseas buyers may take up to anything from 27 to 80 days to pay for goods and services supplied. Each European country differs greatly in terms of their accepted payment terms so exporters should make themselves familiar with these. In addition, using credit insurance as protection against payment defaults can remove the worry from this waiting period.

As each European country has different commercial terms and practices, there is no one 'European' matter or issue that an exporter needs to consider; exporters should treat EU customers the same as any other international customer.

Importantly for exporters is the network of on-the-ground resources available through global credit insurance companies. This network can not only visit a potential customer and offer excellent local market knowledge including cultural and commercial traditions, it can also offer local debt collection services which may be very valuable for exporters dealing with a large number of different countries and separate political, legal and commercial risks in each market.

Typically, insurance costs less than half a per cent of a company's total insured sales and customers in European markets are well accustomed to working with partners who have credit insurance.

Insurance can also provide additional benefits to the bottom line by giving a business the ability to extend more credit to customers and expand sales without expanding risk. It can also allow them to use insured accounts receivable as collateral when negotiating better costs of financing your business.

*The information that an exporter needs to provide to Atradius if they decide to take out credit insurance to cover transactions to a firm in an EU country*

To take out credit insurance against customers in Europe, companies need to provide the following to Atradius:

- turnover and bad debt history for the last four years
- spread of risk – usually involves an aged receivable listing showing current clients' balances
- contractual terms of payment available to clients
- list of clients to be covered
- current recovery procedure, that is, debt chasing timeline.

*Variations in cover for different types of risk and different countries*

Companies can choose the level of protection to offset credit risks. The most common and widely accepted type of cover is 'Whole of Turnover'. This offers the most comprehensive coverage, protecting a client's whole ledger.

Atradius also offers a 'Named Risk' option where companies can choose which customers to protect against. For example, a company may choose to only cover their top ten trading partners or only those customers they perceive as high risk.

The final option is 'Single Risk' coverage. This protects companies to a minimum exposure of A$1 000 000.

Some countries may carry specific conditions such as letter of credit only; however these tend to be outside of Europe. Underwriters may also impose specific conditions to individual companies, that is, maximum terms of payment or shorter reporting of overdues on specific clients.

*The procedure that Atradius adopts in processing the exporter's application for credit risk insurance*

There are a number of things that are assessed in the application for credit insurance. These include:

- previous bad debt history
- spread of risk
- trade sector involved
- current payment performance on account ('Day Sales Outstanding')
- individual accounts being considered.

*Important information relating to claims*

To make a claim, companies need to provide the following:

- a copy of the invoices under the claim
- proof of delivery or confirmation of services performed
- a six-month statement of account so we can review the payment history
- proof of debt chasing up to the point of claim
- proof of insolvency, if applicable.

## FACTORING

Factoring is a further alternative for exporters wishing to protect against losses when sales are made on an open account or documents against acceptance basis. The process begins with the exporter agreeing with a factoring firm in their own country as to which debts the factor will agree to collect. This will involve the factoring firm liaising with a correspondent factoring firm in the buyer's country to assess the credit risk. If the factoring firm agrees to take on the debt collection, the exporter assigns the rights to payment to them and provides them the invoice for the goods after the goods have been shipped. The factor then takes on the risk of collecting the debt. The factoring firm will pay the exporter up to 80% of the value of the invoice upon presentation of it to them. The factoring firm then forwards the invoice to a correspondent firm in the buyer's country and that firm collects the invoice amount from the buyer. It then transmits the funds to the exporter's factoring firm and the exporter is paid the remaining amount due less the factoring firm's fees.

Factoring has significant advantages for the exporter in that they are able to receive a considerable portion of the funds from the sale immediately the goods are shipped. The website of Factors Chain International[8] suggests that the overall costs of factoring are lower than for letters of credit. It is also particularly useful for exporters selling into a number of EU countries because it is more frequently the case that the one correspondent factoring firm will cover debts on an EU-wide basis. However, there are a number of possible problems for the exporter. First, if a dispute exists between the exporter and the buyer relating to the quality of the goods, for example, then the factoring firm will not pay the balance of the money due until the dispute is resolved. The factoring firm in the buyer's country will often assist with this as it is in the interests of the factoring firm as well as the seller and buyer that disputes are resolved speedily. Second, factoring firms

[8] See <http://www.factors-chain.com>.

might not agree to take on debts from all buyers. Much will depend on their assessment of the risk to themselves. Third, while the costs and risks may be less than for letters of credit, the exporter has to wait to receive the balance of the funds due to them until they have been received by the exporter's factoring firm. Many factoring firms will agree that if this period exceeds 120 days then the exporter is guaranteed payment regardless of whether the factoring firm has received the funds.

## FOREIGN EXCHANGE RISK

As of 1 January 2008, the euro is the currency of 15 of the 27 members of the European Union. Those that have not yet adopted it include the UK, Denmark, Sweden, the Czech Republic, Slovakia, Hungary, Poland, Estonia, Lithuania, Latvia, Bulgaria and Romania.

In order to secure a sale, exporters entering into agreements with customers in the EU may find it necessary to have the contract amount stated in either euros or the currency of the customer's country. The risk that this poses for the exporter is that if their currency appreciates against the euro or other relevant currency between the date of contract and the date when payment is due, they may lose a considerable amount. This risk is present when there is a delay between the date that the contract amount is agreed and the date for payment and applies whether payment is by letter of credit, documentary collection or open account and is expressed in the currency of the buyer. With small profit margins, exchange rate losses can quickly erode the profit on any particular sale. On the other hand, exchange rate gains can also lead to greater profits for the exporter.

To illustrate this, Table 5.2 shows the highest and lowest amounts of US dollars, Canadian dollars, Australian dollars and Japanese yen that would have been required to purchase one euro during the period from 1 October 2007 to 31 December 2007.

The table shows that not only do various currencies tend to fluctuate quite widely against the euro but that each currency fluctuates somewhat independently. Thus a Canadian exporter who was receiving payment on 7 November 2007 for goods sold under an earlier contract for €1 million would receive CAD$1.34 million upon conversion into Canadian dollars on that day. Yet if the same exporter received payment on 4 December and converted to Canadian dollars that day they would receive CAD$1.49 million. Conversely if a Canadian businessperson was importing from an EU firm they would have needed more Canadian dollars to buy the goods on 4 December than they

*Table 5.2 Highest and lowest exchange rates for the euro during the period 1 October 2007 to 31 December 2007 for selected currencies*

| Currency | Highest value of currency to euro during 1 October to 31 December 2007 | Lowest value of currency to euro during 1 October to 31 December 2007 |
|---|---|---|
| US dollar | 1.41 (9 October) | 1.49 (26 November) |
| Canadian dollar | 1.34 (7 November) | 1.49 (4 December) |
| Australian dollar | 1.56 (31 October) | 1.70 (21 November) |
| Japanese yen | 160.4 (23 November) | 167.5 (11 October) |

Source: Table compiled from data supplied on the website <www.x-rates.com>.

would have needed on 7 November. The same applies in the case of the Australian and US currencies due to the international strengthening of the euro at this time against these currencies. However, the table shows that the euro actually weakened against the yen during this time and accordingly Japanese exporters and importers would have been in the reverse position to those from the other three countries in terms of exchange rate gains and losses for earlier negotiated contracts.

In order to obtain some certainty about the amount that they will receive when time for payment arrives, exporters use a variety of currency hedging techniques to guard against exchange rate movements. The simplest of these is the forward exchange contract. A forward exchange contract allows the exporter to obtain, in advance, the rate at which they will buy currency at the time that payment is due. From the exporter's point of view, a simple forward contract is intended to guard against their own currency appreciating against the contract currency. Thus the risk with forward contracts is that if the exporter's currency depreciates in the period between the date of contact and the date for payment, the exporter would have been better off not entering into a forward exchange contract. Table 5.2 shows that the Australian, Canadian and US currencies mentioned actually depreciated against the euro during the period under consideration. Thus, taking out a forward exchange contract would not have been to the exporter's advantage during that period. On the other hand, exporters from Japan would have benefited from taking out a forward exchange contract because their currency apprenticed against the euro.

There are a variety of other hedging instruments that can protect an exporter whether their currency moves either favourably or adversely to them between the date of contract and the payment date. These include open dated forward contracts, currency options, flexible forwards and participating forwards. An explanation of these various hedging techniques can be found at <www.tdcommercialbanking.com>. Exporters' banks are most often in the best position to advise as to the most appropriate type of hedging instrument for any particular transaction or series of transactions.

# 6 Sales to the EU using an EU representative

## INTRODUCTION

MANY FIRMS exporting goods to the EU find it beneficial to have a representative in one or more of its member countries. How many representatives and where they are located will depend upon the market that the exporter has found for its goods. The most common types of representative are agents and distributors. Agents act on behalf of the exporter to find customers for the goods or services being sold. Those customers then contract directly with the exporter as in a direct export transaction. The agent receives a commission for having found the customer and carrying out other duties that the agreement between the agent and the exporter might specify. Distributors, on the other hand, buy directly from the exporter and then on-sell to end customers. Because there is a long-term relationship between the exporter and the distributor, there is often a master agreement between them setting out the obligations of each and usually the terms of sale for the ongoing shipments of goods.

It should now be apparent that all of the issues covered in the previous chapters relating to contract terms, delivery obligations, transport, customs and payment when an exporter sells directly to a customer in an EU country will also be applicable in agency and distribution arrangements. In the case of agency, while the agent finds customers for the exporter, the agent will most often refer the customer on to the exporter for the final negotiation of the contract of sale. Each contract of sale with a customer found by the agent will need to include terms regarding the delivery of the goods and the transport of the goods and will involve either the customer or the exporter arranging customs clearance. In the case of a distribution agreement, the exporter's master agreement with the distributor also needs to include provisions relating to the delivery of the goods, their transport, and clearance of the goods through customs. Because distributors in the EU tend to have considerable bargaining power in relation to smaller exporters from outside the EU, an exporter may often be faced with a situation where they will have to accept terms requiring them to deliver the goods to the distributor's warehouse within the EU. Thus the exporter will be confronted with all of the issues raised in the previous chapter.

This chapter begins with some observations on the usefulness of having an EU representative. It then proceeds with a discussion of the general considerations involved in selecting an agent or distributor. Many of the factors to be considered are common to both arrangements. Where there are some factors that are peculiar to either arrangement, this will be indicated. The chapter then discusses the main terms that an exporter is likely to want to include in an agency agreement and the limitations that Directive 86/653/EEC[1] (referred to in this chapter as the 'Commercial Agency Directive') imposes on the types of obligations that an exporter can require of an agent in the EU. This directive dates from 1986 and is required to be implemented by all EU member countries in their laws that deal with commercial agents. It therefore applies to actions of agents within all member countries. This is followed by a section dealing with the impact of EU competition laws on agency agreements.

The chapter then makes some observations about the provisions that an exporter will want to include in a distribution agreement, emphasising those provisions that differ from an agency agreement. The final section of the chapter deals with distribution agreements and more particularly the restraints that EU competition laws impose on them. EU competition laws are enshrined in the EU Treaty and are aimed at preventing anti-competitive arrangements as well as curbing abuse of a dominant position. In many cases smaller exporters from outside of the EU will not be greatly affected by these laws. The reasons for this will be made clear in the discussion.

## WHY APPOINT A REPRESENTATIVE FOR THE EU MARKET?

The first issue that concerns exporters is whether to appoint a representative for the entire EU market or to divide the market among a number of

[1] [1986] OJ L382/17.

representatives. It has already been noted that one of the overriding objectives of the European Commission is the achievement of a single market for goods. However, major differences remain from country to country and region to region in terms of consumer tastes and preferences and in terms of the degree to which there may be competing products to those of an outside exporter. After having undertaken the relevant market research, an exporter may find that only one or two countries within the EU represent potential markets for their product range. Accordingly, if an EU representative is to be appointed, then to achieve the best results the representative should be based within the country where the market for the goods exists or at least be very familiar with the relevant competing products within that market. If it is considered that there may be several countries in which the product might sell, the exporter is then faced with a choice of either appointing one representative for the entire market or alternatively segmenting the market and appointing different representatives for each segment. This is often a key decision for an exporter and underlines the importance of thorough market research.

The second issue concerns the logistical advice and assistance that a representative can provide. A representative familiar with EU transport providers and costs as well as the various national and EU-wide regulations that apply to the product can boost the profits of exporters to a greater degree than the costs involved in having that representative. In all likelihood, the sales representative appointed by the exporter will not be able to handle any customs clearance issues that need to be resolved given that customs agents tend to specialise in this area. However, a knowledgeable agent can give advice about which customs agents have expertise in relation to the product in question.

A third reason for appointing a representative, whether agent or distributor, is the ongoing knowledge that the representative can provide about competing products and how the exporter might best tailor their product range to meet the competition. The expansion of the EU market in recent years to effectively 30 countries and the diversity of those countries have significantly increased the competitiveness of the overall market in global terms. The multilateral agreements that the EU is in the process of negotiating with the Mediterranean countries and other bilateral deals will only increase the competitive pressure. Thus, as the single market policy becomes more widespread, it is to be expected that local producers will have significant advantages over those from outside. This means that exporters need every assistance in order to meet not only the high level of internal competition but also other competing products from outside of the EU. The appointment of a knowledgeable and diligent representative can therefore reduce the risk of failure in the market.

## SELECTING AN AGENT OR DISTRIBUTOR

Selecting the right representative is an all-important step for the exporter. While most prudent exporters enter into formal agreements with their chosen representatives, it can be argued that no agreement can substitute for a carefully cultivated relationship based upon trust. The following discussion provides an explanation of some of the issues that need to be considered.

Most exporters will aim to find a representative who has some experience within the relevant industry. This is important not only in terms of the representative's ability to locate customers for the product but also in terms of the representative being able to provide accurate advice about competing products and relevant regulations affecting the entry of the product into the EU.

Following on from this is the reputation of the representative within the industry. This is much harder to establish but a prudent exporter will want to be satisfied that the representative will be able to keep trade secrets and intellectual property rights related to the product confidential. Additionally, it is useful to establish if the representative has shown commitment in terms of selling the products of firms that they might have represented in the past and provided adequate after-sales service if required. It would also be useful to know if the proposed representative has been engaged in any litigation arising out of their duties as representative for prior principals.

The business capability of the representative needs to be assessed to ensure that they have adequate staff, financial capability and record-keeping systems to be able to deal with customer requests and advise the exporter in a timely manner of updated sales and product information.

In the case of a representative who is a distributor, the financial strength of the distributor is important to the exporter because the distributor may well be the exporter's biggest customer. If the distributor encounters financial difficulties, this may well place the exporter in financial difficulties as well. Closely tied to this is the logistics capability of the distributor. Distributors commonly sell to retail outlets. If their distribution systems are not well managed and their customers not well served in a timely manner, this may lead to those customers going elsewhere with the consequent adverse effect on the exporter's business.

# Case study

## Using a distributor to sell into the EU market

Ozkleen is a family-owned business producing cleaning products. Its well-known brands include Shower Power (Bath Power in the UK), Shower Power Pine, Carpet Power, Pre-wash Power, Grease Monkey, Power Wipes, Power Cloth, Oven Power and Drycleaners Secret. The philosophy behind its market-leading product, Shower Power, was to develop a product that was technologically superior to its rivals, environmentally friendly, user-friendly, contained no chlorine, required no scrubbing and had a pleasant fragrance.

The company commenced operations in 1995 and full distribution was achieved in Australia in 1997. By October 1997, Shower Power was ranked the number one household cleaner in Australia. In 1998, the company commenced planning to enter the export market, targeting the UK first. The company received considerable assistance from the Queensland Government Office in London in developing its initial strategy and making contacts. By 2000, it had its product on the supermarket shelves of Sainsbury, followed quickly by Tesco, also in 2000, and Waitrose, in 2001. It has subsequently been successful in having its product placed on the shelves of Carrefour, France's leading supermarket chain and a global player in the supermarket business.

The Ozkleen experience in entering the EU market provides valuable insights into the process of achieving sustained sales of the product there. These include the need for a successful distributor; the role that a representative of the exporting company located in Europe can play; the financial and managerial commitment required when exporting into the European market; and the extremely competitive yet segmented nature of this market. Each of these matters is dealt with in more detail below.

### *The need for a successful distributor*

Without a successful distributor it is almost impossible to get products onto supermarket shelves. Supermarkets are often reluctant to deal with individual product suppliers, preferring to deal with the larger distributors in order to reduce the number of their suppliers; they may elect to consolidate suppliers. In addition, supermarkets are reluctant to stock any more than three or four brands of competing products and it is often necessary to wait until one of the existing product lines drops out before there is a chance for a new entrant. Consequently, the choice of a distributor that has considerable power and good relations with supermarket chains is vital.

Ozkleen first engaged a distributor for the UK market in 1998. The distributor was one of the UK's largest distributors and dealt in no competing products to those produced by Ozkleen. Despite its large size, the distributor ran into financial troubles in 2005 due to intense competition within the distribution sector. This was a setback for Ozkleen but the success of its products made the search for a new distributor easier. A new approach was adopted and a distributor was chosen that specialised in the non-food household sector and had excellent connections with supermarket chains but at the same time did not handle products directly competing with Ozkleen's range. This experience demonstrates that an exporter must be flexible enough and have sufficient financial commitment to be able to withstand difficulties with distributors that often arise quite independently of the exporter's control regardless of the care which has been taken in their initial selection.

### *The need for a representative of the exporter in the EU*

Many exporters might think once a distributor has been found then all marketing matters will be seen to by the distributor. However, the Ozkleen experience demonstrates the opposite. A representative of the exporting company is often necessary to ensure success in the EU market. First, it may not always be easy to convince a distributor to take on a company's product and, second, the company itself, rather than the distributor, often has to be involved in marketing the product. Having an Ozkleen representative in Europe has performed a vital role in both of these tasks.

In the UK, the opportunity for accessing supermarkets came when one of the competing products was no longer stocked by the supermarket. A clever marketing campaign was launched by Ozkleen by getting members of the public to trial the Ozkleen product and have them contact the supermarket requesting that it be stocked. Still, supermarkets were not that easily convinced. It was necessary for the Ozkleen representative and the distributor to convince the supermarkets that it was worthwhile for them to stock the product on the basis that consumers demanded it and it would provide a healthy rate of sales along with a decent margin.

In terms of marketing the product, Ozkleen has found it necessary to market directly. Supermarkets tend to change their range of products quickly if a product is not performing. Ozkleen has undertaken television advertising campaigns both in France and the UK. While filming in Europe is extremely expensive, the costs have been kept down by recruiting people to volunteer to be in the television advertisements based on their experience with using the products.

### *Financial and management commitment*

Too frequently exporters have the view that if a distributor is appointed, exporting costs will be kept to a minimum and stocks that are surplus to the domestic market can easily be disposed of by the overseas distributor. The Ozkleen experience belies this view. First, there has been a significant commitment of management time and expense in sustaining an in-country presence in Europe to first of all get the product into the supermarkets and then to maintain and increase sales. Without these efforts and attention, success in supermarkets would have been unlikely. Second, the terms of sale that exporters must accept both from distributors and supermarkets are generally not advantageous. Distributors will generally require exporters to use 'Delivered Duty Paid' incoterms, thus requiring exporters to clear goods for customs at the EU end. Ozkleen initially used a customs agent but, in order to get goods delivered to replenish stocks so that strict supermarket delivery deadlines could be met, turned to DHL, a major logistics provider that could handle all aspects of the transport and customs clearance procedures. Supermarkets insist that 99% of their requests for product must be met on time. Retaining a logistics company that can meet these demands involves significant costs to the exporter, and care has to be taken when adding these costs to the cost of production to maintain the products' competitiveness.

Transport and production costs are not recovered quickly when supplying supermarkets. Exporters will frequently have to wait for payment from the distributor until after the distributor has been paid by the supermarket and are thus out of pocket in the meantime. This can be a considerable cost given that transport time from Australia to the EU can be around 8–9 weeks and 9–13 weeks of stock are generally required by the distributor at all times to meet supermarket demands. In addition, some supermarkets will require that a set minimum of a product be sold and will adjust their payments if such minimum is not reached.

*A competitive and segmented market*

It has been noted above that the success of the product in the UK was, in itself, insufficient to convince French supermarkets to stock the product and separate campaigns had to be launched in France. In addition, labelling and packaging has to not only meet language requirements but must be tailored to suit nuances of the particular market. In the case of France, this required a greater appeal to the environmental attributes of the product.

The market for those goods produced by Ozkleen is a very competitive one. While the company has its trademark registered in all countries throughout Europe, it has faced attempts to trade off its successful use of the word 'power' for its products and has also found that its successful marketing strategies are now being copied by some competitors. The role of the company's representative in Europe is therefore an essential one in terms of anticipating and dealing with competitive threats. Such matters cannot normally be left to distributors alone.

## APPOINTING AN AGENT

When entering into an agreement with a prospective agent in EU member countries, an exporter needs to be aware of the Commercial Agency Directive[2] which contains several mandatory provisions that are likely to apply to the agreement. At the outset it needs to be noted that the directive provides that either party can ask the other for a statement in writing of the terms of the agreement[3] and, accordingly, most exporters appointing agents tend to have a formal written agreement. The following discusses the common terms that are included in agency agreements and how those terms are affected by the Commercial Agency Directive. Decided cases are used to illustrate the points made.

## PARTIES TO THE AGREEMENT

Representatives who are intending to act as agents are usually careful to insist that the agreement between them and the exporter contains a term that specifically states that the representative will be a 'commercial agent'.

[2] Ibid.
[3] Article 13.

The Commercial Agency Directive sets out the characteristics of a commercial agent in Articles 1 and 2. In summary, Article 1 states that a commercial agent is a 'self-employed intermediary who has continuing authority to negotiate the sale or the purchase of goods on behalf of another person (the principal) or to negotiate and conclude such transactions on behalf of the principal'.[4]

Article 2 states that representatives who are not paid for their services are not considered commercial agents. Commercial agents operating on commodity exchanges or in the commodity market are also excluded from the definition. Article 2 allows member states to provide in their legislation implementing the directive that if a representative's activities as a commercial agent are considered to be 'secondary', then they will not be considered to be commercial agents in that member state. It is therefore important to check the legislation implementing the directive in the member state in which the agent is to be appointed in those cases where the representative will perform other activities for the principal other than what is normally considered to be agency activities – as defined above.

There have been a number of cases where representatives have sought to bring themselves within the definition of 'commercial agents' in order to attract the other provisions of the directive, particularly the one relating to compensation upon termination of the agreement. However, the courts have taken the approach that they will look beyond the words used by the parties in their agreement to the actual facts concerning the relationship.

In *Blanc Canet v Europecar* [2005] ECC 34, the representative's agreement stated that she was an 'independent commercial agent' on behalf of Europecar. However, on an examination of the facts, the court found that she was not able to negotiate contracts on behalf of Europecar, did not carry out her activities independently and could not enter into contracts on Europecar's behalf. Consequently, despite the wording used, she could not be considered a commercial agent in terms of the directive.

In *Smith v Reliance Water Control* [2004] ECC 38, the plaintiff Smith requested the defendant that he be permitted to cease his employment with the defendant and became a commercial agent instead. The reason for the plaintiff's request was that, as an employee, child support payments could be deducted automatically from his salary. Such was not the case with commission payments made under an agency agreement. The lower court took a dim view of the plaintiff's motives in converting his relationship from one of employee to one of commercial agency and refused to

[4] Commercial Agency Directive, Article 1(2).

find that he was a commercial agent. On appeal Smith was successful. The appeal court said that it was necessary to look at all of the facts of the relationship regardless of the motive. The court found that the agreement provided that Smith had a sales target that had to be met; he had a 'no competition clause' in his agreement; he had to ensure adequate margins for any sales that he negotiated on the company's behalf; he had to regularly provide information about his activities to the defendant; and he had to follow up any leads that the defendant gave to him regarding potential customers. He was paid a commission of 4.5% and the commission was paid within two weeks of the sale being made. In essence, most of the common terms of an agency agreement were found in his agreement with the defendant.

In *Mercantile International Group PLC v Chuan Soon Huat Industrial Group Limited* [2003] ECC 28, the claimant was the sole representative of the Singaporean defendant for the UK for over 20 years. The claimant entered into contracts as 'agent' for the defendant and the original agreement between them had been entitled an 'agency agreement'. The practice of the parties was that the claimant would enter into agreements with customers on behalf of the defendant but would charge the customers a higher price than the claimant notified to the defendant. The defendant was aware of this practice. The claimant was not paid a commission. Its sole basis of remuneration was the difference between the prices it charged customers and the amount that it notified to the defendant as the sales figure. Upon termination of the agreement, the claimant asked for damages. The question was whether it was a 'commercial agent'. The court found that regardless of the fact that different prices were charged to customers than were notified to the defendant and regardless that there was no commission as such, the claimant was still a commercial agent as defined in the commercial agent's directive. However, representatives will not always be successful in claiming that their relationship is truly one of agency even if they are paid a commission. For example, in *AMB Imballagi Plastici v Pacflex Limited* [2003] ECC 381, the court found that the true relationship between the parties was that the claimant actually bought the goods from the defendant and on-sold them to customers. Although the claimant was paid commissions, the nature of the relationship was more akin to a distributorship than an agency.

Thus, the cases make it clear that courts will look at all of the circumstances of the parties' relationship before deciding whether the relationship is in fact one of commercial agency within the definitions provided within the Commercial Agency Directive.

## AGENT'S BASIC OBLIGATIONS

Article 3 of the Commercial Agency Directive provides that a commercial agent must 'look after his principal's interests and act dutifully and in good faith'. In particular, the agent must make proper efforts on the principal's behalf in negotiating transactions (or, if authorised, entering into transactions), must make all necessary information available to the principal and comply with the principal's reasonable instructions. Article 5 of the directive states that the parties cannot derogate from the basic obligations as stated in Article 3.

It is advisable to fill out these obligations in more detail with specific provisions such as, for example, what must be communicated to the principal and what constitutes proper efforts on the principal's behalf. It is also advisable for the parties to make it clear that the agent cannot enter into contracts on the principal's behalf but merely negotiate and refer potential customers on to the principal. Such a provision is in the interests of both parties because under continental EU law, if an agent enters into a contract with a customer and does not disclose the fact that they are acting as an agent, then the agent themselves will be liable to the customer and the customer also will only have rights against the agent. This type of provision is even more significant under UK law because, in the absence of such a provision, if an agent acts on behalf of an undisclosed principal but acts otherwise within the scope of their authority, then the customer may elect to either claim against the agent or against the principal if the contract is not fulfilled.

## PRINCIPAL'S BASIC OBLIGATIONS

The primary obligation of the principal is to pay the agent commission. This is discussed in more detail below. However, Article 4 of the Commercial Agency Directive also provides that a principal must act dutifully and in good faith. In particular, the principal must assist the agent by producing all documentation relating to the goods so that the agent is able to carry out their sales obligations. In addition the principal must inform the agent within a reasonable time of the acceptance or rejection of orders passed on by the agent to the principal. Agents may well wish to see a clause included in the agreement that extends this obligation by stating that the principal cannot unreasonably refuse to accept orders.

Article 4 also contains a somewhat unusual provision in that it requires the principal to advise the agent if the principal has reason to believe that there is likely to be a significant decrease in the volume of transactions that the agent could normally have expected to occur. Failure to advise the agent will amount to a breach of the agreement and may lead to termination by the agent. Along with the other obligations in Article 4, this obligation is reinforced by the fact that Article 5 provides that the parties are not able to derogate from any of the obligations in Article 4.

## TERRITORY AND PRODUCTS

It is usual for the parties to agree on the specific products for which the agent will arrange sales on behalf of the principal and the geographic territory in which the agent is responsible for arranging those sales. Provision needs to be made in agency agreements for cases where the principal develops new products and whether those can be sold directly by the principal into the agent's territory or whether they will automatically be added to the list of products that the agent can sell on behalf of the principal.

## COMMISSION

One of the key objectives of the Commercial Agency Directive is to protect the rights of commercial agents. An examination of the provisions in the directive relating to commission and compensation for termination make this apparent. This section examines the provisions relating to commission while a later section looks at termination payments. Articles 6–12 of the directive relate to commission. The issues covered in these articles include the agent's basic right to remuneration; transactions concluded during the term of the agency for which the agent is entitled to commission; transactions concluded after the termination of the agency for which the agent may be entitled to commission; and when commission becomes due and when it has to be paid.

Article 6 of the directive provides that 'any part of the remuneration (of the agent) which varies with the number or value of business transactions shall be deemed commission'. It is usual for the parties to have specific provisions in their agreement that set out the formula for calculating commission. It is possible for the parties to either have a set rate of commission or to vary the rate of commission depending on the volume of sales in total or the volume of sales to specific customers. In the absence of specific provisions relating to the rate of commission, Article 6 provides that, subject to individual member countries' laws about the level of remuneration, the commission will be calculated in accordance with industry standards or, if none, on the basis of what is reasonable.

Article 7 of the directive provides that an agent is entitled to commission where the transaction has been concluded as a result of his action or where the principal concludes a transaction with a customer that the agent has previously found for the principal. This is subject to the range of products as covered by the agreement. The second part of Article 7 refers specifically to the agent's territorial rights to customers. It provides that when implementing the directive, member states must specify in their legislation that commercial agents are entitled to commission on one of two bases. Either the agent is always entitled to commission if he is entrusted with a specific geographical area or group of customers, or the agent is only so entitled if he has an exclusive right to a specific geographical area or group of customers. Thus, when drawing up the terms of agency agreements for agents in a particular country, it is necessary to check the legislation for that country implementing the directive to see if agents only have an automatic right to commission if they are appointed on an exclusive basis or if they have an automatic entitlement whether or not the word 'exclusive' is used.

Article 8 provides that the agent will also be entitled to commission on transactions concluded after the termination of the agency if the transaction has resulted from the agent's efforts during the life of the agency relationship and if the transaction occurs within a reasonable time after the conclusion of the agency relationship. It may be advisable to be more specific about what amounts to 'reasonable time' when drawing up agency agreements. Article 9 adds to the provisions of Article 8 by stating that a new commercial agent in the territory will not be entitled to commission on any transaction that results in payments to the previous agent.

Article 10 provides that commission becomes due either when the principal has executed the transaction or should have executed the transaction in accordance with his agreement with the third party or the customer has executed the transaction. Thus commission is payable both in cases where the transaction has been completed and where it would have been completed if the principal had not defaulted. Article 11 makes this even clearer by stating that the right to commission can only be extinguished if it is established that the contract between the principal and the customer will not be executed and the principal is not to blame. These provisions are clearly to protect the agent's rights to be remunerated for the work done in negotiating a transaction which falls over through the fault of the principal. Transactions which fall over as a result of the customer are not protected. This is because the agent should take responsibility for the selection of customers and if a bad choice is made the agent should not be entitled to be remunerated because if it.

The timing for the payment of commission is no later than the last day of the month following the quarter in which it became due. Article 12 requires principals to give agents a statement of all commission no later than the last day for the payment of commission. The agent is entitled to be provided by the principal with all information to enable them to check how the commission has been calculated. The directive does not specify whether the commission is calculated according to the net price of the goods (excluding transport costs if paid by the principal) or whether it is the full amount of the transaction. When drafting an agency agreement this point needs to be clarified by specifying which price shall form the basis for the payment of commission.

Many exporters may commence agency relationships within the EU with an appointment of an agent for only one country. This may lead to a situation where customers outside of the territory find out about the product and make contact with the agent. This issue needs to be clarified in agency agreements so that the agent is compensated for their expansion of the principal's business in those instances while at the same time allowing the principal the right to develop this business themselves and maintain the freedom to appoint another agent for that other territory if need be.

## MINIMUM SALES TARGET

It is usual to include a provision in the agreement that requires the agent to reach a certain performance level. This can either be in terms of a minimum sales volume in terms of quantity, a minimum sales amount in monetary terms or a minimum number of customers. It is a matter for the parties to decide what performance level is acceptable. However, as noted below, attempts by a principal to terminate agency agreements for failure to reach minimum targets will be examined closely by the courts to determine if this arose due to the failure of the agent to adequately carry out their duties or for reasons over which the agent has little control.

## REPORTING REQUIREMENTS

While there is a general obligation on the part of agents to act diligently and in the best interests of the principal, it is useful to also specify the type of matters that must be reported to the principal to allow the principal to make an assessment of the agent's performance of their duties. These might include updates on competing products in the territory, changes in regulations that affect the product, or general market conditions within the territory.

### ADVERTISING AND PROMOTION OBLIGATIONS

The parties must decide which of them is responsible for the promotion of the products within the agent's territory, who will produce any promotional material and who will be responsible for the costs of doing so. With highly technical products it is likely that the principal will wish to produce all promotional material themselves to avoid any possibility of misrepresentation occurring in relation to the products. If the agent is to produce promotional material, then the principal will want to be assured that any trademarks used in it will be used correctly.

### CONFIDENTIALITY

When negotiating agency agreements, it is frequently necessary for the principal to divulge considerable information about their product to ensure that the agent has the capability to sell it. Since there is no formal agency agreement in place at this stage, it may be necessary for the principal and the prospective agent to enter into a confidentiality agreement requiring the potential agent to keep confidential any information that the principal has disclosed during negotiations. It is also usual to include in the formal agency agreement an obligation on the agent not to divulge to others or seek to appropriate to themselves the intellectual property of the principal.

### NO COMPETITION

If the agent is representing competing products to those of the principal on behalf of some other party, the agent is likely to find themselves in a conflict of interest situation and will be unable to adequately carry out their duties to act in the best interests of either of the principals for whom they are acting as representative. For this reason it is usual to provide that the agent cannot represent competing products to those of the principal without the principal's formal agreement. In order to ensure the effectiveness of such a clause, it will be necessary to define carefully those products for which the agent is responsible. It may also be necessary to have the agent declare in the agreement the range of other products for which they currently act as representative on behalf of other parties. However, if the agent is precluded from representing any other products of any kind for any other principal, it may lead to the conclusion that the agency is simply a part of the principal's business located in the country concerned. This may lead to tax authorities deciding that the principal has a permanent establishment in that territory and imposing tax on any profits made in that territory. In addition, it is possible that such an arrangement might lead to the agency not being considered a 'genuine agency' for the purposes of the block exemption for vertical agreements discussed below.

## DELEGATION

Implicit in the selection and appointment of a particular agent by a principal is the understanding that the agent will act personally and not delegate their functions or assign the obligations and rights under the agreement to some other firm. Accordingly, there is frequently a provision in agency agreements that only allows the appointment of sub-agents, delegation to another firm or assignment of the agency with the express permission of the principal.

## DURATION OF THE AGENCY AGREEMENT

The parties can decide to have an agency for a fixed term or for an indefinite term. Where an agency for a fixed term expires but the arrangement continues on an informal basis, Article 14 of the Commercial Agency Directive deems the agency to be converted into one for an indefinite term. In *RII Diffusion v Relais Informatique Diffusion Sarl Compain* [2005] ECC 21, an agency agreement that stated that it 'continues from year to year unless three months notice is given' was held to be an agency for an indefinite term.

## TERMINATION OF THE AGENCY AGREEMENT

Termination can occur in two situations. The first is where neither party is at fault and simply wishes to terminate the arrangement. In this case, if the agency is terminated by the principal, then compensation may be payable to the agent – see below. The second is where there has been a breach of the agreement by one of the parties and the other wants to terminate it.

Turning first to the situation where there is no breach by either party, if the agency agreement is for a fixed term it will expire at the end of that term. An agency agreement for an indefinite term may be terminated by either party provided that notice is given. The period of notice required is set out in Article 15 of the Commercial Agency Directive. Essentially, the notice period is on a sliding scale, being one month if terminated during the first year of the contract, two months if terminated during the second year and three months if terminated during the third year. The parties cannot contract out of these periods of notice. Member states are able to provide in their implementing legislation for continuation of notice periods on this sliding scale for agreements that have been in existence up to six years. Periods of notice to be given by the principal cannot be shorter than those required of the agent. In order that commissions due can be calculated in accordance with the provisions on commission, the end of the notice period must occur at the end of a calendar month.

The second situation in which an agency agreement can be terminated is where there has been a breach by one of the parties. Article 16 of the Commercial Agency Directive makes it clear that nothing in the directive shall affect member countries' laws regarding termination of the agency agreement for breach or termination of the agreement because of exceptional circumstances. Because the directive is not more specific than that and because individual countries' laws vary slightly in relation to termination for breach of contract, it is advisable when drafting agency agreements to spell out in detail the type of circumstances that will allow termination. These are often couched in terms of a breach of the 'fundamental' or substantial obligations of the agent or of the principal and those obligations considered fundamental are frequently listed. However, the case of *Laboratories Arkopharma SA v Gravier* [2003] ECC 33 discussed below suggests that such an attempt might not always be effective.

It comes as no surprise that there have been a number of cases on the point of whether the agent has committed a breach significant enough to allow for termination by the principal. Several of these cases revolve around the question of the principal's rights to terminate the agreement because of an agent's failure to achieve results. An analysis of the cases tends to suggest that the courts are somewhat reluctant to deny an agent's rights to compensation in line with the intent of the directive which is to protect agents.

In *Laboratoires Arkopharma SA v Gravier* [2003] ECC 33, the issue was the termination of the agreement for alleged 'serious misconduct' of the agent. The agency agreement had defined 'serious misconduct' as, among other things, failing to achieve minimum targets. The principal argued that the parties should be free to determine what defined 'serious misconduct' and the court should be prepared to give effect to their intentions. However, the court took the position that it was not up to the parties to decide what serious misconduct was but that the court should decide this in all of the circumstances. The court affirmed that in the circumstances of this case that failure to meet targets did not amount to serious misconduct and, further, that attempting to define it in such a way offended the relevant French law and was therefore null and void. A similar decision was reached in the case of *Re an Agreement to Exclude an Agent's Right to Compensation* [1992] EEC 238 where the court also took the view that it is a matter for the court to decide whether failure to reach sales targets was sufficient to entitle the principal to terminate the agreement for breach. Further, it may well be the case that the principal bears the onus of proof if they want to terminate on these grounds. In *Accodim Sarl v Establissements Rabaud* [1992] ECC 82, the principal argued that the agent breached the agreement because it did not obtain results. The agent claimed that its failure to do so was because of economic circumstances existing at the time. In upholding the agent's appeal, the court said that it was up to the principal to prove that the failure to perform was in fact the agent's fault and in this case the principal had failed to do this.

However, in the case of *Scandia Diffusion Sarl v Sopenkorpi* [1990] ECC 159, the court found that where an agent's sales had fallen by half from one year to the next, an important customer had been lost and the agent had failed to represent the principal at trade fairs and canvass customers, then the principal was within its rights to terminate the agency agreement by restricting the agent's territory without payment of compensation.

The question of what amounts to a termination was addressed in *Cooper v Pure Fishing (UK) Limited* [2005] ECC 6. Here the plaintiff had acted as an agent for the defendant for the sale of fishing gear. The arrangement was an ongoing one with renewal of contracts every six months. The agent also acted for another principal but the products of that firm did not compete with those of the defendant. The defendant brought out a new range of fishing gear and the plaintiff refused to sell it because of the conflict with its other agency arrangement. The defendant refused to renew the agent's contract on the basis that the agent was in breach of their agreement because they refused to sell the new product range. The plaintiff argued that the failure to renew amounted to a termination for which they were entitled to compensation. The court found for the plaintiff because it was of the view that a failure to renew cannot be described as equivalent to a termination for breach.

## COMPENSATION FOR TERMINATION

Article 17 of the Commercial Agency Directive requires member states to include in their implementing legislation either a right to an indemnity for the agent upon termination of the agency or a right to compensation. 'Termination' is likely to include the expiry of a fixed-term contract. The UK has interpreted the provisions as meaning that member states must, at *a minimum*, include either the indemnity basis or the compensation basis. Because of its interpretation, the UK allows both alternatives. Parties can choose which of these is to apply in their agency agreements. If no choice is made the compensation basis will apply. Article 18 provides that compensation will not be payable where the termination was for breach of the agreement by the agent.

Where member states have elected to include the right to an indemnity, the directive does not state how much the indemnity should be but rather gives guidelines as to how it should be determined. The amount of the indemnity should take into account the extent to which the agent has brought in new business and improved existing business relationships along with what is equitable having regard to the amount of the commission that the agent will lose because of the termination. In any case, the amount of the indemnity should not exceed one year's commission. In addition to obtaining an indemnity, the agent is also entitled to seek damages if the agency has been wrongfully terminated. However, if the member state has elected the compensation basis for determining how much the agent should receive, then the court cannot use the indemnity basis. In *DSR Senator Agency v Maritime Union Sud Oeust* [2003] ECC 27, the agent asked for a termination payment based on the number of customers he had brought to the principal's business. A lower court had allowed compensation to be calculated on this basis. However, on appeal, the appellate court said that because France had adopted the compensation basis for calculating termination payments, it could not use the number of customers in assessing the compensation that the agent should receive.

Where member states have elected to provide a right to compensation for termination, then the compensation is to be assessed in accordance with the damages that the agent has suffered as result of the termination. Guidelines are given as to how the amount should be calculated. Article 17(3) provides that damage shall be deemed to occur particularly when termination takes place in circumstances leading to deprivation of the agent of commission that they otherwise would have received but for the termination. Damages will also include the extent to which the agent has been unable to recoup the costs that they have incurred in setting up their agency business on behalf of the principal.

In the case of *King v Tunnock Limited* [2001] ECC 6, the appellant had been a commercial agent of the defendant for the sale of cakes and biscuits for many years. The appellant's father had held the agency business before him. The respondent principal went out of that line of business and therefore terminated the agency relationship. They argued that because they had now gone out of that line of business the agent would not suffer a loss of commission in the future and therefore no compensation was payable. However, the court found that at the time of termination the agency had considerable commercial value mainly attributable to the goodwill built up by the agent and his father. Accordingly, the court assessed the damages as being equivalent to the last two years of commission. The court made it clear that Article 17 does not state that damages can only be assessed with regard to future loss of commissions. The court seemed to take the view that the use of the words 'particularly when the termination takes place' does not preclude other means of assessing damages. The quantification of the damages was very much in line with the approach of French courts that tend to adopt compensation equivalent to two years of commission based on the average of the last three years of commission as the basis for calculating damages.

However, in *Ingmar GB Limited v Eaton Leonard Inc* [2002] ECC 5, the English High Court declined to follow the French method for assessing compensation because it would result in 'an injustice to the defendants and an excessive windfall to the claimants way above the value of the agency'[5] and instead assessed compensation on the basis of 'the length of time of the agency (eight years), the inevitable lack of profitability in the early years, the high degree of engineering and sales expertise required in obtaining, nurturing and developing the customer base and the degree of profitability of the agency at the time of its rupture'.[6] The end result was an award of approximately £183 000 as opposed to an award of £211 000 which would have been the figure under the French method. This departure from the French method was followed in *Lonsdale v Howard and Hallem* [2007] UKHL 32.

[5] [2002] ECC 5 at 11.
[6] Ibid.

Regardless of which alternative has been adopted by member states, the agent shall not lose their right to compensation if the agency is terminated by the death of the agent or where termination by the agent is justified by age, ill health or infirmity and that because of this, they are no longer able to carry on their business as agent. However, it is the responsibility of the agent to prove that it was in fact their ill health, age or infirmity that led them to terminate. In *Exbanor SA v Patrigeon* [2005] ECC 35, the agent failed to advise the principal of their ill health at the time of termination and was denied compensation. Agents must make a claim for an indemnity or compensation within one year of the termination of the agency. Article 18(1) of the Commercial Agency Directive makes it very clear that if the principal has grounds to terminate the agency because of a breach by the agent, then no indemnity or compensation will be payable. Article 19 provides that the parties cannot derogate from the provisions of Articles 17 and 18 to the detriment of the agent. For this reason, standard agency agreements tend to follow closely the provisions of Articles 17 and 18 in that part of the agreement that relates to compensation for termination.

## RESTRAINT OF TRADE

After termination of an agency relationship a principal will want to ensure that the agent does not immediately start to act for a competitor or, alternatively, establish a competing business themselves. Consequently, it is usual to provide that the agent cannot engage in a competing business in the territory in relation to the products for a set period. Article 20 sets two years as the maximum time for restraining an agent from engaging in a competing business.

## APPLICABLE LAW

Where a principal appoints an agent in an EU country, it seems likely that the Agents Directive will apply to the contract. However, two cases where this question has arisen have reached opposite conclusions.

In *Allium SA v Alfin Incorporated* [2001] ECC 35, the agency agreement was concluded by a principal based in New York and an agent in France. The contract was expressly stated to be governed by New York law which did not provide for compensation in the event of termination. Consequently, the agent sought to argue that the Commercial Agency Directive should apply. The French Supreme Court came to the view that because the contract was an international one and made expressly subject to New York law, the French law implementing the directive could not apply to the agreement.

However, in the later case of *Ingmar GB Limited v Eaton Leonard Inc* [2002] ECC 5, the court had to decide whether an agency agreement between a Californian principal and an EU agent which expressly provided that it was governed by Californian law was in fact governed by that law or by the Commercial Agency Directive. A lower court had referred this question to the European Court of Justice. The European Court of Justice held that 'it was essential to the development of the community legal order that a company established outside of the EC, whose commercial agent carried on its activity within it, could not evade the provisions [of the Commercial Agency Directive] by a choice of law clause'.[7] The English judge applied this finding and added that the activities of a commercial agent appointed in the EU are closely connected with the EU and that, accordingly, the Commercial Agency Directive should be applied regardless of the choice of law clause inserted by the parties.

## DISPUTE RESOLUTION

The parties frequently insert a provision setting out how any disputes under the agreement will be dealt with. Choices include informal dispute resolution, arbitration or the more formal process of litigation. Chapter 9 deals with dispute resolution in some detail and the reader is referred to that chapter for consideration of the issues that arise in selecting the most appropriate method for the resolution of disputes.

## AGENCY AGREEMENTS AND COMPETITION LAW

Article 81 of the EC Treaty prohibits agreements between undertakings that seek to restrict competition. An agency agreement is an agreement between undertakings – the principal and the agent. Moreover, it could be classed as a vertical agreement in the sense that the principal and the agent are at different levels of the distribution chain for the distribution of goods or services. However, many vertical agreements are considered to promote rather than restrict competition because they in fact facilitate the distribution of goods and services throughout the EU. Because of this, a block exemption regulation was promulgated in 1999 to exempt a range of

[7] [2002] ECC 5 at 6.

vertical agreements from the operation of competition laws.[8] The lengthy guidelines[9] set out by the Commission to aid in the interpretation of the block exemption make clear that in ordinary circumstances where all that the agent does is refer customers on to the principal (i.e. genuine agency agreements), these agreements will be exempted from the operation of EU competition laws by the block exemption regulation. The following explores those situations where an agency agreement might not fall within the exemption so that parties from outside of the EU can avoid those types of agency arrangements that might offend EU competition laws.

The Guidelines on Vertical Restraints suggest that agency agreements might not fall within the exemption if the agent bears significant financial or commercial risk in relation to the sales that they make on the principal's behalf. In genuine agency arrangements, the principal bears the risk of the sales and, accordingly, even though the agency is a separate undertaking, the selling or purchasing is considered to be primarily part of the principal's business. The key defining characteristic of genuine agency agreements is that property in the goods does not vest in the agent or the agent does not themselves supply the contract services and, in addition, the agent does not

- contribute to transport costs of the goods
- invest in sales promotion of the goods or services
- maintain stocks of the goods at their own expense and can return unsold stocks to the principal at no expense to the agent
- operate after-sales service at their own expense
- make specific investments (such as premises or equipment) at their own expense to assist in the sale of the goods or provision of the services
- have liability for defective products
- take responsibility for non-payment or default by a customer unless caused by the agent's default, in which case the agent should only lose their commission on the sale.

The point has been made that it is reasonably common for agency agreements to contain some obligations on the part of the agent that could be said to fall within the above list. However, the question is whether they involve a *significant* financial or commercial risk to the agent. Only if the risks are significant will the agency be considered to be a non-genuine agency for purposes of the application of Article 81(1) of the EC Treaty.[10]

[8] Commission Regulation (EC) No. 2790/1999, [1999] OJ L336/21.

[9] Commission Notice, Guidelines on Vertical Restraints [2000] OJ C291/1.

[10] For a further discussion of these grounds, see M. Mendelsohn and S. Rose, *Guide to the EC Block Exemption for Vertical Agreements*, Kluwer Law International, The Hague, 2002, pp. 81–3.

On the other hand, the guidelines also set out some provisions of agency agreements which are 'allowable' because they relate to the principal's commercial strategy. These include territorial limitations; limitations on customers the agent is to contact; prices at which the goods or services will be sold by the principal to the customers that the agent finds; exclusive agency arrangements; limitations on the agent acting for a competitor; and non-compete provisions after the termination of the agency provided that those non-compete provisions do not 'lead to foreclosure of the relevant market where the contract goods or services are sold or purchased'.[11]

If an agency arrangement does not fall within the provisions of the block exemption, then it may be caught by Article 81. A number of issues need consideration here. First, if the agreement is one in which the agent actually takes title to the goods, then it is more likely to be a distribution agreement and should be considered in relation to the block exemption regulation's provisions on distribution agreements (see below). Second, even if the agency agreement contains some of the features that characterise it as a non-genuine agency, those provisions of the block exemption regulation that exempt from the operation of competition law those agreements where the market share is less than 30% are likely to apply provided no hard-core restrictions are contained in the agreement (see below). Third, even if a particular agency arrangement appears to offend Article 81 because, for example, the agent takes on the credit risk of some customers, the parties still have the option of attempting to use the general exemption provisions of Article 81(3) to show that it leads to benefits in terms of efficiency gains due to the improved distribution of goods and services within the EU.

## DISTRIBUTION AGREEMENTS

A distribution relationship differs from an agency in that in a distributorship, the exporter sells the product to the distributor who then on-sells to the customer. However, when framing a suitable agreement for the appointment of a distributor, many of the same issues arise as for an agency agreement. The following discussion details provisions which are similar between the two agreements and provisions where the two types of agreements diverge.

[11] See Guidelines on Vertical Restraints, para. 19.

As is the case in an agency relationship, an exporter will frequently wish to define carefully the territory into which the distributor should on-sell the goods and the products which the distributor is to on-sell. Thus, provisions here between the two types of agreement are similar with the exception that, in distribution agreements, clauses which limit territory need to framed carefully so as not to offend EU competition clauses. This is discussed more fully below.

Distribution agreements will also seek to impose obligations on the distributor not to distribute competing products without the consent of the exporter; to achieve minimum targets; to report regularly on sales matters to the exporter; to share the expense of advertising the product; to keep information relating to the exporter's business and products confidential; and to use the exporter's intellectual property rights only for the purposes of the distribution agreement. Standard agreements also include provisions on the length of the agreement, how it can be renewed and the circumstances in which it can be terminated early. Early termination provisions need to be framed carefully given that one frequently finds in the civil and commercial codes of European countries provisions that require the termination of agreements only for just cause. Many standard agreements reflect this with a general duty on the parties to deal with each other fairly and in good faith. Further, some standard agreements provide for an indemnity for the distributor after termination of the agreement.

As in agency agreements, there are also provisions regarding the resolution of disputes and the law that will apply to the agreement. While parties have flexibility to determine the governing law of the contract, regard must be had to each country's conflict of law rules which may have the effect that mandatory laws, such as EU competition laws, and other specific laws that countries may have regarding distribution agreements and contracts that are carried out within their territories apply regardless of the parties' choice of law.

Because of the different nature of distribution relationships, there are also provisions found in distribution agreements that do not have their counterpart in agency relationships. Many of these relate to the resale of the goods purchased by the distributor from the exporter. A distribution agreement will spell out clearly that the distributor buys the goods from the agent and will often annex the standard terms and conditions that will apply to each shipment. While there is a master agreement between the exporter and the distributor that covers matters concerned with the ongoing relationship, the terms and conditions of each particular sale need to take into account the matters discussed in detail in earlier chapters dealing with terms of delivery, transport and insurance, payment and clearance of the goods through customs.

Further provisions in the master agreements that relate to the on-sale of goods often require the distributor to maintain an adequate sales organisation to perform their duties in on-selling the goods; to carry out after-sales service; and perhaps to have regard to maximum prices subject to the provisions of competition law (as discussed below). It is also possible to find provisions that a distributor is able to be paid a commission should they increase the business of the exporter by more than a set margin. Unlike agents, distributors are often free to appoint sub-distributors of the goods as long as they inform the exporter that they are doing so. Again, this is because exporters may be limited in restricting the parties to whom goods will be on-sold due to competition law. Finally, exporters need to have regard to the provisions of the EU Product Liability Directive. It is discussed in more detail in the following chapter.

The question of EU competition law as it applies to distribution agreements is an important one and, accordingly, the following discusses in some detail how it may affect a distribution arrangement between an exporter from outside of the EU and an internal EU distributor.

## EU COMPETITION LAW AND DISTRIBUTION AGREEMENTS

In the simplest form of distribution arrangement between a firm outside of the EU and a distributor located within the EU, the outside firm will sell to the distributor with no restrictions as to how the distributor will on-sell the product and the agreement will impose no restrictions on other distributors that the outside firm might wish to use. However, in order to increase their market share and profitability, firms exporting to the EU market and distributors operating within that market might enter into particular types of distribution arrangement that seem, at first glance, to be restricting competition and accordingly might offend EU competition laws. The following first explores some of the more common distribution arrangements of this type[12] and then discusses some of the more important EU competition law issues that need to be considered when entering into arrangements of these types.

[12] The Commission's Guidelines on Vertical Restraints discuss these types of distribution agreement in some detail at paras. 137–229. However, the guidelines make it clear that these are only examples of the various types of vertical restraints that can exist and that all of the principles set out in the guidelines will apply in assessing other types of vertical restraints that may arise.

## COMMON RESTRICTIVE DISTRIBUTION ARRANGEMENTS

The first example of a distribution arrangement that might offend EU competition laws is one in which a firm outside of the EU attempts to ensure that the EU distributor purchases all of its supplies from the one supplier. This has the effect of restricting the distributor from buying and reselling competing goods and services. This is known as 'single branding' because the distributor is in effect confined to selling just one brand of the product. This type of arrangement has the potential to offend competition laws because, among other reasons, it precludes suppliers of competing products from dealing with the distributor and it means that customers of the distributor are limited to only one choice for that type of product when buying from the distributor.

The second common type of restrictive agreement is the exclusive distributorship. Here, the arrangement is that the supplier has only one distributor for a particular territory. Since each national market in the EU has its own characteristics and already has its own distributors with a long history of major customers in that market, it is common for outside firms to attempt to appoint one well-known distributor for an entire country market. In larger countries in which there are distinct regional variations, a single distributor might be appointed for each region. At the same time, each exclusive distributor is prohibited from selling into the territory of another distributor. One of the major problems with exclusive distribution arrangements, as far as competition law is concerned, is that customers are faced with only one source for the product within their country or region. Different distributors might charge different prices for the product depending upon the purchasing power within that market, thus defeating competition on an EU-wide basis. A variation on the exclusive distribution arrangement is where a supplier appoints different distributors for different classes of customers. As is the case with exclusive distribution arrangements, those customers will be faced with only one supplier for the product and accordingly this has the potential to offend competition laws.

A third possibility is that of selective distribution. Here suppliers are selective in which firms they will use as distributors based not on territorial considerations but on the qualities of the distributors themselves. These might include the level of training of the distributor's staff and hence their ability to adequately market the product or their ability to provide after-sales service. There might also be a limit on the number of distributors for a particular market territory as in the case of exclusive distribution arrangements. In this type of arrangement suppliers will agree not to sell to any 'unauthorised' distributors, thus limiting the number of firms within the EU from whom final customers can buy the product in question and accordingly having the potential to offend competition laws.

A fourth possibility is the exclusive supply arrangement. Here an EU distributor will seek to impose on a firm supplying from outside the EU the condition that the supplier will sell all or most of their output to just one firm within the EU or alternatively that all of their output that is destined for the EU market will only be sold to that distributor. It can be seen that in the situation where the supplier is forced to supply all of the output to the distributor (quantity forcing), this arrangement is the opposite of the single branding case where the distributor is forced to purchase all or most of their supplies from the one supplier. In situations where the supplier only deals with one distributor within the EU, it can be seen to be an extreme form of exclusive distribution arrangement. It has the potential to offend competition laws because there is only one distributor from whom final customers can purchase the product and hence a lack of competition.

## HOW DOES EU COMPETITION LAW AFFECT THESE AGREEMENTS?

At the outset it needs to be pointed out that where a firm from outside appoints a distributor in only one country within the EU, the agreement is unlikely to be subject to EU competition law. This is because EU competition law only applies to agreements that affect trade between member states. However, because most member states of the EU have sought to harmonise their own national competition laws with those of the EU, an outside firm may find that restrictive distribution agreements may fall foul of national laws on much the same basis as they would if EU competition law applied. In any event, most firms outside of the EU want to share in the broader EU market and not only in one particular country. For that reason they are likely to have distributors in at least two countries or one EU-wide distributor and this would accordingly bring their arrangements within the realms of EU competition law. Thus the following discussion focuses on competition law at the EU level.

The starting point for any discussion of the types of arrangement discussed above in the context of EU competition law is Article 81 of the EC Treaty. In summary, Articles 81(1) and 81(2) provide that agreements between undertakings that affect trade between member states and that have as their object or effect the prevention, distortion or restriction of competition within the common market shall be void. In particular, it prohibits agreements that seek to fix prices; limit or control markets; share markets or sources of supply; apply dissimilar trading conditions that place some firms at a competitive disadvantage; or bind parties with supplementary obligations that have no connection with the subject matter of the contract. A first reading of Article 81 suggests that all of the distribution arrangements outlined above would be void.

However, it is recognised that there may be some benefits to restrictive agreements between undertakings, even if at first glance they might seem to restrict competition. For example, without some form of incentive for distributors to be given a particular market share, they may simply not take up the opportunity to distribute products and, accordingly, consumers would be worse off than if there were some restrictions.[13] For that reason, Article 81(3) of the EC Treaty allows agreements that improve the distribution of goods or services provided that such agreements fulfil four conditions. The relevance of these four conditions to any of the types of distribution agreements mentioned above is that the agreement must contribute to the improvement of production or distribution of goods or services; consumers still get a fair share of the benefit; the agreement must not allow the firms to eliminate competition or a substantial part of it for the products in question and that the restrictions are vital for the attainment of the goals of improving the distribution of goods or services. Detailed discussion as to how these criteria should be applied is contained in the Guidelines on Vertical Restraint. Most arrangements made by smaller and medium firms outside of the EU appointing a distributor within the EU will most likely be covered by the more specific block exemption for vertical agreements[14] discussed below. However, an understanding of the more general provisions of Article 81(3) is important for those arrangements that might fall outside of the block exemption.

The block exemption regulation was promulgated to set out the circumstances where vertical agreements will gain the benefit of exemption under Article 81(3) and therefore not offend the provisions of Article 81(1). The block exemption applies to all of the types of agreement mentioned in the preceding section. This provision exempts the types of agreements mentioned above from offending Article 81(1) provided that the relevant

[13] A discussion of some of the reasons for exempting some vertical agreements from offending competition laws is found in paras. 115–118 of the Guidelines on Vertical Restraints.

[14] Commission Regulation (EC) No. 2790/1999 [1999] OJ L336/21 ('the block exemption regulation').

market share is below 30%, provided that the agreements do not contain any hardcore restrictions[15] and provided that the agreements do not contain certain non-compete clauses. As this regulation is most relevant for smaller and medium firms entering into distribution arrangements with EU distributors, each of these three criteria are discussed in detail below.[16]

The first issue therefore that needs to considered by firms in determining if their arrangement with distributors is covered by the block exemption regulation is the market share for the product or service in question. In the case of single branding, exclusive distribution, exclusive customer allocation and selective distribution arrangements, the market share of the supplier for the product or service in question cannot exceed 30% if the agreement is to be exempted by the block exemption. This is the case because, in these types of arrangement, it is the supplier that is attempting to limit competition within the marketplace. In the case of exclusive supply agreements, the market share of the buyer cannot exceed 30% if the block exemption is to apply. This is because in exclusive supply arrangements it is the buyer who is trying to limit competition. In both cases, the market share is determined by an assessment of both the relevant product market and the relevant geographic market. The relevant market has been defined as follows:

> The relevant product market comprises any goods or services which are regarded by the buyer as interchangeable, by reason of their characteristics, prices and intended use. The relevant geographic market comprises the area in which the undertakings concerned are involved in the supply and demand of relevant goods or services, in which the conditions of competition are sufficiently homogenous, and which can be distinguished from neighbouring geographic areas because, in particular, conditions of competition are appreciably different in those areas.[17]

This definition is taken from the Commission notice on the definition of relevant market for the purposes of Community competition law.[18] This

[15] Block exemption regulation, Articles 2 and 3.

[16] It should be noted that there are other block exemptions that apply to specific industries and also to horizontal agreements between firms. However, because the 1999 block exemption regulation is the most relevant to the type of distribution agreements mentioned above, the discussion focuses on it.

[17] Guidelines on Vertical Restraints, para. 90.

[18] [1997] OJ C372/5.

document is used to define relevant product and geographic markets not only for the purposes of Article 81(1) but also for determining whether firms are in a dominant position (Article 82) in a market and where mergers between firms will adversely affect competition. In simple terms, the notice proposes that the test to determine whether goods or services fall within the same product group and the extent of the geographic market can be determined by analysing the effect of a small change in prices. Accordingly, if a 5–10% change in the price of product A which is alleged to be a substitute for, or interchangeable with, product B would in fact result in consumers switching to product B and away from product A, then the goods are in fact interchangeable and in the same product market. Similarly, if a 5–10% increase in prices by a firm in country A would lead to consumers switching their source of supply to a competing firm in country B, then countries A and B would be the relevant geographic market. However, it is a complicated matter to get the evidence to decide if in fact consumers would switch in response to a change in prices. The notice proposes various ways in which this can be achieved. Firms running the risk of offending EU competition laws should seek expert advice as to the determination of their relevant product and geographic market. Article 9 of the block exemption regulation sets out the time frame during which the data to determine market share will be applicable.

The second criterion to qualify for the benefit of the block exemption is that the agreement must not contain any 'hardcore restrictions'. Hardcore restrictions are set out in Article 4.[19] These hardcore restrictions will render the whole of any agreement containing any of them void. Because of this, it is necessary to deal with each of them in turn.

The first hardcore restriction prohibits the fixing of prices or the setting of minimum prices for goods or services. The second is more complicated and prohibits restrictions on the territory or the customer group to which goods or services can be sold. However, territorial restrictions are allowed for exclusive distribution and exclusive customer allocation agreements provided that those agreements do not attempt to restrict sales by customers of the buyer and provided that only active sales into the territory of another distributor or territory reserved to the supplier are prevented. This means that a distributor in territory A cannot actively seek out customers in the territory of distributor B but that if customers from distributor B's territory place an order with distributor A, then they must be supplied. It

[19] See Guidelines on Vertical Restraints, paras. 4–56, for a detailed explanation of hardcore restrictions.

is also permissible to restrict wholesalers from selling to end users, sales to unauthorised distributors in a selective distribution system, and the sale by the buyer to other manufacturers for components that were supplied to the buyer for purposes of incorporation into final products.

The third hardcore restriction means that selective distributors operating at the retail level cannot be prevented from either active or passive sales to end users but can be prevented from operating out of an unauthorised establishment. In other words, in this type of selective distribution system, all distributors must be free to seek out customers or to service customers who approach them.

The fourth hardcore restriction outlaws any agreement that seeks to prevent distributors in a selective distribution system from obtaining supplies from each other. The final hardcore restriction prohibits agreements that seek to allow buyers of components that they use in the manufacture of products preventing the supplier of those components from supplying them to any of the buyer's authorised repairers.

As noted above, the third issue that needs to be considered is any non-compete obligations on the part of the distributor. Non-compete obligations will not void the entire agreement but only the clause imposing them will be struck out. Article 5 of the block exemption regulation provides for three types of non-compete arrangements that will be struck down. The first of these is that the distributor should not be prevented from dealing in competing goods for a period that exceeds five years including agreements that are for an indefinite term. The only exception here is where the supplier owns the premises from which the goods are distributed and then the non-compete period cannot outlive the period of tenancy. While this provision appears to make it difficult for the types of agreement mentioned above to be entered into for any more than five years, it is necessary to have regard to the guidelines that suggest that agreements beyond five years will be permissible provided that renewal requires the explicit consent of both parties and there are no obligations that prevent termination by the distributor at the end of the five-year term.[20]

The second restriction on non-compete clauses prohibits the supplier from preventing the distributor dealing in competing goods for more than one year after the termination of the agreement. There are some very limited circumstances where the one-year period can be exceeded. Third, selective distribution agreements cannot ban the distributor from selling

[20] See Guidelines on Vertical Restraints, para. 58.

the products of *particular* competing suppliers. In other words, while it is possible to prevent the selective distributor from dealing in *all* competing products, it is not permissible to single out particular competing suppliers and prevent the selective distributor from selling their brands.

While distribution arrangements that meet these criteria will normally be exempted under the block exemption, the benefits of the exemption can be withdrawn in cases where they are found to be incompatible with any of the conditions set out in Article 81(3).[21] The Guidelines on Vertical Restraints set out in detail circumstances where distribution agreements that might otherwise meet the criteria might still be incompatible with Article 81(3). This will be the case primarily where while an individual agreement relates to less than 30% of the market share, there are parallel distribution agreements that have a cumulative negative effect on competition in the marketplace. Thus, while an individual supplier's market share is less than 30% under one of the distribution agreements mentioned above, it is possible that most of the suppliers within the industry have their own vertical agreements. In these cases, the cumulative effect of the agreements within the industry may limit competition and accordingly the benefits of the block exemption may be withdrawn.

In summary, firms from outside of the EU entering into single branding, exclusive distribution, exclusive customer allocation, selective distribution or exclusive supply arrangements need to look carefully at the specific provisions of the block exemption regulation and, if it does not apply, to the more general Article 81(3) exemptions to determine if their type of arrangement will avoid being caught by EU competition laws. If the agreement is not exempted by either the specific provisions of the block exemption or the general provisions of Article 81(3), there is the possibility that it will be challenged either by the Commission, the competition authorities of an EU member country, or in the courts of a member country.[22]

The above discussion has not canvassed the possibility that such distribution agreements, while not offending Article 81, might offend Article 82. This article proscribes conduct that amounts to an abuse of a dominant position. To offend Article 82, a firm must be in a position of dominance; it must abuse that position; and there must be an effect on trade between member states. Given that most smaller and medium firms engaging

21 Commission Regulation (EC) No. 2790/1999 [1999] OJ L336/21, Articles 6 and 7.

22 Council Regulation (EC) No. 1/2003 [2003] OJ L1/1 allows the provisions of the block exemption regulation to be enforced by either EU courts or the courts in member states.

distributors in the EU are not likely to gain dominance in the EU market, this issue will not be canvassed in any greater depth. The reader is referred to general works on EU competition law or EU law generally.

The foregoing has provided a very introductory outline to the relevant law. The expertise of a lawyer well versed in EU competition laws is essential when drafting these agreements.

# 7 Entering the EU market via franchising arrangements

## INTRODUCTION

FRANCHISING IS A form of licensing arrangement where the owner of intellectual property (trade marks, patents, copyrights and designs) authorises another person to make use of those intellectual property rights in exchange for a fee. The difference between franchising and other types of licensing arrangements is that the grant of the intellectual property rights is frequently accompanied by a comprehensive manual that not only sets out how the intellectual property rights are to be used but also the manner in which the business in which they are used is conducted. It is increasingly common for franchisors to impose their entire business system upon the franchisee, so that each franchised unit is essentially a clone of the original. This allows the franchisor to achieve ready recognition of their brand name and product or service that accompanies it and provides some business certainty to potential franchisees by reducing the risks of business failure that might otherwise occur if the potential franchisee had sought to develop and market a completely new product or service themselves.

Franchising typically starts with success in the domestic market before the franchisor will consider internationalising the franchise operations. However, smaller domestic markets soon become saturated and, in order to ensure growth of the business, a franchisor may have little choice but to look for opportunities overseas. A survey of Australian franchisors in 2008[1] found that the top three reasons for international expansion were to increase the size of the organisation (52.7%); there had been approaches

1 L. Frazer, S. Weaven and O. Wright, *Franchising Australia 2008*, Griffith University, <http://www.griffith.edu.au/_data/assets/pdf_file/0008/101051/fa2008-web-version.pdf>, p. 59.

from investors in other countries wanting to become franchisees (25.4%); and the business had been successful in the domestic market (16.4%).

The EU is an important destination for outside firms seeking international expansion of their domestic franchising operations. A survey of 109 franchisors in the USA in 2006[2] found that more than half of them had franchisees in one or more countries of the EU. In terms of countries where those franchisors had the most franchise operations, the survey found that more than half of the respondents nominated the UK as the country where they had the most units. Only 12% of respondents indicated that they had the most units in Germany and 8% in France. Cultural similarities matter when it comes to successful international franchising and this may well explain why more than half selected the UK as the most attractive target country.[3] The *Franchising Australia 2008* survey found that around 30% of them had franchise operations in the EU. The UK was the most popular destination, with 20% of respondents having outlets there. A further 11.5% indicated that they had operations in other countries in the EU.[4]

It is likely that the EU will be an increasingly popular franchise destination. The US survey referred to above found that of the franchisors that did not have operations somewhere in the EU, two-thirds of these planned to do so in the future. Part of the reason for this may be that 92% of existing franchisors were either satisfied or very satisfied with their European operations, thus providing an impetus to those not already established there to plan to do so. The countries targeted by most potential franchisors were the UK, Germany, France and Spain.

Some statistics regarding the extent of franchising in various European countries appears in Table 7.1. It shows the number of franchise systems in various European countries along with franchising growth rates (where provided) and the approximate amount of royalties that franchisees have to pay to franchisors. No information is provided regarding the breakdown between purely national and international franchise systems in each case. The table draws on information provided by the Eurofranchise Lawyers Group in a publication on the web.[5] The publication is a useful reference for all legal aspects of franchising into the various countries covered.

[2] U. Schlentrich et. al., *International Franchising: The European Union*, report presented on behalf of Rosenberg International Centre of Franchising, International Franchise Association 46th Annual Convention, Palm Springs, California, 25–28 February 2006, <http://www.unh.edu/news/docs/RCIF_EU2006.pdf>.

[3] A. Schultz and S. Kozuka, 'The Importance of Cultural Differences When Expanding a Franchise Internationally' (2008) 6 *International Journal of Franchising Law* 5.

[4] *Franchising Australia 2008*, op. cit., p. 55.

[5] See Table 7.1 source note.

*Table 7.1 Franchising in various European countries*

| Country | Number of franchise systems per year | Approximate growth rate per year | Percentage of turnover as royalties |
|---|---|---|---|
| Austria | 330 (2002) | 8% | 2–6% |
| Belgium | 100 franchisors | Not available | 3–8% |
| Finland | 146 (2006) | 8–20% | 3–10% |
| France | 835 (2004) | 7% | 2–8% |
| Germany | 845 (2004) | 6% | 2–6% |
| Greece | 420 (year unknown) | 90% (over last 10 years) | 2–10% |
| Italy | 735 (2005) | 10% | 2–7% |
| Netherlands | 480 (2004) | 7% | 4–6% (goods) 10–40% (services) |
| Norway | 250 (2004) | Not available | 2–4% |
| Poland | 506 (2005) | 15–20% | 5% |
| Portugal | 347 (2003) | Not available | 6–41% |
| Spain | 712 (2005) | 9–12% | 3–6% |
| Sweden | 300 (2004) | 10% | 2–43% |
| Switzerland | 220 (year unknown) | 5% | 2–10% |
| UK | 718 (2005) | Not available | 10% |

Source: Eurofranchise Lawyers Group, 'Franchising Europe: Comparative Survey' (2007), <http://www.eurofranchiselawyers.com/pdf/Comparative_Table_05_05_08%20printable.pdf>.

The aims of this chapter are to provide the reader with an overview of types of franchising arrangements; legal issues that need to be considered before entering into a franchise agreement with an EU franchisee; the franchise agreement itself; and finally some EU-wide laws that affect the operation of the franchisee's business but that might also have an impact on the entire chain if disregarded by the franchisee.

## TYPES OF FRANCHISE ARRANGEMENTS

The most common form of franchise arrangement is the 'master franchise' in which the franchisor selects a head franchisee in the intended franchise territory and then allows that franchisee (the master franchisee) to in turn select and supervise sub-franchisees. The *Franchising Australia 2008* survey found that over 64% of franchisors used master franchising as a method for entering overseas markets.[6] No comparable figures are provided in the US survey referred to above.

The relationship between the franchisor and the master franchisee can take a variety of forms. The master franchisee might be permitted to select sub-franchisees independently or they might require the approval of the franchisor for each sub-franchisee. The franchisor might allow the master franchisee to run some outlets themselves in addition to appointing sub-franchisees. The terms of remuneration of the master franchisee can also vary. They may be paid a set fee for each sub-franchisee that they establish within the territory or they may receive a percentage of the profits from each sub-franchisee. The franchisor is also likely to receive a percentage of the profits within the territory directly from the master franchisee.

While the arrangements between franchisor and master franchisee may vary, it is usual that the agreements between the master franchisee and the sub-franchisees follow the standard format for all agreements within the franchise network to ensure the uniformity and hence quality standards of the entire network. Most often the agreements will take the form of a business format franchise in which the operator of each individual franchise outlet agrees to meet strict requirements concerning the way in which the business is to be run; the range of products and services that are provided; the sourcing of supplies; the training of personnel; and the layout and appearance of each store or outlet. As the franchisor is often not in direct contractual relations with each sub-franchisee and therefore has limited opportunity to monitor each sub-franchisee's operations, it is common in master franchising arrangements for each sub-franchisee to be provided with a detailed manual of operations. Franchise agreements will provide that failure to operate the business in accordance with the manual will be a breach of the agreement.

A second alternative strategy for franchisors when expanding into international markets is direct franchising. Here the franchisor will contract directly with each franchisee whether they are located in the home country of the franchisor or overseas. The terms of agreement between the franchisor and the franchisee will again usually follow the business format franchise arrangement as described above. There are considerable administrative costs associated with international expansion via direct franchising. The franchisor will bear significant expense not only in negotiating and setting up each outlet but also in providing ongoing supervision to ensure that quality standards are maintained. As culture, business practices

6 *Franchising Australia 2008*, op. cit., p. 60.

and regulations vary in each country in which the franchisor wants to establish operations, the administrative overheads of direct franchising on an international basis may well outweigh the risk of appointing a master franchisee. However, where there will be only a few outlets in each country and considerations of quality are paramount, franchisors might opt for direct franchising.

A third method of international expansion is via the joint venture. In countries where there is little experience with franchising and where business practices and culture are very different to that which exists in the home country of the franchisor, the joint venture can be a means of expanding internationally while at the same time being able to directly monitor and train franchisees. Joint venture arrangements might occur as a precursor to the later establishment of a master franchise arrangement once the franchisor is sufficiently confident of the business environment and capability of potential master franchisees within the territory. Joint venture arrangements are most suited to countries and products where only a few outlets will be operated. If a number of outlets are to be established, consideration needs to be given to whether the same joint venture partner will be selected for each outlet or whether different joint venture partners will be needed who have local knowledge of the market in the area in which they will be operating. However, managing a large number of joint ventures across a number of countries is likely to create even more administrative difficulties than managing a large number of direct franchises because of differences in management culture and organisational practices between the two partners. The *Franchising Australia 2008* survey found that 15% of respondents used the joint venture as a method of international expansion.[7] By way of contrast, the US survey revealed that only 4.93% of the total overseas units of all franchisees in the survey were of the joint venture type.[8] However, the US survey also found that of those planning to expand into the EU, 21% planned to use the joint venture option as opposed to 66% who planned franchisee-owned operations and 12% who favoured outlets directly owned by the franchisor.[9]

A fourth method of expansion is either by 100% direct company-owned outlets or by 100% indirect ownership via a wholly owned subsidiary. Here the franchisor will establish and manage their own outlets in the overseas country. This will not only incur high administrative overheads but also require consideration of all of the usual issues that confront a

[7] Ibid., p. 60.

[8] *International Franchising: The European Union*, op. cit., p. 14.

[9] Ibid., p. 21.

firm when establishing a permanent presence in an overseas country. These are discussed in more detail in Chapter 8. Regardless of the potential difficulties, the 2008 Australian survey found that 33% of franchisors had wholly owned operations as a method for conducting their international operations.[10] In the US survey, only 7% of overseas outlets were wholly owned by the franchisor.[11]

## Case study

### Franchising into the EU market

Bartercard is an international network allowing members who join the network to trade with each other without using cash. Bartercard commenced operations on the Gold Coast in Australia in the 1990s. After success in Australia, the concept was launched in other countries with operations commencing in New Zealand in 1993, and in the UK and Sri Lanka in 1996. Bartercard now has operations in 13 countries throughout the world. It has operations in the UK, Australia and New Zealand and Cyprus in the EU and has plans in place to expand to Spain, Italy, Ireland and Germany. The Bartercard system was developed by founder, Chairman and CEO Wayne Sharpe, and has won several awards including the Franchise Council of Australia's best homegrown franchise award in 2001, and best franchise system ($50 000 to $200 000) and best export franchise system in 2002.

A business that is accepted for membership of the Bartercard network is initially given a line of credit to allow it to commence trading with other members. Each new member is also issued with a plastic Bartercard similar to a credit or debit card. When the business wants to obtain goods or services from another member of the network, it uses its card to obtain those goods or services without payment of any cash. The value of those goods or services is debited to its account. When another member of the network wants to obtain goods or services from it, the value of those goods and services is credited to the business's account. Several banks now allow the use of their EFTPOS facilities for Bartercard transactions, indicating the increasing acceptance that this novel concept has reached on a global basis. An example of how the Bartercard system works is contained on the company's website.[12] It is as follows.

[10] *Franchising Australia 2008*, op. cit., p. 60.

[11] *International Franchising: The European Union*, op. cit., p. 14.

[12] At <http://bartercard.com>.

A restaurant wishes to 'barter' for $10 000 worth of printing using meals and drinks. No printer would ever want $10 000 in meals from the one restaurant; however, by selecting a Bartercard printer, the restaurateur pays the printer in 'Trade Dollars', in this case T$10 000. The printer's account is 'credited' and the restaurateur's account 'debited', so the restaurant now owes T$10 000 in meals to the Bartercard network, *not* the printer. This is repaid as various Bartercard members come to the restaurant (new business) over the following months. Hence, the restaurant has paid for its printing requirements with meals, using an interest-free 'line of credit' and at a cost of approximately 30–40 cents in the dollar, in replacement good cost. The printer can now use the Trade Dollars earned to buy office furniture, advertising, car repairs, stationery, courier services, colour separations, accounting and legal services – even a family holiday. These are all commodities for which the printer would normally pay cash. By using Bartercard Trade Dollars, the printer conserves cash and benefits from the extra business.

The Bartercard experience provides some valuable lessons in the *methods that franchisors can use for their international expansion*. Prior to its expansion overseas, Bartercard had trialled and proved the success of its business concept in the Australian marketplace. Two of its first overseas expansions were to the culturally similar New Zealand and UK markets. This experience suggests the importance of success in the domestic market before overseas expansion as well as illustrating the tendency of franchisors to expand to culturally similar countries for their initial international operations.

Bartercard uses a mix of master franchises and wholly owned outlets in its international operations. In the UK for instance, there are 12 offices. Of these, four are wholly owned operations and the remainder are independent, operating as franchises under the control of the UK head office which itself is a wholly owned operation. The UK experience suggests that franchisors need to be flexible in their franchise methods. Initially, the UK office was an independent master franchisee. However, this arrangement failed to produce satisfactory results and, accordingly, Bartercard bought back the licence and the UK head office became wholly owned. Similar experiences have occurred in other countries including the United Arab Emirates. However, the strategy of having some outlets directly owned has its advantages as well as being necessary from time to time. Wholly owned outlets provide a solid training ground for people who wish to pursue a career within the organisation rather than simply running their own independent franchise. Bartercard has found that staff who have managed directly run franchises quickly learn the system and have opportunities for global career development.

In terms of the *advantages of franchising* as a means of international expansion, Bartercard has found a major advantage to be that expansion on a global scale can be achieved relatively quickly because franchisees provide the capital to establish their own operations. In addition, franchisees have better knowledge of local laws, customs and market opportunities than does the franchisor. Local franchisees are permitted to do their own advertising, being more familiar with the best opportunities in their geographic area.

However, there are some *potential disadvantages*. First, franchisors must be rock solid in their home market if they want to make a success of international franchising. Second, they should not underestimate the cost of supporting overseas expansion or the costs that may be incurred when operations have to be bought back. Third, franchisors have to be constantly vigilant so that if an overseas operation is not going well, it can be bought back before the reputation of the franchisor is damaged in the country concerned. This risk can be minimised with the careful selection of franchisees at the outset and over its time of operation. Bartercard has developed its ability to select franchisees that are likely to make the business concept work successfully.

Bartercard provides *extensive training* to its franchisees. Typically, franchisees will require up 5–7 weeks training to become familiar with the various manuals that set out the company's method of operations. Training occurs in sales and marketing, member relationships management, administration systems and business management as well as in the technology systems upon which Bartercard relies. In the UK, this training is provided through the UK head office, and partially in Australia. After a franchise is established in a country, there will be ongoing in-country support given to new franchisees in that overseas country. Head office within each country (whether wholly owned or master franchisees) also provide much ongoing support in all of the areas mentioned above. So that the system can be maintained and other support given, franchisees generally not only pay an upfront franchise fee but also pay a considerable percentage of their profits to the head franchisee. Yet even though some 30–40% of profits may be paid as a royalty, both the head office within the country and the individual franchisee remain profitable.

Profits are earned through fees from businesses that want to become part of the network and from transaction fees.

Bartercard has sought to *protect its intellectual property* in a number of ways. Its trade mark is now registered in some 67 countries worldwide and pending in a further 50. Its information technology systems are protected by various copyright laws. Companies that have attempted to copy the Bartercard system have not been successful. What they see from the outside is not enough to enable the system to be easily copied. In addition, there are at least 20 or 30 major things and many minor things that Bartercard does better than its competitors, thereby enabling it to maintain its market lead with this business concept.

Bartercard is not only useful for domestic transactions but can also be used by members worldwide for export and import. In times of difficulties in international payments and financial uncertainties, the Bartercard system offers major advantages for those engaging in international business transactions.

## MATTERS FOR CONSIDERATION PRIOR TO ENTERING INTO A FRANCHISE AGREEMENT

Before entering into a franchise agreement, there are number of matters that the franchisor needs to consider. First, the franchisor needs to aware of methods of registering and protecting their intellectual property rights in the overseas territory. Second, they need to have regard to any pre-contract disclosure requirements that exist in the overseas territory. Third, they need to make an assessment of whether their franchise arrangements will offend competition laws in the relevant overseas jurisdiction. Finally, regard must be had to any codes of ethics for franchising. Each of these matters is now discussed in relation to establishing franchise operations in an EU member country.

## REGISTRATION OF INTELLECTUAL PROPERTY RIGHTS

A franchise operation can involve the licensing of a range of different types of intellectual property to the franchisee. The most common of these are trade marks that identify the brand name of the product. Fast food chains, auto shops and car rental companies provide examples of franchises involving brand names. However, where a novel invention is an essential part of the franchised business, then the right to use that invention might also be licensed to the franchisee. An example might be a car wash company that uses a novel piece of machinery that differentiates its service to that of its competitors. It is also possible that designs are an integral part of the franchise operation. For example, a fast food chain may have developed and use a specific type of furniture in its outlets and the shape of this might be an important part of its marketing strategy. Here design protection may be sought. Finally, many business format franchises involve the handing over to the franchisee of a comprehensive manual of operations for which the franchisor will hold the copyright. While it is not necessary to register copyright for it to be protected in the EU, the other forms of intellectual property can be registered. It is therefore necessary to point out the important features of each of these forms of intellectual property, applicable registration procedures and the protection that registration affords.

## TRADE MARK PROTECTION

The key component of a successful franchise operation is the ready recognition of the brand name of the franchise by members of the public. Many franchisors therefore seek to protect their brand name through registration of a trade mark. A trade mark's essential features are that it identifies the origin of the goods or services to which it is applied; it represents a guarantee of the quality of the goods or services; and it allows the trade mark owner and its licensees to use the trade mark to advertise the product or service. It can be a symbol, slogan ('can't believe it's not butter'), figure (501 jeans), name (Kodak), sounds, signature or even a portrait of a person. It can even be registered as a three-dimensional mark that identifies shapes of goods (Toblerone).[13]

The EU made it possible from 1996 to register what is known as a 'community trade mark' that will have effect throughout the entire EU area. This was made possible by the Community Trade Mark Regulation.[14] The office handling registrations is known as the Office for the Harmonization for International Marks (OHIM) and is located in Alicante in Spain. As well as undertaking the registration process, it maintains a register of all trade marks that have been registered and assists in their enforcement. At

13 The examples used here come from *Intellectual Property Law in the European Community: A Country by Country Review*, 2nd edn, World Trade Press, Concord, MA, 2007.

14 Council Regulation (EC) No. 40/94 [1994] OJ L11/1.

the time of writing, there were over three million trade marks registered in the member states of the EU.[15] Not all of these are registered at OHIM because, before 1996, each country had its own trade mark registry and many trade marks remain registered only in national offices and some have elected not to re-register at the EU level.

A franchisor from outside the EU who wishes to register a trade mark needs to begin the process by appointing a trade mark representative from the list held by OHIM to lodge the application on their behalf. In addition, it is useful to have engaged a specialist industrial property adviser who is able to conduct a search to ensure that the mark is not already registered either by OHIM or one of the national offices within the EU and that it is not likely to be confused with any existing mark. Understandably, this can be an involved process given the number of trade marks already in existence.

The next step will involve the trade mark representative lodging an electronic application with OHIM. This application can be found on the OHIM website[16] along with further details of the registration procedure. The application can be filed in any of the languages of EU member countries. However, one of the five official EU languages must be used as a second language. The second language will be a permitted language for those wishing to lodge objections, revocation or invalidity proceedings. If the primary language of the application is one of the five official EU languages, that will be the language for objections and other proceedings.

Once the application is received by the office it will be given priority over any other applications filed later than that date. However, under the provisions of the Paris Convention (Article 4), [17] the applicant will receive the same priority date as in their home country if the application is lodged within 12 months of the application being lodged in their home county. Most often, however, franchisors will have already been operating in their home country for several years before deciding to venture abroad. If another person has the trade mark or a very similar one registered in the EU, then the franchisor may well have to change their mark for EU purposes or, alternatively, explore options for the revocation of the existing mark held by the other person. For these reasons a franchisor who sees potential for international expansion into the EU should register their trade mark at the earliest opportunity.

15 OHIM, 'The Community Trade Mark in Practice. 3.8. How to Register', <http://oami.europa.eu/en/mark/role/brochure/br1en19.htm>.

16 At <http://oami.europa.eu/en/mark/marque/efentry.htm>.

17 Paris Convention for the Protection of Industrial Property, 20 March 1883.

OHIM will conduct its own search to ensure that the proposed trade mark is not already in use. Additionally, Article 7 of the Community Trade Mark Regulation lays down certain absolute grounds upon which registration must be refused. These include marks that have become generic, or are a customary sign in any of the EU member countries, or purport to describe certain features of the goods themselves (such as quantity, quality, geographic origin or value of the goods) as opposed to identifying them as of a particular brand.

Provided that the proposed mark is not refused on any of these grounds, it will be published in the Community Trade Marks Bulletin, with parties allowed to object within a period of three months. Objections can be lodged on several grounds but most particularly that the trade mark will lead to confusion of the public because of its similarity to another mark.[18] It is not only existing registered trade mark holders within the EU who can object to the registration. Any holder of any other international trade mark that has effect in the EU can object, as well as holders of trade marks that are either 'well known' or, while not registered, give the holder a right to prevent the use of the trade mark by any other person by force of the law of the member state where that trade mark has been in use. Prominent examples here include business names and signs. Objections based on any of these grounds will be heard by OHIM and, if they are upheld, the applicant may have their application refused or be required to amend it. There are provisions that allow the applicant to appeal against a decision of OHIM by lodging an appeal to the Office's Board of Appeal, and thereafter application can be made for judicial review on certain limited grounds.

If there are no objections within three months or if any objections are dismissed, then the trade mark becomes registered. It will last for 10 years and can be renewed for further periods of 10 years. Registration will mean that the registered holder can prevent others from using the mark anywhere within the EU. If there are any infringements of the trade mark, the holder or licensee can bring an action against those infringing the trade mark in the European Community's 'Trade Mark courts'.[19] The action may be commenced in the country where the infringement took place or in the country where the holder is domiciled. Decisions of the Trade Mark courts can be enforced in other member states.

Franchisors from outside of the EU also need to be aware that any license for the use of the trade mark must also be recorded in the trade

[18] Community Trade Mark Regulation, Article 8.

[19] Member states designate which courts in their state will hear trade mark disputes pursuant to Article 92 of the Community Trade Mark Regulation.

mark register. If the trade mark is not used for a period of five years in some member country of the EU (one is sufficient) after registration or if its use misleads the public or if it becomes generic, then an application can be made by interested parties to have it revoked. OHIM has exclusive jurisdiction in relation to these applications.

## PATENT PROTECTION

A franchisor with a patentable invention is likely to have taken out a patent on that invention in their own country prior to establishing franchising operations there. It is also likely that they would have been advised by their patent attorney to have the patent registered in any country throughout the world in which they anticipate they might wish to use that invention, at the same time as seeking protection in their own country. The reason for applying for international registration at the same time as national registration is to protect the novelty of the invention, as will be discussed below.

There are three routes by which a patent can be registered within EU member states. These are through national offices, under the European Patent Convention (EPC)[20] or under the Patent Cooperation Treaty (PCT).[21] Registration in three or four national offices will generally be less expensive than taking out a European patent under the PCT because of the need to have various translations done when validating the patent in each national patent office after the grant of a European patent. However, for a potential franchise operation, EU-wide protection may be desirable either through the EPC procedure or the PCT procedure. It is not yet possible to take out a 'Community Patent' but a proposal has been made for a community patent procedure that would operate in a similar way to the community trade mark.

To obtain a European patent, four criteria must be satisfied.[22] There must be an invention. The invention must be novel. It must involve an inventive step and it must be industrially applicable. The criteria requiring 'an invention' is to exclude discoveries of naturally occurring phenomena (e.g. minerals or plants). Novelty is assessed in terms of 'state of the art', meaning that the invention must not form part of existing knowledge in the world. In order to show that it is novel, the invention cannot have been disclosed to anyone with specialised knowledge in the field prior to making

[20] Convention on the Grant of European Patents ('European Patent Convention'), 5 October 1973.
[21] Patent Cooperation Treaty, 19 June 1970.
[22] European Patent Convention 1977, Articles 52–57.

the application. Taking out a patent only in the inventor's home country is considered to be such a disclosure because the patent will have been open to the public during the objection phase. Accordingly, if an invention is to retain its novelty it is necessary to file the application in many countries if it is to be protected internationally. The provisions of the Paris Convention allow inventors 12 months from the date of filing in their own country to file in any other country. If so, the application in those other countries will be given the same priority data as in the inventor's home country. The third criterion for a European patent is that the invention must involve an inventive step. This means that the solution that the invention adopts to the problem that confronted the inventor must not be an obvious one. For this reason, improvements in the functioning of existing products are unlikely to be patentable. The fourth criterion is that the invention must be able to be applied industrially. This excludes theoretical ideas that cannot be implemented.

There are a number of exclusions from patentability. These include computer programs, plant and animal varieties obtained through essentially biological means, and methods for the treatment of humans or animals or diagnostic methods practiced on the human body. However, these exceptions are narrowly drawn so that, for example, pharmaceuticals are not considered to be methods of treatment; biotechnology inventions are not excluded because they are not considered to be purely biological means of obtaining new plant and animal varieties; and computer programs that have a technical effect such as controlling the operation of a technical device are also not excluded.

The various steps for obtaining a European patent are shown in Figure 7.1. A detailed guide to making patent applications has been prepared by the European Patent Office (EPO) and can be found on its website.[23] There is also a further detailed guide as to the examination procedure. The time required to obtain a European patent is usually 3–5 years, although provisions exist for an accelerated application. However, once the patent has been published, provisional protection is granted and there is a right to prevent others from using that invention but any third party can seek to oppose the patent within nine months of it being granted.

The PCT aims to facilitate the taking out of a patent in many countries of the world simultaneously. There are 120 member countries of the PCT. All EU member countries are signatories to the PCT along with most

[23] *How to Get a European Patent: Guide for Applicants, Part 1*, <http://www.epo.org/patents/law/legal-texts/html/guiapp1/e/index.htm>.

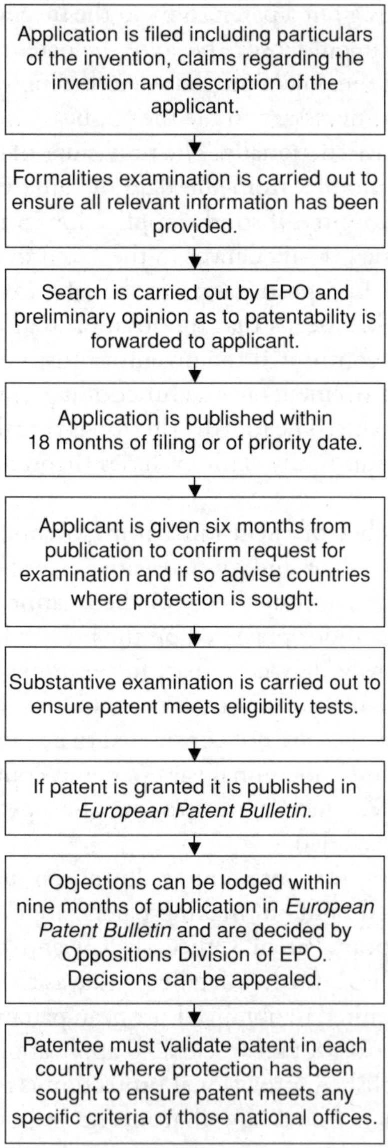


*Figure 7.1 Flow chart of patent application procedure in the EPO*

other industrialised nations including the USA, Canada, Japan, Korea and Australia. When an inventor files an international application under the PCT, they can do so in their own country's patent office. However, the search report must be carried out by one of the patent offices that have been designated as an international search authority. The EPO is one of those.

As with a European patent, the search report also contains an opinion on patentability of the invention, allowing the inventor to decide whether or not to proceed with the application. If a decision is made to proceed, then an international preliminary examination is carried out and the application is published by the World Intellectual Property Organization in the relevant patent journal. This occurs as soon as possible after 18 months from the time of filing of the application.

After publication, the application enters what is known as the 'national phase'. Accordingly, for inventors wishing to register within the entire EU, the application would be sent to the EPO for it to then undertake its processes to determine if the invention is patentable within the EU. Because there will already be an international search report and opinion of patentability, the process undertaken by the EPO is somewhat more expedited than with an ordinary application to it. The application to the EPO must be made within 31 months from the date of filing of the original international application. A useful guide to the PCT procedure can be found on the website of the World Intellectual Property Organization (WIPO)[24] and a comprehensive guide to the role of the EPO in relation to PCT applications can be found on the EPO website.[25]

## DESIGNS

Franchisors may also wish to protect the design of the products associated with the franchise. Registration of a design grants protection in relation to the outward appearance of a product as opposed to trade marks that protect the symbol or other mark that identifies the product as belonging to a particular firm or patents that protect the way in which a product functions. An example of a design that a franchisor might wish to protect is the packaging in which the product is contained that has a distinctive shape and helps consumer recognition and therefore sales.

A franchisor from outside of the EU who is already using a design in their home country may gain protection for that design by registration pursuant to the provisions of the Community Designs Regulation.[26] There are two basic requirements for registration. These are novelty and individual character. The latter requirement means that the design must create a

[24] WIPO, *Protecting Your Inventions Abroad: Frequently Asked Questions about the Patent Cooperation Treaty*, April 2006, <http://www.wipo.int/freepublications/en/patents/433/wipo_pub_433.pdf>.

[25] *How to Get a European Patent: Guide for Applicants, Part 2*, <http://documents.epo.org/projects/babylon/eponet.nsf/0/7c5ef05581e3aac0c12572580035c1ce/$FILE/applicants_guide_part2_en.pdf>.

[26] Council Regulation (EC) No. 6/02 [2002] OJ L3/1.

different impression on the person viewing it to that created by any other existing design. Novelty means that a person will only be able to register the design in the EU if it has not already been disclosed there. If interested parties within the EU could reasonably be expected to be aware of the design of the product, then it will be considered to have already been disclosed and, accordingly, will not meet the novelty requirements for registration as a design. However, in the EU, those wishing to apply for design protection have a grace period of one year after disclosure to make their application for registration without destroying the novelty criteria that needs to be satisfied to register a design. The reason here is that the person inventing the design may wish to test it on the market before going to the expense of registering it. Although this grace period applies to the novelty requirement, if the owner of the design wants the same priority date as applies in their home country, they will need to have filed the application within six months of filing for registration in their home country.

The first step in seeking registration for a design in the EU is to file an application following the procedure on the standard form that can be found on the website of OHIM.[27] An important part of the application is the detail of the design itself. Thus the application should be accompanied by 'views' of the product to show its novel character. Up to seven different views are permitted and most often these will be drawings or other pictorial representations of the product. The application is then examined but only for formalities and to ensure it is not contrary to public policy or morals. Assuming there are no problems, the design is then registered and published immediately. However, in order to protect the design itself, only minimum details are provided in the publication of it. Applicants can request that publication of the design be delayed for up to 30 months from the date of filing of the application if they are not ready to exploit the design commercially. If another party contests the right of the person to register the design, they are able to file an application for invalidity with OHIM who will then organise a hearing of the matter and make a decision.

While any person from inside or outside of the EU can file an application for registration of a design, about 90% of applications are filed by professional representatives who are familiar with the EU design legislation. If there is any dispute concerning the design, a professional representative will need to deal with this on the applicant's behalf.

[27] See <http://oami.europa.eu/en/design/form.htm> for the guide to completing an application for a design.

Once a design is registered then the registered holder can take action against any party infringing it. The period of protection by registration is five years and this can be extended every five years up to maximum of 25 years. It needs to be noted that the EU design legislation also protects 'unregistered designs' from unauthorised copying. However, attempting to enforce an unregistered design requires the owner to prove, among other things, not only the date of disclosure in the EU but also that there has in fact been such a disclosure. The evidence to prove this can be difficult and expensive to gather.

## PRE-CONTRACT DISCLOSURE

In line with international trends, an increasing number of countries within the EU have decided that franchisees, being in a generally weaker bargaining position to powerful international franchisors, need some protection when entering into franchising agreements. This protection is most often provided by requiring the franchisor to disclose certain matters to the franchisee prior to entering into a franchise agreement. The EU member countries where specific pre-contractual disclosure laws exist include Belgium, France, Italy, Romania, Spain and Sweden. Pre-contract disclosure laws are also being considered by a number of other countries. The contents of the disclosure laws differ significantly from country to country. The following provides a summary of the major issues that are covered. Franchisors need to consider each country's disclosure laws carefully along with the penalties for failing to comply with them before entering into franchise agreements.

The first matter that the various laws require to be disclosed to potential franchisees relates to the *franchisor and its business*. The extent to which information must be provided varies from country to country, but most countries require franchisors to disclose information about their operations within the country where the franchisee will conduct its business. For example, the information that a franchisor in the Belgian market must provide includes a summary of the state of the market for the product or service, the number of other franchisees that the franchisor has in the country, and the number of agreements that have been entered into, renewed and terminated over a set number of previous years.[28] Italy, France and Spain have similar requirements in their pre-contractual disclosure

[28] See C. Wormald, 'Belgian Franchise Law' (2005) *International Journal of Franchising Law* 3–5.

requirements. Italy also requires a summary of any judicial or arbitral disputes concerning the network over the past three years.[29]

The second type of information that franchisors are frequently required to disclose relates to *the franchise agreement* itself. Some countries require the franchisor to disclose the important terms of the proposed agreement to the potential franchisee. Belgium, for example, requires the franchisee to be told the key obligations; the consequences of failing to meet them; how royalties will be calculated; the term of the agreement; its termination and renewal; the extent of non-compete clauses; and the rules for the determination of the value of the business if the franchisor has the right to repurchase.[30] Other countries such as Italy[31] and Romania[32] go further and specify a list of matters that must be contained in the franchise agreement itself. In those cases careful regard must be had to the relevant legislation when actually drafting the agreement.

A number of observations can be made about these disclosure obligations. First, because of the extensive nature of disclosure laws in those countries that have adopted them, many franchisors might come to the conclusion that in order to ensure that they have fully complied, they should provide potential franchisees with a copy of the entire proposed agreement at the same time as providing the other required information such as the nature of the business and other franchisees.

Second, it is readily apparent that if a franchisee elects not to proceed they will have in their possession a considerable amount of confidential information regarding the business of the franchisor that could be potentially harmful to the franchisor if disclosed to competitors. For this reason, several countries specifically provide in their franchise disclosure laws that any information provided to potential franchisees as a part of the franchisor's disclosure obligations must be kept confidential by the potential franchisees. In those countries that have not specifically incorporated this into their disclosure laws, other provisions regarding the protection of trade secrets may be applicable.

Third, the disclosure laws of most countries apply equally to both domestic franchisors as well as those from outside of the country. However, Italy requires a foreign franchisor that has not previously operated in Italy to disclose a range of information about the franchisor's overseas operations.

[29] See A. Frigani, 'Franchise Disclosure Legislation in Italy' (2004) 2 *Journal of International Franchising Law* 3–8.

[30] See Wormald, op. cit.

[31] See Frigani, 'Franchise Disclosure Legislation in Italy', op. cit.

[32] See M. Mendelsohn, *Franchising Law*, 2nd edn, Richmond Press, 2004, London, pp. 404–7.

This includes the number of franchisees in the network; a list of outlets directly run country by country; upon request by the franchisee the location and contact details of at least 20 franchisees; and the variation in the number of franchisees year by year and country by country for the last three years.[33]

Fourth, apart from complying with disclosure obligations, there is no requirement for franchisors to register the franchise with authorities in most countries. Spain seems to be alone in maintaining a register of all franchise activities within the country and has regulations concerning what information must be provided to the registering authorities.[34]

Finally, it needs to be noted that while franchising is not a regulated type of contract pursuant to the civil and commercial codes of many countries within the EU, often there are general provisions in those codes that require parties entering into agreements to disclose matters that are considered to be material. For example, in Germany and other countries that have adopted close variations of the German civil and commercial codes, there is a general duty to disclose information that a person knows or should know is crucial in the decision-making processes of the other party. However, this does not extend to contract risks such as an awareness of general market conditions. The general duty of disclosure has been held to apply to franchise agreements by German courts.[35]

## EU COMPETITION LAW

Most franchising arrangements will not be caught by EU competition laws provided that the relevant market share of the franchisor does not exceed 30%. As explained in the previous chapter, this is because the EU block exemption regulation specifically permits vertical restraints provided that the market share of the supplier does not exceed 30%. The Guidelines on Vertical Restraints[36] specifically refer to franchising when discussing the various types of vertical restraints such as exclusive or selective distribution arrangements (paras. 199–201), the use of intellectual property rights to assist in the distribution of goods or services (paras. 30–41) and the determination and calculation of market share (paras. 95 and 97).

[33] Decree No. 204/2005 of the Ministry for Production Activities, Italy. See the discussion of this regulation in A. Frigani 'Regulation Setting up Franchise Rules in Italy: Commentary and Unofficial Translation' (2006) 4 *International Journal of Franchising Law* 3–8.

[34] See A. Echarri, 'Spain – New Regulations on the Spanish Franchisor's Registry' (2006) 4 *International Journal of Franchising Law* 3–4.

[35] See the discussion in A. Schultz, 'Fundamental Changes to the German Civil Code' (2003) 3 *International Journal of Franchising Law* 25–26.

[36] Commission Notice, Guidelines on Vertical Restraints [2000] OJ C291/1.

Most franchising arrangements involve some vertical restraints on competition that could include exclusive distribution rights, selective distribution arrangements and non-compete obligations.[37] An example of exclusive distribution arrangements is the allocation of a specific territory to the franchisee. An example of selective distribution is strict selection criteria to be admitted as a franchisee and a limit on the number of outlets that will be opened in a particular geographic area. An example of non-compete clauses occurs where the franchisee agrees not to sell competing brands of the product. The latter is particularly applicable to distribution franchises as exist in the case of auto parts for example. The guidelines make it clear that provided that the market share of the franchisor does not exceed the 30% level, then such restraints are permissible in franchising arrangements.[38]

However, franchising also involves the franchisor allowing the franchisee to use intellectual property rights. The guidelines contain five specific criteria that must be met in relation to intellectual property rights (referred to in the guidelines as 'IPRs') if agreements are to qualify for exemption from competition laws under the block exemption.[39] First, the IPR provisions must be part of a vertical agreement. The definition of vertical agreement includes one where there are terms containing conditions upon which the parties may purchase sell or resell certain goods or services and not pure licensing agreements.[40] Most franchising agreements are vertical agreements because of the restrictions that are imposed in the way in which goods or services are to be sold – in compliance with the franchisor's manual of operations for example. Second, the IPRs must be assigned by the supplier for the use of the buyer and not the other way around. In franchising this is fulfilled by the use of the franchisee of the franchisors trade name for example. Third, the IPR provisions must not constitute the primary object of the agreement. The point here is that the IPRs assigned must be assigned primarily for the purpose of assisting in the sale and distribution of goods or services. This is the case with franchising agreements. Fourth, the IPRs assigned must be directly related to the sale of the goods or services. Again, the use of the franchisor's brand name suggests that the use of the franchisor's trade mark is directly related to the sale of the goods.

Finally, the assignment of the IPRs must not contain conditions that have the same or similar effect to the 'hardcore restrictions' that are not permitted under the block exemption. These hardcore restrictions have

[37] Guidelines on Vertical Restraints, paras. 199–201.

[38] Guidelines on Vertical Restraints, para 200.

[39] Guidelines on Vertical Restraints, paras. 30–41.

[40] Examples of licensing agreements which do not qualify for exemption under the block exemption are given in para. 32 of the Guidelines on Vertical Restraints.

been discussed in the previous chapter. Thus, franchising agreements along with ordinary distribution agreements cannot contain any of the hardcore restrictions if they are to qualify for exemption from competition provisions under the block exemption.

The guidelines provide some examples of clauses in a franchising agreement that would usually be considered necessary to protect a franchisor's IPRs. These include obligations on the franchisee not to engage in a similar or competing business; not to disclose the franchisor's know-how or any experience gained in the operation of the franchise; to only use the know-how only for the purpose of the business; to obtain the franchisor's consent to any transfer of the business; and to advise the franchisor of any infringements by third parties of those IPRs.[41]

The guidelines specifically refer to what amounts to market share in the case of franchising.[42] In the case of simple distribution franchises, the franchisor's share of the market where the goods are sold determines whether or not the 30% threshold is met. In the case of business format franchises, the issue is more complex. Here the franchisor needs to look at their market share in the market where the business format is exploited. In other words, what share of the market does the franchisor have in supplying the services through the business format? The franchisor will need to consider not only other competing franchises but also the supply of other goods that are provided to the public other than through franchised operations. Given this wide definition of competitors, the franchisor should be able to meet the 30% test in most instances. Where goods are supplied to the franchisee to be sold under a business format arrangement, the franchisor needs to calculate their market share in relation to the sale of those goods as well. For example, in the supply of goods by a franchisor to a franchisee in a fast food chain, the franchisor has to assess their market share in relation to the supply of those types of goods. In all cases, it is the value of goods and services that is used to calculate market share.[43]

## EUROPEAN CODE OF ETHICS FOR FRANCHISING

The European Franchise Federation has a long-established code of ethics[44] for franchisors within European countries. All European member-country

[41] See Guidelines on Vertical Restraints, para. 44.

[42] See Guidelines on Vertical Restraints, para. 95.

[43] See Guidelines on Vertical Restraints, para. 97.

[44] European Franchise Federation, European Code of Ethics for Franchising, <http://www.eff-franchise.com/spip.php?rubrique13>.

franchise associations are members of the European Federation. The Code of Ethics is not a binding legal instrument. However, it has been noted that its provisions may well be used by courts in some countries as general standards that apply within the industry should it become relevant to examine the conduct of franchisors.[45] For that reason, a brief explanation of some of the more important aspects of the code are given here.

The code sets out three fundamental obligations of a franchisor in a franchising relationship and three fundamental obligations of a franchisee. A franchisor is obliged to have successfully operated the business that it intends to franchise for a reasonable time and in at least one pilot unit before embarking on the process of recruiting other franchisees. The franchisor should also have the ownership or, at least, legal rights to the intellectual property that are vital to the franchise and is obliged to provide training to any franchisees that it recruits. A franchisee must use its best endeavours in operating its business to ensure the overall growth and reputation of the business. It should also be prepared to supply the franchisor with relevant information as required and allow for inspections of its premises to ensure operating standards are being maintained. There is also an obligation to keep confidential the trade secrets and intellectual property rights of the franchisor. There is an obligation on both parties to deal fairly with each other and to resolve disputes in good faith. The franchisor should give the franchisee a reasonable time to remedy any alleged defects in performance.

The code also contains provisions concerning the way in which advertising for potential franchisees should be conducted and standards that should apply when selecting potential franchisees. It is noteworthy that the code requires franchisors to give full disclosure of all information relevant to the franchise relationship in a reasonable time prior to entering into any formal agreement and that a pre-contract can be required with regard to the information that is disclosed. Advertising for potential franchisees must be free of misleading information. There is a list of essential terms that franchising agreements should contain. This list largely parallels the list of terms that are discussed below.

## THE FRANCHISE AGREEMENT

This section deals with the matters to be considered when drawing up the agreement between the franchisor and the franchisee that operates an

[45] See A. Frignani, 'Disclosure in Franchise Agreements', paper prepared for a conference in Brussels on 31 October 1995, <http://www.jus.unitn.it/cardozo/Review/Business/Frignani-1997b/Disclosr.htm>.

individual outlet. These agreements have tended to become standardised. The following discussion makes clear that most of the matters to be considered will involve obligations on the part of both the franchisor and the franchisee. Where some matters are more the responsibility of one party rather than the other, this will be indicated. As noted above, agreements between franchisors and master franchisees are generally more complex and subject to variation. However, many of the matters covered in the following discussion will also require consideration in the framing of an agreement between a franchisor and a master franchisee.

## INTELLECTUAL PROPERTY RIGHTS

The underlying basis of a franchising agreement is the grant of intellectual property rights from the franchisor to the franchisee. Standard form agreements[46] typically set out in detail the intellectual property rights that the franchisor will allow the franchisee to use. Most often these are trade marks but can also involve patents, copyright and designs. The agreement will provide that the franchisee is able to use these rights in exchange for a fee (royalty) and further that the franchisee must only use these rights within the context of the franchised business and must surrender the right to use them upon termination of the franchise. The franchisee will also be obligated to keep confidential not only all intellectual property of the franchisor but also any trade secrets and other matters concerning the operation of the business that may give the franchisor its competitive edge in the marketplace. Further, franchisees will often be obligated to inform the franchisor if any third party is breaching the franchisor's intellectual property rights, so that the franchisor can take appropriate action by way of seeking an injunction to prevent the unauthorised use of those rights. Both parties may also be obligated to inform the other if either of them develops any suggestions for improvements to the franchise system so that the whole chain will gain the benefits and uniformity will be preserved.

## RUNNING THE BUSINESS

Clauses regarding operation of the business will involve obligations on the part of both the franchisor and the franchisee. In the case of a business

[46] The International Chamber of Commerce (ICC) has a standard franchise agreement that can be purchased. In addition, guidance for clauses to include in a franchise agreement can be found in M. Hesselink et. al. (eds.), *Principles of European* Law, Vol. 4, *Commercial Agency, Franchise and Distribution Contracts*, Oxford University Press, Oxford, 2006.

format franchise, the franchisor will be obliged to provide the franchisee with the operations manual and the franchisee will be obligated to follow it. Franchisors maintain the right to inspect the business from time to time to ensure that operations are being carried out in accordance with the manual and other provisions of the agreement. In addition, the franchisor will often assume some responsibility for initial training of staff but thereafter this may become the responsibility of the franchisee. The franchisor may also assist the franchisee in obtaining premises and may even assist the franchisee to obtain the necessary capital to finance the start up of the business. Most often the franchisor will be responsible for advertising and marketing of the business to ensure a uniform message is portrayed throughout the territory. However, franchisees may often be charged a levy to cover those expenses.

## TERRITORY

Franchisees will want to ensure that they are the only outlet in a given geographical area so as to protect their customer base. However, franchisors will want to maintain the right to open more outlets in the territory if demand warrants it. Often a compromise is reached so that the franchisee has the first right to purchase any additional outlets that the franchisor considers are warranted within a given geographical area. As noted above, territorial exclusivity is not considered to offend EU competition law if the market share is below the 30% threshold.

## ROYALTY AND REPORTING

As noted above, the franchisee will pay a percentage of its takings as a royalty to the franchisor in exchange for the use of the franchisor's intellectual property rights and other assistance that the franchisor gives to the franchisee in the operation and promotion of the business. The franchisee will also be obligated to provide the required information to the franchisor to allow the royalty to be calculated. The franchisee will be obliged to pay the royalty within a given time frame.

## SUPPLIERS AND PRICING

In order to maintain the quality of products and services, the franchisor may require the franchisee to purchase from a given list of suppliers. The franchisor will be obligated to make this list available to the franchisee. However, such clauses need to be carefully considered in the light of competition laws of the relevant jurisdiction.

## TERM OF THE AGREEMENT AND RENEWAL

The parties need to agree on the term for which the franchise is to operate. Given the nature of franchises as business opportunities, potential franchisees will want a long-term agreement. Franchisors, on the other hand, may want to make the agreement subject to renewal on, for example, a five-yearly basis, rather than fixing a longer term at the start. Again the provisions of competition law may be relevant to a franchisee's right with regard to the length of the agreement and its renewal. The ability to enter into agreements beyond five years has been discussed in the previous chapter.

## TRANSFER

Obligations regarding transfer fall upon both parties. If the franchisee wishes to sell the business, they will frequently be obliged to seek the consent of the franchisor to the new owner to ensure that they have the capability of operating the business to the standard required. Such a provision usually states that the franchisor cannot unreasonably withhold their consent. On the other hand, the franchisor may sell the franchise. In this case, the franchisor may have obligations to advise franchisees of an impending change of ownership.

## TERMINATION

The agreement will usually contain a provision that allows the franchisor to terminate for serious breaches of the agreement by the franchisee. To make matters more certain, franchisees will often insist that those breaches that are considered serious enough to warrant termination should be set out in full in the agreement. Termination on the part of the franchisee may be provided for by the giving of a prior notice to enable the franchisor to find another person willing to take over the franchise in the event that the franchisee is unable to sell it. Such a situation might arise in the event of the death of the franchisee and where the franchise involves considerable personal goodwill for its operation. Provisions relating to termination are sometimes the subject of specific laws in the county where the franchisee is located.

It has already been noted that the disclosure laws of some countries require the franchisor to disclose the circumstances in which termination of the agreement can occur. However, there may be general provisions in civil and commercial codes that apply to the termination of agreements including franchise agreements. The German Civil Code, for example, provides that contracts can only be terminated without notice if there is good cause. The German Federal Court of Justice declared invalid a clause in a franchise agreement that provided for very short notice of termination of the agreement on the grounds that there had been a breakdown of trust because it was too general to indicate 'good cause'.[47] Accordingly, regard must be had to general contract laws and their effect on a party's ability to end the arrangement when drafting franchise agreements.

## RESTRAINT OF TRADE

In the event that a franchise agreement comes to an end, the franchisor will wish to prevent the franchisee from utilising the knowledge they have gained in a similar business. Again, restraint of trade provisions are governed by EU competition laws and have been discussed above.

## OPERATION OF THE FRANCHISE BY THE FRANCHISEE

Franchisees must abide by relevant laws in their own country when operating the franchise. Failure to do so will not only incur problems for the individual franchisee but may tarnish the entire brand name. Accordingly, potential franchisors need to have an understanding of relevant business laws in any country in the EU where they are intending to establish franchise operations. The best source of advice is a local lawyer. However, there are some areas of EU-wide law that need to be discussed here that have particular relevance for overseas franchisors. These are EU laws relating to product liability and unfair commercial practices.

## PRODUCT LIABILITY

Franchisors need to be aware of the EU Product Liability Directive 85/374/EEC[48] as amended by Directive 1999/34/EEC[49] which extended the definition of products to include agricultural products. The directives impose strict liability on, inter alia, persons putting their name, trade mark

[47] See the discussion of the *Apollo* cases in A. Schultz and B. Kubala, 'Important Developments in German Franchise Law through Far-reaching Court Decisions' (2004) 2 *International Journal of Franchising Law* 21–24.

[48] [1995] OJ L210/29.

[49] [1999] OJ L141.

or other distinguishing feature on the product where the product causes damage to a person as a result of a defect in the product. The person whose trade mark appears on the product has a limited number of grounds of escaping liability including they did not put the product into circulation; that the defect occurred after the product was put into circulation by that person; that the product was not manufactured or distributed in the course of their business; that the defect was caused because of mandatory requirements imposed for the manufacture of the product by public authorities; or that at the time the product was made, the state of scientific knowledge was not such as to enable the defect to be discovered.

It would seem that this directive could have application to franchisors because their trade mark is on the product in question and it may be difficult for them to argue that they did not place the product into circulation. The matter of product liability may therefore need to be addressed in any agreement between an overseas franchisor and a master or direct franchisee.

## EU UNFAIR COMMERCIAL PRACTICES DIRECTIVE

As noted earlier, franchisors often have responsibility for advertising the product or service for the entire franchise group. For this reason, overseas franchisors need to be aware of the EU Unfair Commercial Practices Directive 2005/29/EC[50] which proscribes misleading practices, aggressive practices and other unfair commercial practices. This directive aims to harmonise consumer law throughout the EU in furtherance of the single market objective. The directive was enacted in 2005 and was to be incorporated into the laws of each member state by the end of 2007. As at the beginning of 2009, six EU member states still had to implement it.[51]

The directive makes it very clear what type of practices fall into these categories by setting out a list of practices that are absolutely forbidden (the 'black list'). The black list is not exhaustive and, accordingly, misleading, aggressive or other unfair practices might also be actionable by consumers against the persons engaging in them. The following provides an overview of what amounts to a misleading, aggressive or other unfair commercial practice and then deals at some length with those items on the black list that seem most likely to apply to franchisors.

50 [2005] OJ L149/22.

51 See <http://ec.europa.eu/consumers/rights>.

Misleading practices can be either actions or omissions. A commercial action is misleading if it either

- contains false information and is therefore untruthful, or,
- in any way, including overall presentation, deceives or is likely to deceive the *average consumer* even if the information is correct
  and
- causes or is likely to cause him to take a transactional decision that he would otherwise not have taken.[52]

It is misleading to

- omit material information that the average consumer needs, according to the context, to take an informed transactional decision;
- hide or provide material information in an unclear, unintelligible, ambiguous or untimely manner;
- fail to identify the commercial intent of the commercial practice if not already apparent from the context.[53]

A commercial practice is aggressive if 'the average consumer's freedom of choice or conduct is significantly impaired'.[54] The most common examples of this occurring are when a trader exercises undue influence so as to apply pressure to the consumer to enter into the transaction.

Other unfair commercial practices that do not fall into the category of misleading or aggressive are also prohibited. However, there are two criteria that the directive uses to identify these other unfair practices. First, if the practice is contrary to the requirements of professional diligence it may be an unfair practice. Professional diligence is defined as

> the special skill and care which a trader may reasonably be expected to exercise, commensurate with honest market practices and/or general principle of good faith in the trader's field of activity.[55]

The second criterion for evaluating other practices is whether 'the practice materially distorts or is likely to materially distort the average consumer's economic behaviour'[56] in the sense that the practice

[52] Health and Consumer Protection Directorate-General, *The Unfair Commercial Practices Directive*, Office of Official Publications of the European Communities, Luxembourg, 2006, <http://ec.europa.eu/consumers/cons_int/safe_shop/fair_bus_pract/ucp_en.pdf>, p. 11.

[53] Ibid., p. 12.

[54] Ibid., p. 14.

[55] Ibid., p. 14.

[56] Ibid., p. 15.

impairs the ability of the consumer to make an informed decision and enter into a transaction that would not otherwise have been entered into.

The black list of practices that will automatically be regarded as misleading or aggressive is set out in Annex 1 to the directive.[57] The following discusses only those items that are most likely to be relevant to franchisors in their advertising practices. However, franchisees operating the actual business units need to be familiar with the entire black list. An action against a particular franchisee for misleading or aggressive practices may well harm the overall reputation of the franchise chain.

The black list prohibits the use of trust marks, quality marks or similar when the trader is not authorised to use the mark. Likewise, it is not permissible to claim to be a signatory to a code of conduct if such is not the case. Thus, if a franchisor discovers that someone other than an authorised franchisee is using the trade mark of the franchisor, authorities charged with enforcing the directive in the country concerned may take action against the person or firm using the mark. Related to this is a prohibition against misleading consumers into believing that a product has been made by a particular manufacturer when it has not. Again, this is relevant in instances where a franchisor discovers that someone other than a franchisee is promoting their products as 'franchised products'.

Bait advertising is also prohibited by the black list. Accordingly, those franchisors engaged in advertising for their franchises (distribution franchises in particular) should not issue invitations to the public to buy products at a certain price unless the franchisor undertaking the advertising knows that the franchisees will be able to supply those products at that price for a period that is reasonable in the circumstances.

It is also illegal to market after-sales service in one language but, when the time comes for the after-sales service, it is only available in another language. Franchisors with networks throughout Europe need to be careful to ensure that their advertising for after-sales service is in the same language as the after-sales service will be delivered. Related to this is the prohibition on creating an impression that after-sales service is available in a country of the EU other than the country where the consumer purchased the product if this is not the case.

Many businesses attempt to have their product or service endorsed by way of 'advertorial'. In other words, an article in a magazine is written about the product or service which appears to be an independent recommendation of it, leading consumers to be attracted to it. If there has been

[57] See also the discussion of the black list in ibid., pp. 20–5.

payment for the 'advertorial', this must be disclosed in the content of the article in the magazine.

Claiming that a product is able to cure illnesses, dysfunction or malformations when, in fact it cannot, is also a prohibited practice. This may be relevant to franchisors in the cosmetic or natural therapy industries. Any claims made in advertising for the franchise group must be able to be substantiated.

A range of aggressive marketing strategies are also contained in the black list. Included here are marketing strategies claiming that a product is 'free' when in fact the consumer must buy another product to get the free gift; enclosing in mailed-out advertising material an invoice for the product leading to the impression that the consumer has already ordered it; and making persistent and unwarranted solicitations to attempt to make a sale.

The consumer protection authorities of each member state are required to enforce the directive. Penalties apply to those people who are found to be in breach of it.

# 8 Establishing a permanent presence in the EU

## INTRODUCTION

PREVIOUS CHAPTERS HAVE dealt with selling goods into the EU market either by direct exporting or via the intermediate step of having an agent or distributor as an on-the-ground presence. Alternatively, those with a successful business model for delivering either services or goods may decide to embark upon franchising within the EU. However, many exporters of services and those with regular customers for their goods may find it necessary to have a permanent presence in order to satisfy customer demands effectively and remain competitive.

Most firms wishing to set up a business presence within an EU member country do so by forming the equivalent of a private limited company in the European country where they intend to carry on their business. Frequently, the person or firm establishing the private limited company will wish to own 100% of the shares, making the new business a wholly owed subsidiary. In this way the firm maintains control of the operation while at the same time achieving the advantages of the new company being a separate legal entity. The disadvantages of forming a private limited company are that it cannot call on the public to subscribe capital, thus limiting capital contributions to amounts that the founders can raise. In addition, there are detailed procedures that must be followed to form a company and associated expenses such as legal fees, registration expenses and, in some cases, taxes on contributed capital. There are two main sources of law relating to the establishment of private limited companies. These are directives at the EU level and the company laws of individual countries. The EU directives attempt to establish some common elements that should be included in each country's individual company law. The more significant directives in relation to forming a private company are discussed below.

An alternative means of establishing a business presence is to establish a branch of the parent company in an EU member country. A branch is not a separate legal entity from the parent company, meaning that the parent company will be liable for all of the debts and obligations entered into by the authorised person running the business of the branch. There are also detailed procedures for establishing a branch in any European country and obligations to disclose the accounts of the parent company so that persons dealing with the branch are aware of the financial position of the parent. In this respect, the establishment of a branch does not allow for 'separateness' of the two businesses. As is the case with a private limited company, laws relevant to the formation of a branch also exist at both the EU and individual country level. The EU branch directive is discussed below.

A third means of establishing a business presence is to set up a public company, list it on the stock exchange and invite members of the public to subscribe for shares. It is rare for smaller businesses and those setting up a new business to begin by incorporating a public company. It is more usual for a firm to begin as a private limited company and then later convert to a public company as the business grows and, with it, the need for wider sources of capital. Until recently, a firm wishing to trade in several different countries within the EU using a public company structure was obliged to establish a separate public company in each country in which they wished to have a presence or establish a branch to carry on business there. There has been considerable activity at the EU level in regulating public companies. Some of the more important EU directives will be mentioned below but given that the private limited company is a business vehicle much more frequently utilised by firms wishing to set up a permanent presence in an EU member country, the following discussion focuses on it.

A fourth option is to set up what is known as a 'European Company' or 'SE' ('Societas Europeanas'). The European Company can operate in more than one country within the EU without having to separately establish itself in each jurisdiction. It is most suitable for larger public companies. As yet, there is no 'European Private Company' option but the European Parliament has passed a resolution calling for legislation to establish this type of business vehicle to enable small and medium firms to set up EU-wide operations without the need to register separate private companies or branches of the parent company in each country in which they want a presence. Both the European Company and the proposed European Private Company are discussed below.

The remaining alternative for establishing a business within an EU member country is to acquire or merge with an existing business there. Again, the law relating to mergers and acquisitions is split between the EU level and the individual country level. The main focus of the EU-level law is to ensure that the entity that results from the acquisition or merger does not limit competition and also that stakeholders in the merged or acquired entity are protected. The regulation that deals with mergers and acquisitions is discussed below. Individual country regulation of mergers is becoming more harmonised, particularly given the advent of the European Company. Some comments will be made below on regulation of mergers at the private limited company level.

Prior to commencing operation, it is also common for companies to have to obtain some form of business licence. The type of licence required will depend on the country concerned and the nature of the business being conducted. Once the company is established and operating, it is of course bound by all of the laws within the country where it is established. The most significant of these include local labour laws, taxation laws, environmental laws, contract laws and consumer protection laws. In a work of this length, it is impossible to deal with all of the individual laws that affect a company's operation in all of the EU member states. Each member country provides a considerable amount of information about business laws on the internet. However, it is almost always necessary to have a local lawyer in the country where the business is operating to advise on local laws that affect the operation of the business and how these work in practice. There still remains considerable variation within the EU regarding taxation law, environmental law and aspects of labour law.

It is also common to find on the websites of the various member states' investment agencies throughout the EU that many countries offer incentives to establish in certain locations or in certain industries. The matter of incentives is subject to those provisions of the EC Treaty that relate to state aid. Nonetheless, member states have been very creative in developing a range of incentives while ensuring that they come within the conditions set out in the treaty and subsidiary legislation. Relevant state aid legislation and examples of incentives offered will be discussed below.

This chapter discusses relevant EU regulation regarding each of the alternative company forms mentioned above: the private company, the branch, the public company, the European Company and finally establishment through merger or acquisition. It then examines licensing procedures and incentives that exist. However, prior to that discussion it is necessary to make some observations about the major provisions of the EC Treaty that allow firms from one EU member country to establish in another through any of the forms mentioned above. That provision is known as the 'right of establishment' and is one of the four fundamental freedoms of the EC Treaty. While that provision applies to firms from EU member states, some discussion is needed about the extent to which it also applies to firms from outside of the EU.

## RIGHT OF ESTABLISHMENT

EU member countries have taken the view that in order to achieve the overriding goal of a single market within Europe, there needs to be freedom for any person within any country to establish a business in any other member country. This is accompanied by the three other essential freedoms for achieving a single market. These are freedom of movement of goods, capital and labour. It is apparent that in many instances the successful establishment of a business in another country will require capital transfers across borders along with the movement of key personnel to run the business. It may also be necessary for physical goods to cross boundaries as a part of the business's operations, as in a distribution outlet for example. While this chapter deals primarily with how freedom of establishment is implemented in practice across the EU, it needs to be borne in mind that, in practical terms, the successful operation of the business will depend upon the implementation of the other three important freedoms.

The right to establish a business is laid down in Article 43 of the EC Treaty. This article has the effect that member countries must modify any laws that restrict persons from other member countries from establishing a business. In addition, member countries are not permitted to enact new laws which conflict with the right to establishment. This not only includes a prohibition on measures that discriminate against persons from other member states wishing to establish a business. It also prohibits member countries from maintaining measures that, while not specifically directed against nationals from other states, nonetheless have this effect because they might, for instance, make it more costly or more difficult administratively for persons from other states to establish a business than for local persons. Thus, persons from other member states have the same right as nationals of the host country when wishing to establish a business. This is often referred to as a 'right to national treatment' and is fundamental to the right of establishment as enshrined in the EC Treaty. Exceptions to the right to establishment can be made on the grounds of public policy, public security or health[1] and in activities concerned with the exercise of a state's official authority.[2]

The European Commission is given the power to enforce the right to establishment by Article 226 of the EC Treaty by taking infringement proceedings ('IP'). The Commission must first bring the matter to the attention of the state concerned and give the state an opportunity to submit its observations. If the Commission remains of the view that the matter is in breach of the treaty provisions, it can send the state a reasoned opinion requiring it to amend its measures so that they comply. Failure of the state to do so can result in the Commission bringing the matter before the European Court of Justice. Failure of the state to comply with the ruling can result in the matter again being referred to the Court of Justice for the imposition of a penalty under Article 228 of the EC Treaty.

Details of the cases where enforcement action has been taken can be found on the Europa website.[3] An examination of recent cases leads to the following observations. First, the Commission is not deterred by the size or power of member states when taking action. For example, both Italy and France were required to amend the manner in which they awarded contracts for hydroelectric concessions and, after having done so, infringement proceedings against them were dropped.[4] Germany and Portugal have been referred to the European Court of Justice for failing to amend their requirements for organisations that could be authorised to conduct vehicle inspections.[5] Second, most of the action taken by the Commission has resulted from measures that have indirectly given an advantage to local businesses. Thus, for example, onerous procedural requirements for the establishment of distribution centres in the Catalan region of Spain had to be amended after the Commission's investigation of them found that the relevant laws gave an advantage to locals over foreigners.[6] France and Poland have been requested to amend their requirements for the setting up of shops that allowed for participation of existing retailers in the

[1] EC Treaty, Article 46.

[2] EC Treaty, Article 45.

[3] At <http://ec.europa.eu/internal_market/services/infringements/index_en.htm>.

[4] See IP/07/912 and IP/08/1793 at <http://ec.europa.eu/internal_market/services/infringements/index_en.htm>.

[5] See IP/06/1795 and IP/08/332 at <http://ec.europa.eu/internal_market/services/infringements/index_en.htm>.

[6] See IP/08/507 at <http://ec.europa.eu/internal_market/services/infringements/index_en.htm>.

decision-making process.[7] There have also been a number of instances where countries have been required to amend their laws relating to the establishment and running of pharmacies.[8] Third, the above examples demonstrate that a wide range of sectors has been involved in Commission action including distribution and retail industries, broadcasting and media industries, electricity generation, and ownership of pharmacies.

Thus, the EU Treaty gives a clear right to persons in any member state to establish a business in any other member state. This right is actively enforced. However, the right to establishment is only extended by the treaty to persons within the EU. This leaves open the question as to what rights persons from outside the EU have to establish a business in any one or more of the member countries. There is no EU-wide approach to this matter and it is left to individual states to regulate it. Most states have a foreign investment promotion agency that seeks to attract investment into their country. An examination of the websites of these authorities shows that member countries of the EU do not lay down any special requirements for firms from outside of the EU wishing to establish a new business in their country as compared to the requirements for other firms from within the EU or local persons wishing to establish a corporate presence. Thus firms from outside of the EU only need to comply with the same requirements as firms from other EU countries when establishing a new corporate presence in a member state. However, as will be noted below, the acquisition of an existing business may be more difficult for firms from outside of the EU than for firms from within it. Consequently, any businessperson from outside of the EU needs to obtain appropriate advice as to the particular country and particular industry in which they wish to invest.

Finally, it needs to be noted that once a firm from outside the EU establishes a new corporation within an EU member state, that corporation will be treated as a national of that state.[9] Accordingly, the newly created firm can avail itself of the right to offer services to the citizens of other EU member states[10] as well as establish branches or agencies within other member states and take advantage of any favourable EU regulations on mergers and acquisitions.

[7] See IP/06/1794 and IP/08/121 at <http://ec.europa.eu/internal_market/services/infringements/index_en.htm>.

[8] See for example IP/06/858 at <http://ec.europa.eu/internal_market/services/infringements/index_en.htm>.

[9] EC Treaty, Article 48.

[10] The offering of services is regulated by Articles 49–55 of the EC Treaty and the various directives that have been made pursuant to those provisions.

## LEGAL AND PROCEDURAL ISSUES ARISING IN THE FORMATION OF A PRIVATE COMPANY

There are a number of legal and procedural considerations that arise when forming a private limited company. At the outset, it needs to be noted that each member country has its own company law that sets out detailed procedures for the formation of private companies as well as registration processes. It is impossible to deal with all of the variations to the form of private companies and their incorporation processes here and, accordingly, the following discussion raises the more significant matters requiring consideration. It also deals with the more important EU directives that relate to the formation of private companies.

The first concern in forming a private company is the basic company statutes.[11] These have two main purposes. The first is to set out the objects or purposes of the company, the details of the persons who are forming it and the share capital of the company. The second is to set out the rights of members and the governance arrangements for the company. The company law of individual EU member countries will also contain provisions about the rights of members and governance arrangements and, accordingly, the basic company documents need to be drafted with these in mind. Some jurisdictions in Europe allow a single company statute or constitution containing these matters. Others require separate instruments – one for the objects and another for the other matters set out above. It is usual to appoint a lawyer familiar with local company law and the relevant EU directives to draw up these documents. In some jurisdictions the company documents need to be approved by a notary public.

Before the basic company statutes can be drawn up, several matters need to be decided upon. First, the founders of the company must decide how much capital the company will have, how it is to be divided into shares, how many shares are to be allotted to each member and how those shares can be transferred. Some EU countries' company law provides that private companies should have a certain minimum level of capital upon formation while others allow the company capital to initially be as low as one pound. There are also differences as to how much of the capital needs to be paid in at the time of incorporation. Many countries have a provision in their

[11] The names of the company statutes vary from jurisdiction to jurisdiction. In some jurisdictions they are referred to as the memorandum and articles of association and, in others, the company constitution.

law that requires approval by shareholders representing 75% of the share value of the company to transfer shares.

Each country's company law will also set out the minimum requirements for governance structures and the obligations and powers of each of the required company organs. Here there is considerable variation in Europe because of the different histories of company development. In the UK, for example, the bodies which are of primary importance are the shareholders meeting and the board of directors. The board of directors includes some members who are involved in the day-to-day management of the company and other 'independent' directors who provide objective views of the company's activities. In Germany and countries which have adopted German-style company laws, the board is split into two levels – the board that oversees the day-to-day management of the company and a separate supervisory board that supervises the management board. In the Netherlands there is an additional body called the 'works council' which represents the interests of workers. These variations highlight the need for local legal expertise in drafting the company statutes.

In some EU member countries it is possible to avoid the need to draw up company statutes and go through the registration process by the purchase of a shelf company. Shelf companies are already incorporated companies with standard company constitutions and usually a minimal share capital. In some countries there are businesses that specialise in the incorporation and sale of shelf companies. A person wishing to commence a business need only purchase the shares from the incorporators and will then have a business vehicle ready to start trading after obtaining any necessary licences to operate. Of course, it needs to be pointed out that certain guarantees need to be given and due diligence needs to be carried out to ensure that the company being purchased has not incurred any binding legal obligations because, given the perpetual succession of companies, these liabilities will carry forward to the new owners. One disadvantage of shelf companies is that those acquiring one may need to go through a process of amending the statutes of the company to suit their own business needs, particularly in relation to the governance of the company.

After the company statutes are drafted, it is necessary to formally lodge these with the body required under the company law of the relevant country. Some EU countries have a registry of companies where the documents are filed. Others require them to be filed in a court as well as in a company registry. Once the documents are filed, the relevant body usually issues a document to evidence the fact that the company is an incorporated legal body in that country.

Most EU member country websites give clear guidance as to what is required to form a company within their jurisdiction. The following case study sets out what needs to be done to incorporate a company in Estonia.

## Case study

### Establishing a private company in Estonia

Foreign firms wishing to establish a subsidiary in Estonia have two options. The first is to purchase a shelf company and the second is to go through the following procedures to incorporate a company in Estonia. The following information on the incorporation option has been compiled from information on the Estonian investment website.[12] The primary law relating to private companies in Estonia is contained in Articles 135–220 of the Estonian Commercial Code 1995 (as amended).

*Step 1*

A foreign company wishing to establish a subsidiary in Estonia must obtain a notarised copy of its certificate of incorporation in the foreign country and the resolution of the foreign company to establish a subsidiary in Estonia. The notary must be one who is recognised by both the Ministry of Foreign Affairs of the foreign country and the Estonian embassy in that country. Prior to notarisation, the documents must be translated into Estonian by either a translator at the Estonian embassy or, alternatively, if there is no translator available then the documents must be sent to Estonia by the Estonian embassy for translation and subsequent notarisation.

*Step 2*

The foreign company must prepare a memorandum of association that includes the following information:

- the name of the Estonian subsidiary to be formed
- its location and address in Estonia
- the area of business activity of the Estonian company

12 <http://www.investinestonia.com>.

- the name of the foreign company and the company's registered office in its country
- the amount of share capital (the minimum share capital is approx. €2500)
- the number of shares and their nominal value
- the names of the persons to whom shares will be issued (the foreign company if a 100% owned subsidiary)
- the amount to be paid for the shares and the time for payment
- any non-monetary contribution and its value (the value of any non-monetary contribution is to be valued by an auditor if it exceeds one half of the value of the share capital or exceeds €2500 approx.)
- the names and places of residence of the management board (the residence of at least one half of the management board must be in the EU or Switzerland)
- the name and address of the auditor
- the amount of foundation expenses (calculated by reference to fees required by Estonian registration authorities) and how these will be paid.

The foreign company must also prepare articles of association that set out the governance procedures of the company including the amount of share capital, rights attaching to shares, members of the management board and the amount of reserve capital. They are annexed to the memorandum. In a private company the general meeting of shareholders and the management board are the governance bodies. A supervisory board is also required if the share capital of the company is greater than €25 000 (approx.).

The memorandum (including the annexed articles) must be signed by the duly authorised persons of the foreign company. They must be translated into Estonian and notarised in the same way as the documents in Step 1.

*Step 3*

The foreign company must open a bank account in Estonia and pay in the minimum share capital.

*Step 4*

All members of the management board of the new Estonian company must sign and then submit a petition for registration of the company with the Central Commercial Register within six months of signing the memorandum. This petition must also contain the following particulars which will be entered in the commercial register:

- the name of the company
- its address and area of activity
- the amount of share capital
- the date of signing of the memorandum and articles of association
- the name and addresses of the management board
- other required information.

The petition must be accompanied by the signed memorandum with articles attached, a bank notice evidencing payment of the capital into a bank account, and specimen signatures of the management board along with the names, addresses and contact details. The registration process will take 2–3 weeks if all documents are in order.

We now turn to the various EU-wide regulatory requirements for establishing a private limited company. The disclosure directive,[13] first promulgated in 1968, requires member countries to make it obligatory for all companies incorporated within their territory to abide by minimum disclosure requirements. It was amended by a further directive in 2003[14] which essentially provided that the documents that are required to be disclosed should be available electronically. The disclosure directive (as amended) contains some important provisions relating to the formation of companies. Article 2 of the directive provides that all companies must disclose the following:

- the key documents of their constitution
- any amendments of their constitution
- the entire new constitution as amended
- appointments and termination of officers authorised to represent the company and take part in the administration, supervision and control of the company
- the amount of capital subscribed (to be reported every year)
- balance sheets and profit and loss statements (to be reported every year).

In addition, the directive sets out a range matters that must be disclosed on the transfer of the seat of the company, its winding up or liquidation or a declaration of the nullity of the company by the courts.

[13] Directive 68/151/EEC [1968] OJ L065/8.
[14] Directive 2003/58/EC [2003] OJ L221/13.

Article 3 sets out how these matters are to be disclosed. All member states are required to have a file for each company incorporated in their jurisdiction containing the information set out above. The file has to be kept in a central register, a commercial register or companies register, depending on the individual arrangements for the keeping of records by individual member states. Members of the public must be able to obtain copies of these documents and the public are to be advised that such documents are held by notification in the country's gazette for reporting such matters.

Article 4 provides that documents issued by the company such as letters and order forms need to show the legal form of the company (private, public etc.) as well as the location of its seat. In Articles 7 and 8, the directive contains provisions that allow for third parties and the company itself to rely on the documents that are disclosed and the validity of obligations entered into by the company before and after the disclosure of the documents.

The formation of private companies has also been assisted by the EU directive on single member companies.[15] This directive requires member states to provide in their company laws for the formation of single member private companies (and optionally public companies). Where a single member company is formed either on incorporation or by acquisition of shares, the fact that it is a single member company and the name of the sole shareholder must be recorded on the company file kept by the registration authorities in the country concerned. The directive also provides that the sole member shall exercise the power of the general meeting and that decisions taken must be recorded in the company minutes.

## BRANCH

An alternative means of establishing a business presence in an EU member country is through the formation of a branch of the parent company. The branch will not have legal personality of its own, with the result that the parent company will be responsible for obligations that the branch enters into. For this reason, the selection of the branch manager is an important company decision given that the branch manager will be authorised to enter into obligations on behalf of the branch and therefore the company at large.

The procedural requirements for the formation of a branch are simpler than for the incorporation of a local private company as the following

[15] Directive 89/667/EC [1989] OJ L395/40.

discussion of the branch directive[16] makes clear. However, as will be noted, the accounts of the parent company need to be disclosed in the country where the branch is operating. For this reason, some companies who do not necessarily want the full extent of the company's financial information disclosed in the country where the branch is situated might prefer instead to incorporate a subsidiary company which will be a separate legal entity.

A branch structure may well suit companies that simply wish to have a sales and marketing presence in the overseas country. For example, a company may have its European headquarters in the UK but also wish to distribute its products in Sweden. For that purpose it wants a permanent presence in Sweden that can take orders for its products and assist with the physical distribution of them to outlets within Sweden including arranging any customs clearance procedures that might be necessary. Similar considerations apply to some service companies. For example, information technology companies might wish to have an on-the-ground presence to manage the provision of their services in a particular country. While Article 49 of the EC Treaty allows the cross-border delivery of services within the EU, for practical reasons it may be preferable to have an actual presence in the country where the services are being delivered. A branch will be preferable to a mere representative office because a representative office will not be permitted to carry on business.

The branch directive seeks to harmonise the information that companies establishing branches need to provide to authorities within the country where the branch is to be established regardless of which EU country that may be. The range of documents required to be disclosed allows those dealing with the branch to satisfy themselves about the financial standing of the branch and its parent company. For companies from outside of the EU who wish to establish a branch in an EU member country, the branch directive requires that the following information be disclosed in the country where the branch is to be established in accordance with the procedure laid down in the disclosure directive discussed above in relation to private companies:[17]

- the address of the branch
- the activities of the branch
- the law of the state by which the company is governed
- the register in which the company file is kept and its registration number
- the company's constitution (memorandum and articles)

[16] Directive 89/666/EEC [1989] OJ L395/36 (the 'branch directive').
[17] Articles 7 and 8 of the branch directive.

- the legal form of the company, its principal place of business and its purpose
- the appointment, termination and particulars of persons who can represent the company, including specifically those who can represent the branch and the extent of their powers
- the winding up of the company
- the accounts of the company.

The accounts of the company that are to be disclosed are the same as those that are disclosed in the company's home state provided that the home state adopts similar accounting requirements to those as laid down in the accounting directives (78/660/EEC and 83/349/EEC). Otherwise, separate branch accounts may be required to be drawn up and disclosed.[18] As is the case with private companies, all branch documents must show the register in which the file for the branch is kept and the number of the branch in that register.[19]

While the branch directive appears to be comprehensive, it is necessary to consult the individual requirements of the particular country where the branch is to be established.

## Case study

### Establishing a branch in Sweden

The information for this case study was obtained from the factsheet guidelines for starting a branch office on the Swedish government investment website[20] and the website of the Swedish company's office.[21]

A company from outside of the EU which wants to establish a branch in Sweden must make an application on the required form to the Swedish company's registration office. Only one branch per foreign company is permitted. The application must be made by the branch's managing director. The application form requires the following details:

- the business name, postal address and registered office of the foreign company
- the business name, postal address and registered of the branch (The name of the branch must include the name of the parent company,

[18] Article 9 of the branch directive.
[19] Article 10 of the branch directive.
[20] <http://www.isa.se>.
[21] <http://www.bolagsverket.se/in_english/forms/docuemnt/pdf/887e.pdf>.

its company form, the nationality of the parent company and have the word 'filial' after its name.)

- details of the managing director
- how the registration fee is being paid
- details of the person authorised to accept service of notices on behalf of the branch (if not the managing director)
- who can sign on behalf of the branch (It must be either the managing director alone or either one of the managing director and deputy managing director.)
- the name of the auditor
- the accounting firm
- the registration number of the foreign company and the foreign registry where it is registered
- the financial year of the foreign company
- the share capital of the foreign company
- the contact person for the foreign company
- the business activities of the foreign company (must be stated in Swedish)
- the business activities of the branch in Sweden (must be stated in Swedish).

There are a number of documents that must accompany the application. These include:

- the power of attorney given to the managing director to conduct the activities of the branch on behalf of the foreign company
- certification that the person giving the power of attorney to the managing director is entitled to do so (The certification document must include the names of the directors of the foreign company and their signatory powers.)
- a copy of the passport of the managing director if they are not a person entered on the Swedish population register
- the power of attorney from the foreign company or minutes of a board meeting authorising a person to accept service of notices on the branch (This is required if the managing director is not resident in Sweden.)
- a certified copy or the original of the certificate of incorporation of the foreign company
- a certified copy or the original of a certificate showing that the foreign company as not been declared bankrupt
- certified copies of the current articles and bylaws or similar document of the foreign company

- annual accounts for the last two years of the foreign company.

Once the required fees are paid and the branch is registered, the branch is given a number and must then register for taxation purposes.

The branch office's letterhead, invoices and order forms shall contain information about the foreign company's legal form and its registered office; the register in which it is registered; its registration number; the branch office's registration number; and the Swedish register in which the branch office is registered.

There are specific requirements in Sweden that a branch of a company from outside the EU must prepare branch accounts annually and submit these to the company's office along with the auditor's report for the branch and the accounts of the company as a whole. These must be in the Swedish language.

All of the foregoing suggests that it is almost a necessity for the branch managing director to be Swedish, although, for citizens of other EU member states, this cannot be required because of the freedom of movement of persons in the EU. However, if the manager is not resident in Sweden, a local manager must be appointed to accept service of process on behalf of the foreign company. If the branch managing director is from a country outside of the EU, special visas and work permits are required.

## PUBLIC COMPANY

The most important directive relating to the formation of public companies is Directive 77/91/EEC, often referred to as the 'capital directive'.[22] Member states are required to ensure that their company law complies with it. Since its promulgation in 1977, two further directives have amended certain sections of it.[23] The following discussion provides an overview of what is covered by the capital directive as amended in order to highlight the extent to which the formation and operation of public companies is influenced by this directive. It also needs to be pointed out that the disclosure directive discussed above also applies to public companies and will naturally be important in formation procedures.

The capital directive provides in Article 2 a list of matters that should be covered in the company's articles of association or constitution. These include the type and name of the company; its objects; the amount of

[22] [1977] OJ L26/1 (the 'capital directive').

[23] Directive 92/101/EEC [1992] OJ L347/64 and Directive 2006/68/EC [2006] OJ L264/32.

authorised capital or, if none, the amount of subscribed capital; the rules relating to the functions and appointments of the governing bodies of the company; and the duration of the company unless this is indefinite. It is noteworthy that the articles of the company only need to set out rules relating to the governing bodies of the company in so far as they are not determined by the company law of individual member states. In addition, the provisions of each member state are to continue to apply with regard to modification of the articles of association or constituent documents of the company.[24] Thus, even at the time of drawing up of the articles of the company, it is necessary to have regard to the law of the state where the company is to be formed.

Public companies are required to have a minimum of subscribed share capital that was originally prescribed as being equivalent to 25 000 European units of account.[25] A method was set out for calculating how any country's currency can be converted to European units of account. The amount of minimum capital was to be revised every five years taking into account economic and monetary trends in the community. This suggests that a common European currency was at least in the contemplation of the drafters of this regulation in the mid-1970s. The capital of the company can only be formed with assets that can be assessed as to their economic value and an undertaking to perform work or supply services cannot form part of the assets.[26] Where assets other than cash are to be contributed, a report must be drawn up by an expert valuing those assets and that report must be published.[27] In addition, where any person involved in the formation of the company transfers an asset to the company within a certain time period after formation and equivalent to at least 10% of the company's subscribed capital, this must be disclosed and published along with the report on value of assets other than cash as well as being approved by the general meeting of the company.[28] The detail of these original provisions regarding the drawing up of expert reports and transfers of assets by founders have been extensively amended by Directive 2006/68/EEC to restrict the circumstances in which valuation reports need to be obtained.

The directive deals in some detail with what must be disclosed relating to the capital of the company. Matters include the registered office

[24] Article 14 of the capital directive.
[25] Article 6 of the capital directive.
[26] Article 7 of the capital directive.
[27] Article 10 of the capital directive.
[28] Article 11 of the capital directive.

of the company; the nominal share capital for each class of shares; subscribed capital for each class of shares; the amount of paid-up capital; shares issued for consideration other than cash; names of the founders of the company; special conditions for the transfer of shares; any special advantage gained by anyone involved in its formation; and the estimated costs of the company's formation. These matters must be disclosed in the company's articles of association or alternatively in a separate document published in accordance with the disclosure directive. Shares that are issued by the company must be paid up at not less than 25% of their nominal or par value[29] and shares cannot be issued at a price below their nominal or par value.[30] Shareholders cannot be released from their obligation to pay contributions other than through an authorised reduction of capital.[31]

These are the major matters covered in the directive relating to company formation. However, the directive also deals extensively with operational aspects of the company including distributions to shareholders;[32] a company acquiring its own shares;[33] increases in capital;[34] reductions in capital;[35] redeemable shares;[36] and liability for obligations entered into before the company was authorised to commence business.[37]

While the capital directive as amended is the most significant instrument dealing with the formation of public companies, there are numerous other directives that affect company operations generally or in specific industries such as finance for example. In this general category, the EU has been particularly active in financial information disclosure by public companies. Consequently, we find several directives relating to accounting and auditing standards[38] as well as transparency of information.[39] This is in line with the philosophy of the earliest directives – the disclosure directive and the capital directive – which was to protect members of the public contributing share capital to public companies.

29 Article 9 of the capital directive.
30 Article 8 of the capital directive.
31 Article 12 of the capital directive.
32 Articles 15–16 of the capital directive.
33 Articles 19–23 of the capital directive.
34 Articles 25–29 of the capital directive.
35 Articles 30–38 of the capital directive.
36 Article 39 of the capital directive.
37 Article 4 of the capital directive.
38 See Directive 78/660/EEC [1978] OJ L222/11; Directive 83/349/EEC [1983] OJ L193/1; Directive 84/253/EEC [1984] OJ L126/20; and Directive 2006/46/EC [2006] OJ L224/1.
39 See Directive 2004/109/EC [2004] OJ L390/38 and Directive 2007/14/EC [2007] OJ L69/27.

## MERGERS AND ACQUISITIONS

When a company from outside of the EU establishes a presence in an EU member state by takeover or merger with an existing company, the main source of law that the foreign company will need to consider will be the law of the member state where the target company is located.[40] While there is a directive in place that sets out procedures that member countries should adopt to facilitate mergers between two EU-based companies,[41] this directive will not apply when a company in an EU member state is either merged with or acquired by an outside company. There is also a takeover directive that sets out procedures that member states should adopt when framing their own takeover laws in relation to takeover bids.[42] However, it will be the takeover law of the individual member states themselves that have most relevance for an outside purchaser of a company.

Thus, the primary source of EU-level law that is relevant for outside purchasers of companies within the EU is EU competition law as elaborated upon in Regulation 2004/139/EEC.[43] This regulation only applies where there is a merger or an acquisition and where the merger or acquisition has a community dimension. There are detailed criteria for determining whether or not there is a community dimension. The most significant of these is that the regulation will not be applicable to any merger or acquisition where the worldwide turnover of the merged entity is less than €2.5 billion. Accordingly, the regulation only applies to the largest of transactions. If it is applicable, then the European Commission must sanction the merger or acquisition. It has been noted that there have been some 3000 transactions notified since 1990.[44]

Accordingly, the regulation is unlikely to apply to small and medium businesses that wish to establish an EU presence through buying an already existing company.

A foreign acquirer of a company in an EU member state will therefore need to have most regard to individual country laws that have relevance for

[40] A very useful reference for the individual country merger and acquisition laws is M. Whalley and F. Semler (eds.), *International Business Acquisitions: Major Legal Issues and Due Diligence*, 3rd edn, Kluwer Law International, Netherlands, 2007.

[41] Directive 2005/56/EC [2005] OJ L310/1.

[42] Directive 2004/25/EC [2004] OJ L142/12.

[43] [2004] OJ L24/1.

[44] See M. van de Hel, 'European Union – EU Merger Control' in Whalley and Semler (eds.), op. cit., p. 516.

the merger or acquisition being contemplated. Local legal advice is essential not only on the general laws relating to business within the country but most particularly on the following: any specific laws relevant to the type of activity in which the target company is involved; individual country's competition laws; company laws that may stipulate requirements involved in the takeover procedure; employment laws that have an impact on how the foreign company must deal with workers in the acquired entity; and tax laws.

Each EU member state will have its own laws regulating specific areas of economic activity. Foreigners wishing to acquire companies engaged in sensitive service sectors such as finance or media will often be required to obtain special government approval before they can embark on a takeover or merger. In addition, it is commonplace for many types of business activity to be regulated by means of a licence to operate. When a foreigner acquires a business that is subject to specific licensing, they may need approval from the relevant government authority to transfer the licence to the acquiring entity. To get this approval, they will frequently need to meet the specific statutory requirements that are laid down for licence holders for that activity.

Competition laws of EU member states often specify that where a merger or acquisition results in a worldwide turnover of the merged entity in excess of a specified amount and a turnover in excess of a specified amount in the country of the target, then competition authorities must approve the merger. In addition to exceeding threshold amounts, some countries also require that the acquisition must amount to more than a set percentage of the target company's shares or that the acquisition results in a market share beyond a set amount. Laws throughout the EU are far from uniform in this regard and local legal advice is essential.[45]

Foreigners will also need advice on the applicability of company laws that will specify the way in which offers are made for target companies' shares; liability for any obligations incurred by the target company; how shares are to be transferred; and whether there are any requirements regarding minimum numbers of shareholders and other requirements (such as residence requirements) for office holders in the newly formed entity. Obligations to the employees of the target company are often the subject of employment-related legislation and tax laws govern the taxation implications of the takeover.

[45] See the various country chapters in Whalley and Semler (eds.), op. cit.

## THE EUROPEAN COMPANY

It took more than 30 years to bring about a form of business that could operate in more than one state of the EU without having to go through registration procedures every time the business wanted to set up a presence in a different member state. This form of business is the 'European Company' and the regulation establishing it finally entered into force in 2004. The 'European Company Statute',[46] as the regulation is known, provides that a European Company can be formed in one of four ways:

- through a merger of two public limited companies from different member states
- through the formation of a holding company by public or private companies from different member states
- through the formation of a joint subsidiary by companies from different member states
- through the conversion of a public limited company into a European company.

In addition, the regulation provides in Article 2(5) that member states may provide in their legislation that companies with their head office outside of the EU can participate in one of the above four ways in the formation of a European Company.

A European Company must have minimum capital of at least €120 000 and have its registered office in the place where its central administration is situated. The registration process involves disclosure of the prescribed information in the Official Journal of the European Communities as well as registering with the national authorities in the state where its central administration is located.

The main governance organs of the European Company are the general meeting of shareholders and a management board plus supervisory board. No person can be a member of both the supervisory and management boards except where a causal vacancy exists on the management board which can be temporarily filled by a representative from the supervisory board. Alternatively, the main organs can be the general meeting of shareholders and an administrative board. For those companies that adopt the management plus supervisory board model, the management board has the power to legally represent the company and carries on the company's business. However, as the name implies, the supervisory board maintains

[46] Council Regulation (EC) 2157/2001 [2001] OJ L294/1.

oversight of major company decisions including major projects, establishment or closing down of business operations or taking on major debts or loans.[47]

In accordance with corporate governance models in several major European countries, the statute requires that the company has in place a means of employee participation. A directive on employee participation[48] was enacted and was finally implemented in all member states by the end of 2007. The European Company has three choices in implementing employee participation. First, employee participation can be through representation on the supervisory board. Second, a separate body to represent employees can be created by the company and that body must be provided with sufficient resources to be able to function to channel the input of employees into major company decisions. The third alternative is a general 'catch-all' provision that allows employees and management to agree on some other form of employee participation. The company cannot be registered until one of these three alternatives exists. Member states may elect to opt out of the employee participation rules for SE companies formed by merger. However, if they do so, then the SE will not be able to be registered in their state unless none of the employees in the merged company previously had a right to participation or unless some agreement has been reached between management and employees regarding participation.[49]

Article 15 of the directive provides that the European Company will be subject to the laws relating to public companies in the place where it establishes its registered office. In addition, it will be subject to all of the EU directives that apply to public companies as well as to the law of the countries in which it does business.

The European Company Statute has now been in place long enough to make some assessment of its use as an alterative form of business within the EU. Its obvious advantage is that companies wishing to carry on business in several countries can do so through one entity (formed as above) rather than having to separately register a subsidiary in each country where it wishes to carry on business. In some jurisdictions, including Germany, it is even possible for companies who wish to form a European Company to buy a European shelf company that is already set up with the minimum capital and standard governance arrangements.

47 See 'Statute for a European Company', <http://europa.eu/scadplus/leg/en/lvb/l26016.htm>.

48 Directive 2001/86/EC [2001] OJ L294/22.

49 See 'Statute for a European Company', op. cit.

Despite this, statistics show that there are, as yet, only some 90 European companies in existence.[50] Most of these have their registered office in those countries that have tended to have previously had company law governance structures that most closely resemble those of the SE. Thus, as at June 2007, we find 29 registered SEs in Germany, nine in the Netherlands, eight in Austria and seven in Belgium. Those countries without a history of supervisory boards or formal employee participation have relatively few registrations – the UK for example has only three registered SEs.[51] The relatively high number of SEs in Germany is partly explained by the fact that Germany has set up a number of shelf SE companies. It has been estimated that 19% of all existing SEs are in fact mere shelf SEs. In terms of method of formation, it has been noted that around 65% of SEs that actually have operations and employees are formed by corporations that merged subsidiaries in a number of EU states to save on administration costs.

A number of reasons have been advanced to explain the relatively poor uptake of the European Company concept.[52] These include the lack of knowledge about the company by legal advisers; the relatively expensive and time-consuming incorporation processes; the requirements regarding employee participation; the delay in implementation of the directive on employee participation; and, perhaps most significantly, the fact that the SE remains regulated to a large extent by the country's laws where it has its registered office. This has the potential to lead to confusion because outsiders tend to expect a European Company to operate according to the one set of laws regardless of where it has its seat. However, the European Company Statute specifically leaves much of the detailed regulation of the SE to whatever national law applies.

Some authors draw attention to an even more fundamental problem. If two companies are to merge to form an SE which will have its seat in another jurisdiction, there will be a transfer of assets out of the original jurisdiction.[53] In many countries this will attract the attention of tax authorities who will require that an exit tax be paid. For larger companies this could be substantial and outweigh the other advantages of adopting the European Company as the corporate form for their business operations.

[50] P. Pelle, 'Companies Crossing Borders within Europe' (2008) 4 *Utrecht Law Review* 6 at 8.

[51] J. A. McCahery and E. Vermeulen, 'Understanding Corporate Mobility in the EU', paper prepared for the 5th European Law and Corporate Governance Conference, Berlin, 27–28 June 2007, <http://www.bdi-online.de/en/Dokumente/Recht-Wettbewerb-Versicherungen/Panel_I_WorkingPaper_UnderstandingCorpMob.pdf>, p. 22.

[52] See Pelle, op. cit., and McCahery and Vermeulen, op. cit.

[53] See McCahery and Vermeulen, ibid., p. 27.

The European Commission is to bring down an evaluation report at the end of 2009 on the European Company concept.

## A PRIVATE EUROPEAN COMPANY?

The idea for a private European company has been around since the 1990s. However, it was not until June 2006 that the Legal Affairs Committee of the European Parliament held a public hearing on the matter and then drafted a resolution calling on the Parliament to present a proposal. In November 2006, the European Parliament published a detailed report with recommendations to the Commission for a private company statute.[54] This was followed in February 2007 with a formal European Parliament resolution calling for a European Private Company (SPE) statute.[55] In July 2007 the Directorate-General for Internal Market and Services held consultations on a possible statute. The results of the consultation have been published by the Commission.[56] In June 2008 the Commission presented a proposal for a Council regulation for a European Private Company.[57] The following outlines the recommendations made by the European Parliament and then proceeds to examine the proposal by the Commission and the extent to which it reflects the Parliament's recommendations. The extent to which there is an unanimity of views may influence the speed at which the proposal is able to finally become law.

At the outset, the European Parliament recommended that the law that applies to an SPE regardless of where it has its registered office should be the proposed SPE statute. In other words, national laws will not govern this type of company. Thus, for example, all matters related to formation, organisational structure, the powers of company bodies, shareholders' rights, voting majorities, purchase and sales of shares in the company, and minimum standards for those representing the company should all be dealt with in the SPE statute. Further, the statute should have a standard set of articles of association attached that the members may adopt in whole or in part.

This recommendation was supported by responses received in the Commission's consultation process. A majority of respondents said that they

[54] European Parliament report with recommendations to the Commission on the European private company statute (2006/2013(INI).

[55] European Parliament resolution on the 14th company law directive and the European Private Company (B6-0399/07).

[56] At <http://ec.europa.eu/internal_market/company/epc/index_en.htm>.

[57] Commission of the European Communities, *Proposal for a Council Regulation on the Statute for a Private European Company*, Brussels COM (2008) 396/3.

faced considerable difficulties operating in a number of European countries because of the diversity of national company law systems. Three-quarters of the respondents supported the need for an SPE so that smaller companies intending to operate across Europe would face simpler administrative processes, save money and time and not have to deal with company law in 27 different jurisdictions. Accordingly, it comes as no surprise that nearly 80% of respondents to the survey supported a statute that was exempt from references to national law. Those who favoured retaining some reference to national law saw it as the only feasible solution. Persuading member states to surrender power over companies would be too difficult a task.

The European Parliament also recommended that the company should be able to be formed completely anew or 'on the basis of an existing company, or following a merger between companies or in the context of a common subsidiary'.[58] However, if existing private companies could convert themselves into SPEs and this was made relatively easy, then many may do so, thereby significantly weakening the control over corporate citizens by the state in which they are resident. The European Parliament also recommended that the SPE should be able to merge, change its registered office and convert into a public company or convert back into a purely national private company. In these cases the relevant directives of the EU will apply supplemented as necessary by the national laws of the relevant member states. Thus, to some degree at least, the SPE may have to confront national legal regimes. A third recommendation was that the SPE have a minimum capital of €10 000 but that it need not be fully paid in. This proposal is unlikely to sit easily with those countries where the so-called $2 companies are allowed.

There are also several recommendations dealing with the liability of directors. Here, the European Parliament appears to have taken the view that executive directors should have personal liability or at least joint liability with the company for acts which are contrary to the provisions of the civil or criminal code governing the particular activity. Thus, national laws are still intended to apply to company conduct as will, of course, taxation, environmental and labour laws. A distinction seems to be being drawn between matters relating to the company internally which are to be subject to the proposed EU-wide company law and those matters that relate to everyday business conduct which, of necessity, must remain local until harmonised.

[58] See European Parliament report with recommendations to the Commission on the European private company statute, op. cit., p.5.

The European Parliament recommended that the statute sets out a list of the company forms in each of the member states that are regarded as being equivalent to the SPE. The accounting standards that apply to these companies should also be applicable to the SPE. In addition, the liquidation and insolvency rules applicable to the equivalent types of companies should also apply to the SPE. This is a further instance of SPEs being subject to national laws.

The proposal from the Commission for the SPE can be summarised in the following list of points:

- The SPE is a private company with limited liability for its members. Its shares cannot be traded.
- It can be set up by one or more founders whether natural persons or companies.
- It can be formed either as a new entity or by merger or by transforming or dividing an existing company.
- Any company form under existing national laws can become an SPE.
- The regulation builds on the disclosure directive with regard to formation but specifically provides for electronic registration and a list of documents that member states may require for registration.
- The SPE will be governed primarily by the SPE regulation and by its articles.
- National law is only relevant to those matters not covered in the regulation. This includes labour law, tax law and insolvency law.
- Types of shares that may be issued and conditions for transfer are defined in the articles. Minority shareholders must consent to any change in the articles that affects their right to transfer shares.
- The company must keep a list of shareholders.
- The minimum capital will be €1 and capital can be contributed by cash or in kind as regulated by the articles.
- Dividends can only be paid if the SPE satisfies the balance sheet test but the articles can provide for a solvency test before dividends are paid out.
- The SPE can acquire its own shares subject to a balance sheet test.
- There is a list of decisions which must be taken by shareholders. This list can be added to by the articles.
- Shareholders decide on the appointment and removal of directors.
- The regulation lays down a general duty of care owed by directors and directors are liable for losses due to a breach of duty.
- All decisions not required to be taken by the shareholders can be taken by the management of the company.
- Minority shareholders can request shareholder resolutions and have the right to have an independent expert appointed by the court.

- The SPE will be subject to the laws on employee participation in the place where it has its registered office.
- The SPE can transfer its registered office to another state.

It can be seen that the proposal from the Commission closely follows the European Parliament's recommendation. One significant point of departure is the minimum capital requirement.

In March 2009, the European Parliament adopted the Commission proposal but made a significant number of amendments.[59] These included a requirement that the SPE have a cross-border element and that it may only be established with a capital of €1 if the company's owners are able to provide a certificate of solvency to show that the new company can pay its debts. Otherwise, a capital of €8000 is required. The Parliament also amended the proposal in relation to the provisions on employee participation.

The concerns about the SPE being just another company form that is governed by national law have been addressed to some extent by the proposed regulation but, as with the SE, the extent to which national laws apply will become clearer once the statute is passed and companies commence using it.

The proposal for a European Private Company is an initiative that has the potential to significantly ease the burdens on small and medium enterprises wanting to operate across borders and, in this respect, it is clearly in line with the objective to create a single market. However, as is often said, the devil is in the detail and it remains to be seen what results from the process. It has been necessary to draw attention to this proposed company form because, if implemented in the form desired by the Commission, it could well revolutionise business practice in the EU over the coming decades and it certainly presents an attractive alternative for companies from outside of the EU who wish to establish a presence there.

## LICENCES AND PERMITS

Countries vary in the degree to which they require businesses to obtain some form of operating licence. The range of activities that are regulated also varies considerably and depends to a considerable extent on the historical attitudes to freedom of business activity and how far the state is prepared to go to limit this freedom in the interests of protecting the public against unscrupulous operators and those who do not have

[59] European Parliament legislative resolution of 10 March 2009 on the proposal for a council regulation on the Statute for a European private company (A6-0044/2009).

the necessary qualifications to carry out the activity in which they are engaged.

Service-oriented businesses that are considered vital to the economy tend to be the most highly regulated. Accordingly, establishing a business as a financial institution, a utilities provider or public transport operator is likely to be highly regulated in all countries whether the person wishing to commence the business is local or foreign. Likewise, sensitive industries such as media will also attract strict licensing requirements as will professional practice as a doctor, lawyer or accountant for example. Some countries also require a licence to operate a manufacturing business. It is not possible to deal with the licensing requirements for every business activity in every EU member state. The websites of investment authorities referred to earlier generally provide some guidance but nothing substitutes for obtaining local legal advice as to the permits necessary and how to obtain them.

## Case study

### Business licences in Luxembourg

This case study is compiled from information provided on the Luxembourg government's investment website. The extensive *Doing Business* guide available on the website sets out clearly and in detail the requirements for operating licences.[60]

Luxembourg's law relating to the setting up of a business[61] requires a business permit for the carrying on of any form of business. Thus any company or branch that is set up in Luxembourg must obtain a permit. Foreigners from countries outside of the EU who visit Luxembourg occasionally to do business without having a permanent presence there must also obtain a permit. The *Doing Business* guide suggests that the legislators have considered it prudent to maintain a system for licensing of business activity in order to ensure that persons or companies that carry on a business are qualified to do so. The guide states that 'the legislators wished to make it clear that they did not intend to be joining those who were calling for liberalisation at any price nor be influenced for those calling for protectionism at all costs'.[62]

60 *Doing Business in Luxembourg*, 11 November 2006, <http://www.bed.public.lu/publications/doing_business.pdf>, Ch. 2.

61 Act of 28 December 1988 (as amended).

62 *Doing Business in Luxembourg*, op. cit., p. 12.

A business permit has to be obtained from the Ministry of Middle Classes and an application must be lodged on the required form along with payment of the required administrative fee. The form can be downloaded from the Ministry's website.[63] The application must be made by the individual person who will be managing the business. Certain documents must accompany the application. For a company, these include its constitution or charter or for a branch the constitution or charter of its parent company along with documentary evidence of the branch manager's authority to carry on the branch's activities on behalf of the parent company. Persons who have not lived in Luxembourg or have lived there for less than five years must also submit a certificate of non-bankruptcy sworn before a notary public and a document showing any criminal record. In addition, evidence must be provided of the person's professional qualifications.

The Ministry will examine the application to ensure that the person applying is 'of good standing' and is qualified to undertake the business activity which they have specified in the application. In the case of those activities that are not specially regulated (see below), the permit that is issued will specify 'trade'. To obtain this general class of permit, the type of qualifications needed by the person applying are qualifications that show that they are capable of managing a company. Such qualifications can be a university degree; an intensive training course that includes a range of specified skills considered as necessary to properly run a business; on-the-job training for a period of three years; or equivalent qualifications which include having passed an examination in business management.

There is a range of specific business activities that require a special permit. These include real estate businesses; large retail premises; pubs, hotels and restaurants; transport of goods or persons; travel agents; professional training bodies; childcare; landscape gardeners and horticultural pursuits; security and surveillance activities; and any business in the finance sector. In addition, there is a range of professions that require a special permit. These are architects, designers, engineers, accountants, surveyors, advisers in industrial property, doctors, lawyers, pharmacists and economic advisers. The *Doing Business* guide sets out in detail the requirements for each activity or profession. Because of increasing mutual recognition of qualifications across Europe, it will be easier for someone within the EU to satisfy the requirements than for persons from outside.

63 <http://www.mcm.public.lu>.

The nature of the business and permit numbers must be shown on all of the business's stationery including emails and websites. It should be apparent that the permit that is issued is a personal one and also specific to the activities for which it is issued. This means that if the person holding it leaves the company, the company must obtain a new permit for the new manager. Likewise, if the company changes the nature of its business a new permit may be required.

## STATE AID TO INDUSTRY

The provision of state aid to industry is heavily regulated at the EU level. Nonetheless, as the following discussion shows, there are many opportunities for firms engaged in specific activities or in specific locations to obtain assistance in the form of grants, loans, tax concessions, or infrastructure support from member governments. It is therefore important for those contemplating setting up a business in the EU to be aware of the basic principles upon which that aid can be given.

The starting point for any discussion on state aid must be Article 87(1) of the EC Treaty which prohibits aid by member states to industry. Prohibited measures must satisfy four criteria to be caught by the prohibition.[64] These are that any measure must involve a transfer of state resources; it must confer an economic advantage on the recipient that they would not have received in the ordinary course of business; it must be selective in the sense that the administering authorities have some discretion in the granting of the aid; and it must have some effect on trade and competition within the community in the sense that the activity in which the beneficiary is engaged is one in which there is some trade between member states. All of these criteria must be met for the measure to qualify as state aid that is subject to EU oversight. It is not difficult to see that most forms of state assistance to industry would meet these criteria and, accordingly, the Commission has wide authority over state assistance to industry.

However, Articles 87(2) and (3) of the EC Treaty allow certain categories of aid as exemptions. Originally, every measure that a state proposed had to be notified and approved by the Commission before a state could implement it. With increasing numbers of member states, the approval

[64] See the discussion in European Commission, Directorate-General for Competition, *Vademecum: Community Rules on State Aid*, 30 September 2008, <http://ec.europa.eu/competition/state_aid/studies_reports/vademecum_on_rules_09_2008_en.pdf>.

of each measure became unworkable and, accordingly, the Commission has in place regulations that set out in detail the criteria that apply to a particular category of aid. This means, in effect, that for most categories of allowable aid the member states need only provide information to the Commission about the measure and do not have to obtain specific approval to implement it.

This frees up the workload of the Commission, but for firms that are receiving aid there are certain risks. These arise because of Article 88 of the treaty which requires the Commission to recover illegal aid from the beneficiary of that aid. Accordingly, if a firm receives aid that the Commission later finds was not delivered in accordance with the guidelines for that particular category, then the Commission requires the member state that delivered the aid to recover it from the beneficiary. Thus, firms that are wishing to avail themselves of the sometimes quite generous incentives need to obtain local legal advice to ensure that the measure under which the aid is being given is in fact in accordance with the guidelines for that particular category of aid.

This is all the more important because with the freeing up of Commission resources from the approval process, it will allow the Commission to adopt closer scrutiny in cases where it has received complaints about the aid measure (usually from other member states or industry groups) that the aid is not in accordance with the guidelines. The Commission has always been active in policing state aid. At the end of 2007, there were 49 pending cases where recovery was being sought by the Commission.[65] Germany, France, Italy and Spain accounted for 38 of these 49 cases.[66] There were also 25 cases where the Commission had required states to take recovery action and had subsequently taken action in the European Court of Justice against the state concerned.[67] In some cases, press releases are issued by the Commission about the case to apply pressure on the state to recover the money from the firm that received it. The spring 2008 report by the Commission on state aid noted that between 2000 and 2007 the total illegal aid and fines recovered by the Commission was over €7 billion.[68] However, by and large, states comply with the guidelines when developing aid schemes. Of the 629 decisions made by the Commission on aid measures in 2007,

[65] Commission of the European Communities, Report from the Commission, *State Aid Scoreboard – Spring 2008 Update*, Brussels, 21.5.2008, COM9(2008) 304 final, <http://ec.europa.eu/competition/state_aid/studies_reports/archive/2008_spring_en.pdf>, p. 28.

[66] Ibid.

[67] Ibid., Annex 4, p. 55.

[68] Ibid., p. 29.

*Table 8.1 State aid and eligible firms*

| Aid category | Firms eligible |
|---|---|
| Initial investment made by large firms to establish a new business or expand an existing business | Only available to firms in regions of a member state where the standard or living is abnormally low or disadvantaged as defined in Articles 87(3)(a) and 87(3)(c) of the EC Treaty. |
| Initial investment made by small and medium firms to establish a new business or expand an existing business | Medium firms (less than 250 employees and a turnover of less than €50 million annually) and small firms (less than 50 employees and a turnover of less than €10 million). |
| Job creation by large firms leading to a permanent increase in new jobs for persons new to the workforce or who have not lost their previous job | Only available to firms in regions of a member state where the standard of living is abnormally low or disadvantaged as defined in Articles 87(3)(a) and 87(3)(c) of the EC Treaty. |
| Job creation (as described above) by small and medium firms | Medium firms (less than 250 employees and a turnover of less than €50 million annually) and small firms (less than 50 employees and a turnover of less than €10 million). |
| Environmental protection expenditure for such purposes as energy saving, renewable energy sources, energy efficient heating, waste management, remediation of contaminated sites | All enterprises meeting conditions can apply if offered by the member state concerned. |
| Research, development and innovation expenditure including fundamental research, industrial research, and experimental development | All enterprises meeting conditions can apply if offered by the member state concerned. |
| Operating Aid such as salary costs transport costs and rent | Only available in regions of a member state where the standard of living is abnormally low. |

(*cont.*)

*Table 8.1 (cont.)*

| Aid category | Firms eligible |
|---|---|
| Additional transport costs for enterprises located in outermost regions or regions of low population density | Available for firms in outermost regions, or regions of low population density. |
| Risk Capital Aid to promote risk capital investments in small and medium enterprises | Medium firms (less than 250 employees and a turnover of less than €50 million annually) and small firms (less than 50 employees and a turnover of less than €10 million). |
| Important services of general economic interest provided by public authorities that would have not otherwise been able to be provided | Only available to firms in regions of a member state where the standard or living is abnormally low or disadvantaged as defined in Article 87(3)(a) and 87(3)(c) of the EC Treaty. |
| Training Aid for employees to gain qualifications relevant to their present firm or to obtain general qualifications that are transferable | All enterprises meeting conditions can apply if offered by the member state concerned. |
| Rescue and Restructuring Aid for temporary assistance to firms in difficulty | All enterprises meeting conditions can apply if offered by the member state concerned. |

Source: European Commission, Directorate-Generale for Competition, *Vademecum: Community Rules on State Aid*, 30 September 2008, <http://ec.europa.eu/competition/state_aid/studies_reports/vademecum_on_rules_09_2008_en.pdf>.

87% resulted in a finding that the aid measure complied with the relevant regulations.[69]

This lengthy introduction has been necessary to acquaint the reader with the basic framework of EU regulation of state aid. It is now necessary to look in more detail at the more important categories of aid that are exempted by the general block exemption. Table 8.1 sets out the categories of aid that states may offer along with the types of firms eligible to receive it. Most categories of aid have limits applied to the level of aid that can be provided as well as some limitations on sectors of economic activity

[69] Ibid., p. 37.

that are not eligible for aid. In many categories these include agriculture, fisheries, transport, coal and steel industries. There are separate schemes in these areas. The following is a case study of incentives offered in Germany.

## Case study

### Investment incentives in Germany

The German government offers many of the categories of incentives listed above. The following outlines each category of incentive and the more important conditions that apply. The information has been obtained from the Germany Trade & Invest website where more comprehensive information can be found.[70]

*Cash incentives for investment*

Germany offers grants to new investment projects that create long-term jobs and have guaranteed financing from a private bank for that part of the project costs that are not eligible for an incentive grant. There is no nationality requirement attached to the grant of the incentives. The percentage of project financing costs that are available will depend on the region in which the investment project is located. Not all parts of Germany qualify. The most generous incentives exist for locating in the former East Germany, followed by regions that border the former Eastern bloc countries and regions in the far north of the country. For example, small firms setting up an investment in the former East Germany can apply for up to 50% of the project costs, while medium firms can claim up to 40% and large firms up to 30%. Firms investing in the former East Germany can elect to take part of the incentive as an investment allowance. However, the overall sum received from the grant and investment allowance combined cannot exceed the maximum rate of incentives for the region.

*Loans*

Firms establishing themselves in Germany can obtain low-interest loans from the European Investment Bank, Germany's nationally operating development bank or the state development banks. The European

[70] See <http://www.gtai.com/homepage/investment-guide-to-germany/incentives-programs>.

Investment Bank provides loans at below-market interest rates for projects that contribute to the EU's general policy objectives including building up weaker regions and building up the general structure of the EU as a business location. Projects must demonstrate economic, technological, environmental and financial viability. The German Development Bank's main loan types are the entrepreneur loan and the entrepreneur capital loan. State development banks tend to specialise in loans to small and medium start-up companies.

### *Labour incentives*

Labour incentives are available at all stages of the employment cycle, from recruitment to initial training prior to starting work, wage subsidies for employees and on-the-job training of employees. Recruitment services are offered by Germany's 800 local job centres free of charge. Pre-employment training programs for employees required to operate machinery and technical equipment will often be subsidised up to the extent of 100%. Those investors who are prepared to offer long-term employment to persons who have had difficulty finding work may be eligible for a subsidy of up to 50% of the wages of the employee for the first 12 months. This subsidy can be up to 70% if the employee is disabled or elderly. Subsidies are also available for up to 50% of on-the-job training costs.

### *R&D incentives*

Research and development (R&D) grants are available to firms in Germany through a variety of sources. These include EU R&D grants, R&D grants in Germany and further subsidies. Eligible categories of research include fundamental research, industrial research or experimental development. Generally, the grants obtained can be used for expenditure on personnel or relevant instruments and equipment.

An application for an R&D grant has to include the timeline for the project as well as a commercialisation plan showing how the results of the research project will generate additional turnover or employment in the region where the project was carried out.

# 9 Resolving a dispute with an EU firm

## INTRODUCTION

MOST INTERNATIONAL COMMERCIAL DISPUTES ARE able to be resolved by the parties themselves. This is by far the least expensive and most satisfactory outcome. However, for the very small percentage of disputes that cannot be resolved amicably, it is necessary to seek the intervention of a third party. The three options canvassed in this chapter are litigation, arbitration and mediation. Most standard international contracts of sale contain a clause that sets out which option the parties will use if the dispute cannot be resolved by negotiation and also, most importantly, the particular institution and place where any dispute resolution will take place. As noted in Chapter 2, those entering into international contracts are also advised to select the law that any dispute resolution body will use in resolving the dispute.

Litigation, arbitration and mediation each have their strengths and weaknesses as methods for resolving international disputes. Litigation is the most formal method, with strict rules of court procedure governing the conduct of disputes. However, because courts have the power to enforce their decisions, it is often seen as the best method for providing a final resolution of the matter. In addition, the parties can usually be confident of a well-reasoned decision and, if such is not the case, the option exists for appeal to a higher court. In most developed countries, the independence of the judiciary from the other arms of government and the business community promotes impartial decision making. On the other hand, litigation has many disadvantages. Court proceedings can be lengthy, business relationships are often destroyed by the adversarial process and costs tend to be high.

Arbitration has the advantage of the parties having some say as to who will hear their case. They are therefore able to select arbitrators who have particular skill in the subject matter of the dispute. It is also less formal than litigation and cases tend to be resolved more speedily. Arbitration proceedings are most frequently kept confidential, thus avoiding the public scrutiny that high-profile court action often attracts with the consequent damage to the reputation of the litigants. However, arbitrators lack the power to enforce their decisions and thus a party in whose favour an award has been made may have to resort to the court to enforce that award if the other party will not comply. Skilled arbitrators do not come cheaply and parties may find that the costs of arbitration may exceed those of court action.

Mediation is gathering strength as an alternative method for resolving international business disputes. As noted in Chapter 1, the EU has recently lent weight to this method by the enactment of the mediation directive in 2008. Mediation can be a speedy and less formal process for the resolution of disputes than either litigation or arbitration. There is also a much greater chance that the parties will be able to maintain their business relationship if mediation is used effectively to resolve any disputes. It is less costly than either litigation or arbitration. Its main disadvantages are ensuring that those engaged in the process have the authority to enter into binding settlement agreements on behalf of the parties and then having the parties abide by those agreements. This can be made quite difficult in those cases where one of the parties is simply using mediation as a delaying tactic to gain some advantage by putting off court action.

This chapter reviews each of these methods of dispute resolution in a European context. It sets out in more detail the potential problems that can arise in each method when attempting to resolve disputes that arise in international business transactions with European business partners.

## LITIGATION AGAINST PARTIES FROM EU MEMBER STATES

A number of potentially expensive and complex issues arise in any court proceeding against a party who is resident in another state and hence outside of the jurisdiction of the court where the party bringing the action is located. Bringing court action typically involves a series of well-recognised steps. These are as follows:

- A writ or document commencing the proceedings must be filed in the relevant court summoning the party to appear before the court to answer the matter being brought against them.
- The writ must be served on the other party so that they have notice.
- Before trial there may be preliminary hearings before the court, along with the requirements that each party provide to the other side the documents upon which they are relying to plead their case.
- The trial itself will occur where each party has the opportunity to present its case to the court and the court makes a decision based upon the relevant law.
- Judgement will be given either for the party bringing the court action or against them and, if it is in favour of the party bringing the action, then it may be necessary for that judgement to be enforced in the country where the defendant resides.

Each of these issues will now be discussed in relation to a party from outside of the EU bringing an action against someone who is resident in an EU member state. At the outset, it needs to be noted that the EU has regulations that govern matters related to the jurisdiction of courts, service of process, taking of evidence abroad and enforcement of judgements between parties resident in EU member states. However, the effect of these regulations when the litigation is between a party from a country outside of the EU and a party from within the EU varies, as will be seen.

## INITIATING PROCEEDINGS

The first question that confronts the lawyers for the plaintiff is to decide which court should hear the case. Well-drafted commercial agreements will contain a clause stating that in the event of any dispute, the parties agree to submit themselves to the jurisdiction of a particular court. This is known as a 'choice of jurisdiction' or 'choice of forum' clause. Understandably, the negotiation of such a clause is not an easy task for lawyers drawing up agreements. The parties themselves are keen to get on with the business deal and do not wish to consider the possibility that they may end up in court. Even if the idea of such a clause is able to be agreed upon, there is still likely to be hard negotiations about which court is most appropriate – a court in the place where the party from outside of the EU has its place of business or a place where the party from within the EU has its place of business or even a third-country court where, for example, the contract may be being performed.

If the parties have been able to agree on a choice of jurisdiction clause in their contract and if a dispute arises, then one would think that the chosen court would necessarily be the court where proceedings will occur. However, a party initiating the action might choose to ignore the choice of forum clause and commence action in a jurisdiction that they feel is more convenient to them. The question then becomes one of whether that court continues to hear the matter or whether it should decline to hear the case on the basis that the parties have agreed to an alternative forum. Here, the court where the proceedings have been initiated has to carefully balance the clear will of the parties as expressed in their agreement as against the possibility that if the will of the parties was honoured, then one of them might suffer serious disadvantages in obtaining a fair hearing of their case.

Within the EU, if there is a dispute between two parties from different EU member states there is a clear provision that the court agreed by the parties should have exclusive jurisdiction to hear the case.[1] Accordingly, if an action is commenced contrary to the choice of jurisdiction clause, then the court where the action is brought should decline jurisdiction if the party against whom the action is brought asserts their rights in accordance with the choice of jurisdiction clause. If an agreement between a party from outside of the EU and a party from an EU member state provides that the court to hear the dispute will be that of a particular EU member state, then the parties' choice of jurisdiction clause must be given effect should the action be brought in another EU court.

If, however, contrary to the parties' choice of jurisdiction clause giving jurisdiction to a court within the EU, a party brings an action in its own courts, a potential problem arises. The court outside of the EU will use its own national law to determine if it has jurisdiction. Laws as to when a court may decline jurisdiction vary from country to country. It is possible that the overseas court where the action is brought could decide to stay the matter because of the parties' choice of forum clause, or it could decide that since the case was brought before it, it should continue to hear whether it should have jurisdiction. In some circumstances, the overseas court might not give effect to the parties' choice of jurisdiction clause and consider it to be in the interests of justice that it hears the case.

[1] Article 23(3) of Regulation 44/2001/EC ('Brussels Regulation') [2001] OJ L12/1. This regulation has to a large extent replaced the earlier Brussels Convention on Jurisdiction and Enforcement of Judgment in Civil and Commercial Matters 1968 and the later Lugano Convention of 1988 as they relate to jurisdiction in proceedings within EU member states.

Conversely, if the choice of jurisdiction clause designates a court outside of the EU but an action is brought in an EU member state court, then some commentators suggest that the effect of the Brussels Regulation (44/2001/EEC) is that if the matter is brought before an EU court, the court may have the option to decide if it has jurisdiction rather than simply staying the matter because of a choice of forum clause.[2] Understandably, this approach means that if an EU party brings an action against a non-EU party in an EU court, then the defendant could be faced with expensive proceedings in attempting to convince the EU court that the forum selected by the parties should be the one to eventually hear the case.

Because of these difficulties, considerable efforts have been made by the Hague Conference on Private International Law to have countries worldwide adopt a convention on choice of court issues. There is a draft convention but it has not yet been accepted despite clear support for it from important professional bodies. In a survey of American Bar Association members, 98% of those surveyed said that such a convention would be useful, and 70% said it would make them more likely to use litigation rather than arbitration as their chosen means of dispute resolution.[3]

Thus, the first hurdle for potential litigants is the possibility that they might face protracted and expensive proceedings over which court should hear the case even if there is a choice of jurisdiction clause. Understandably, these problems become even more protracted where the parties do not have such a clause in their agreement.

## SERVICE OF PROCESS

The provisions of the Convention on Service Abroad of Judicial and Extra-judicial Documents in Civil or Commercial Matters 1965 ('Hague Convention') will govern the procedure for the service of proceedings and other documents by a party from outside of the EU on a party who is resident in an EU member state provided that both states are signatories to the convention. Under the provisions of the Hague convention, countries designate central authorities who will be responsible for the service of documents and then producing a certificate to provide evidence of such service. However,

[2] See N. Hatzimihail and A. Nuyts, 'Judicial Cooperation between the United States and Europe in Civil and Commercial Matters: An Overview of the Issues' in A. Nuyts and N. Watte (eds.), *International Civil Litigation*, Bruyant, Brussels, 2005, p. 18.

[3] Survey of ABA practitioners by the ABA Working Group on the Hague Convention on Choice of Court Agreements as reported in L. Tait 'Choice of Court Clauses and Third Countries from a US Perspective' in Nuyts and Watte (eds.), ibid., p. 305.

the convention is flexible in that it also allows for service through consular offices provided that the state in which the service is to be effected has not objected to this alternative.

There are only some 60 states that are parties to the Hague Convention, including all states of the EU other than Malta. If a party from a state that is not a member of the convention wishes to have a document served on a party in the EU, then it is necessary to have regard to any treaty that exists between that state and the EU member country concerning the service of judicial documents. Australia, for example, is not a member of the Hague Convention and, accordingly, service of documents will be governed by the particular arrangements in place between the Australian government and the relevant EU member state. As each bilateral agreement is likely to involve slightly different processes, it is not possible here to deal with all possibilities.[4] The more significant matter is to note the need to have regard to the bilateral arrangements.

On the other hand, where both parties are from EU member states, service of documents within the EU internally is governed by Regulation 1393/2007/EC[5] (the 'Service Regulation'). As one commentator has put it, the main difference between the Hague Convention and the Service Regulation is that the Service Regulation offers a speedier procedure.[6]

## COURT PROCEDURE IN PRE-TRIAL AND TRIAL STAGES

There are major differences in the way court proceedings at the pre-trial and trial stages are conducted between legal systems that have a common law origin and those that have a civil law origin. These differences are perhaps most apparent in procedure relating to discovery of documents and evidence gathering. Each of these is discussed below.

In common law systems (UK, USA, Australia), it is a procedural requirement that each party reveal to the other the essential documents on which they will be relying to prove their case. In civil law systems, however, no such formal requirement exists and it is a matter for the judge to decide if a party should be able to have access to essential documents relied on

4 For information on Australia's treaties with individual countries, see <http://www.ag.gov.au/www/agd/agd.nsf/Page/Internationalcivilprocedure_ServiceofAustraliancourtprocessabroad-generalinformation>.

5 [2007] OJ L324/9.

6 J. Forner 'Service of Judicial Documents within Europe and in Third States (Regulation 1348/2000) and the 1965 Hague Convention in International Civil Litigation in Europe and Relations with Third States' in Nuyts and Watte (eds.), op. cit., p. 407.

by the other side if they refuse to reveal them. However, in practice, it is commonplace for each party to include copies of documents upon which they rely in the pleadings that they file with the court.

This difference has its roots in the role of the court under each system. In common law systems, the court leaves it up to the parties to gather the necessary evidence and then present it to the court. The court will decide the case based on the evidence that the parties put before it. In civil law systems, the court itself takes the primary role in deciding what evidence is necessary to decide the case. For example, under the German system, the court itself can require witnesses to be called, experts to attend to give evidence, documents to be produced and allow examination of the witnesses by the parties.[7] Because of these differences, civil law systems tend to hold a number of subsequent hearings to decide the case. In common law systems, some pre-trial applications may be needed but, by and large, the main trial is one event which can last for a day, a week or several months.

The next question concerns the actual process by which the evidence is gathered. Within the EU, Regulation 1206/2001/EC[8] provides mechanisms for the cooperation between the courts of member states in the taking of evidence in other member states. This provides for transmission of requests direct from court to court, specified time limits within which the request must be acted upon and for courts to request a particular procedure for the obtaining of the evidence. In addition, courts from one member state of the EU can travel to another member state to take evidence directly.

However, the matter of evidence gathering in non-member states is subject to the Convention on the Taking of Evidence Abroad in Civil and Commercial Matters 1970. Almost all EU member states are signatories to this convention as are a number of other countries including Australia, China and the US but not Canada or Japan. This convention allows authorities in different countries to cooperate in taking evidence and forwarding it on to the court in the requesting country where the proceedings are taking place. The procedure under the convention is somewhat cumbersome. The court wanting the evidence must transmit the request to the central authority nominated by the state under the convention in the state where the evidence is to be gathered. The central authority will then transmit that request to an appropriate body to gather the evidence. The evidence

[7] See T. Taylor and N. Cooper, *European Litigation Handbook*, Sweet and Maxwell, London, 1995, Ch 4.

[8] [2001] OJ L174/1.

itself usually takes the form of a sworn statement – that is, a statement sworn as the truth by the person giving the evidence in front of a person authorised by the state as being able to take such statements (a commissioner for affidavits for example). The authority taking the evidence should use procedures that are in conformity with the evidence laws of the court requesting it.

Needless to say, if a party from a non-EU member state wishes to obtain evidence from a party that is within the EU, it will reduce costs considerably if the evidence is able to be taken in the EU country. However a number of problems exist. First, the procedure under the convention can move very slowly depending on the country concerned and the degree to which central authorities wish to cooperate. Second, evidence given by way of written testimony has the defect that it does not allow for cross-examination of the persons giving the testimony to test the statements made. In addition, as noted above, a party from outside of the EU who wishes to obtain discovery of documents from a party within the EU may run up against difficulties if the request is directed to a civil law country. It may not be honoured because of differences of opinion about the rights of parties to pre-trial discovery. Further, if the party is from a state that is not a signatory to the convention, then it will be necessary to have regard to any bilateral arrangements that exist between that state and the EU member country concerned.

Accordingly, parties from common law non-EU member states might have some difficulty with the differences in pre-trial discovery matters as well as in the procedure of evidence gathering. This makes the decision to litigate all the more problematic.

## CHOICE OF LAW

It is usual for parties to agree on a choice of law clause in their initial agreement. Such a clause nominates the substantive law that the court hearing the matter will apply in resolving the dispute. Generally, courts will give effect to parties' choice of law clauses. However, if the law that the parties have chosen is not the law of the country where the court hearing the dispute is located, significant costs might be incurred in informing the court of the contents of the law governing the dispute. For that reason, it is usual to have the choice of law clause and choice of jurisdiction clause aligned so that, for example, if the courts of the UK are to hear the dispute, then the choice of law should also be UK law. However, as noted above, the success of such a strategy will depend on the actual choice of jurisdiction clause being upheld if it is challenged by the other party in the ways mentioned earlier. In addition, a court may not apply the parties' choice of law clause in all instances because there might be mandatory laws affecting the case. For example, it was noted in Chapter 6 that if an action is brought against an agent in an EU country, then the courts are likely to apply the EU directive on agency.

## ENFORCEMENT

As with service of process and taking evidence, the European institutions have used their powers under the treaty to bring into effect a regulation on the enforcement of judgements within the EU.[9] However, judgements rendered in an EU member state court that are to be enforced in a third state or vice versa still need to rely on the bilateral agreements entered into by EU member states with third states. Thus, each bilateral agreement will need to be consulted to determine the exact mechanisms by which judgements are to be enforced, and the possible grounds upon which a defendant against whom they are to be enforced can challenge the enforcement proceedings. Once again, the possibility of challenge at the enforcement stage makes international litigation a risky method for the resolution of international disputes.

## MATTERS TO CONSIDER IN AN INTERNATIONAL ARBITRATION

As noted above, litigation is fraught with difficulties both at the time of inserting a dispute resolution clause into a contract and then taking court action should an actual dispute arise. Arbitration has become a well-used alternative not only because it tends to be speedier and more private than court action but also because it may be easier for parties to agree at the time of contract about a suitable arbitration clause and arbitral institution. Arbitration is seen as a less threatening possibility than court proceedings and arbitral institutions are completely independent of the state in many countries. This reduces fears a party might have that a foreign court might have a bias against foreign litigants bringing actions before it. However, arbitration does have its limitations, as will be discussed below.

A number of issues arise for consideration if arbitration is to be used to resolve disputes. These include:

[9] Regulation 805/2004 EEC [2004] OJ L143/15 ('European Enforcement Order').

- the selection of an arbitral institution either at the time that the contract is entered into or, alternatively, when a dispute arises
- how an arbitration is commenced
- how the arbitrators are appointed
- the preliminary steps that the tribunal takes
- establishing the facts and the hearing itself
- the award and costs.

## SELECTION OF AN ARBITRAL INSTITUTION

There are many institutions in the EU that have wide experience in hearing international arbitration claims. Some of the better known of these include the London Court of International Arbitration, the Arbitration Institute of the Stockholm Chamber of Commerce, and the International Chamber of Commerce (ICC) International Court of Arbitration with its headquarters in Paris.

Many considerations influence the parties' choice of an institution, including the parties' own geographic locations, the place where the contract is being performed, the place where the institution can conduct a hearing, the language of the hearing and, perhaps most significantly, the rules of the institution itself and how well suited these are to the parties' own views of how they see an arbitration being conducted should the need arise. Some institutions are more flexible than others in each of these matters. Parties therefore need to decide at the outset what they expect out of a potential arbitration and which institution is most likely to meet those expectations.

### Case study

#### An arbitral institution

The ICC International Court of Arbitration ('ICC Court') was founded in 1923. Its primary role is to oversee the work of individual arbitration tribunals (referred to as 'Arbitral Tribunals') that hear disputes pursuant to the rules of procedure of the ICC. There have been over 14 000 arbitrations conducted by arbitration tribunals under ICC procedures since its foundation. There are three important bodies which make up the ICC court system. First, there are the national committees. Then, there is the court itself, the ICC Court. Finally, there is a secretariat which is a full-time body located in Paris that provides services to the court and arbitrators.

While the ICC is headquartered in Paris, it has branches in over 90 countries of the world making it a truly international organisation. These national committees elect representatives to the governing body of the ICC, the World Council. In addition, the national committees nominate persons to be members of the ICC Court. They are then formally approved by the World Council. In 2005, there were some 124 members of the court coming from 86 countries.[10]

The ICC Court is not a court in the usual sense in which that word is used but an administrative body consisting of a chairperson, several vice-chairpersons and representatives from each of the national committees. The court performs an important supervisory role in ICC arbitrations as will become clear in the discussion later in this chapter. To carry this out effectively, it delegates much of the work to three member committees that meet several times a month to deal with matters that are referred to the court and that are delegated to the particular committee by the court. The court has its own internal rules of procedure for the delegation of these functions to committees including the number of members on the committee and the types of decisions that can be made. Members of the court are all legal professionals. To preserve the independence of the court, they are not permitted to serve as arbitrators on any ICC arbitration. They also receive no remuneration from the ICC or national committees for their work and they must also be independent of the national committees.

The ICC Secretariat plays an important role in the day-to-day administration of arbitrations. It is the secretariat that receives the request for arbitration and deals with the forwarding of documents and files to the court and to arbitration panels that are dealing with each particular case. The secretariat has a full-time staff of over 50 persons.[11]

The ICC Court publishes statistics of arbitrations each year. The number of cases filed with the court each year has increased steadily over the past two decades, from around 250 per year during the 1980s to over 550 per year every year since 2000. The truly international nature of the court is evidenced by statistics for 2006[12] which show that the parties in

[10] See Y. Derains and E. Schwartz, *A Guide to the ICC Rules of Arbitration*, Kluwer Law, Netherlands, 2005, p. 12.

[11] Ibid., p. 25.

[12] See '2006 Statistical Report' (2007) 1 *ICC International Court of Arbitration Bulletin* 5–16.

the 593 new cases filed in that year came from 125 separate countries. European parties accounted for 53% of the total followed by 25% from the Americas and 17% from Asia.[13] Nearly 50% of the cases involved amounts between US$1 million and US$50 million.[14]

The following discussion will illustrate the arbitration process by using the ICC Court procedure as an example.

## COMMENCING AN ARBITRATION

Arbitration before the ICC Court is commenced by the person wanting the arbitration (the 'claimant') making a formal request for arbitration to the ICC Secretariat. There are designated matters as to what the request must contain. The secretariat then sends a copy of the request to the other party (the 'respondent'). There are prescribed means by which notices have to be sent. The respondent then files an answer to the request with the secretariat.

If the respondent simply ignores the request, the matter goes to the ICC Court to decide if there is in fact an agreement to arbitrate. If so, then it can decide that the arbitration should proceed regardless of the failure of the respondent to respond to the request for arbitration by the claimant.

## APPOINTMENT OF THE ARBITRATORS

The court itself supervises the process of appointment of arbitrators. One of the advantages of the ICC arbitration process is that arbitrations can be conducted in almost any location throughout the world and arbitrators appointed from almost anywhere in the world. In 2006, 949 arbitrators were appointed. Of these, 689 were appointed by the parties and 239 by the court. Arbitrators came from 71 different countries in 2006, with nearly 60% coming from EU member countries including Switzerland. The types of cases were wide-ranging. For example, 25% were sale and purchase agreements; 17% were cases related to business structure (joint ventures, share transfers and others); and 8% were intellectual property cases.[15]

The court will appoint only one arbitrator unless the parties have requested a panel of three. In about 45% of arbitral appointments in 2006, a sole arbitrator was appointed. The remainder were panels of three

13 Ibid., pp. 6–7.
14 Ibid, p. 14.
15 Ibid., p. 11.

arbitrators. Approximately three-quarters of sole arbitrators were appointed by the court after consultation with the relevant national committee. In three-party panels, over 95% of co-arbitrators were nominated by the parties themselves while the chairperson of the Arbitral Tribunal was nominated by the co-arbitrators approximately 57% of the time, appointed by the court 34% of the time and nominated by the parties themselves in less than 5% of cases.[16] This shows that while the parties readily agree to appoint one member of the panel each, it requires the intervention of the court or the other two arbitrators to select the chairperson.

In 2006, there were only 27 cases where an arbitrator nominated by a party was not confirmed by the court.[17] Further, there were only 18 cases where the appointment of an arbitrator was challenged and only two of these were successful.[18] The decision of the court will be final on matters of appointment of arbitrators, challenges to a particular arbitrator or replacement of an arbitrator. In appointing arbitrators, the court takes into account the nationality of the parties, the residence of the parties and the place where the parties might have nominated for the conduct of the arbitration. The court can draw on the extensive resources of the national committees of arbitration and their lists of arbitrators to decide an appropriate panel or single arbitrator, as the case may be. Where there is to be a single arbitrator, that person will usually come from a country other than the country of nationality of the parties. This also applies to the chairperson of the panel. The court also decides on the place where the arbitration will occur if the parties have not come to an agreement on this.

## PRELIMINARY STEPS

After appointment issues are settled, the secretariat transmits the file containing the request and answer and other documents to the Arbitral Tribunal. The Arbitral Tribunal can conduct a hearing at any location provided that the parties agree – otherwise, it will take place in the location nominated by the court. The tribunal will also determine the language of the hearing in the absence of agreement between the parties. Similarly, the tribunal will also decide which law will apply to the dispute before it if the parties have not chosen the law of the agreement. In an overwhelming 87% of cases in 2006, parties to the relevant contracts had a

[16] Ibid., p. 9.
[17] Ibid., p. 8.
[18] Ibid., p. 9.

choice of law clause in their agreement,[19] and in 86% of cases, the parties themselves decided where their arbitration would be conducted,[20] thereby avoiding the complexities referred to above regarding choice of jurisdiction in litigation matters.

The Arbitral Tribunal (single member or panel) may initially be called upon to decide if it has jurisdiction to hear the case should the respondent object to the jurisdiction of the ICC. The tribunal has the power to rule on whether it has jurisdiction. If the respondent claims that there is no agreement to arbitrate, the ICC Court has the power to decide if, prima facie, there is such an agreement. It is then up to the tribunal to decide on its jurisdiction. If, however, the ICC Court comes to the conclusion that there is no agreement to arbitrate, it notifies the parties that the arbitration cannot proceed. There is a provision that such a decision by the ICC Court can be referred to any court having jurisdiction. This would usually be the courts of the country where the arbitration is being conducted.

The Arbitral Tribunal is then required to draw up the terms of reference for the arbitration. These must contain a number of specified matters and must be signed by the parties. This is a useful procedure because it makes it difficult for a party to argue later that some issues were not covered if they have already signed the terms of reference.

In consultation with the parties, the tribunal draws up a timetable for the conduct of the proceedings and the dates by which the various steps should occur. The tribunal also notifies the ICC Court of this timetable.

## ESTABLISHING THE FACTS AND THE HEARING

The Arbitral Tribunal then sets about establishing the facts. It is frequently the case that much of the evidence that the tribunal will consider in making its decision is in documentary form including the original submission of the parties. The tribunal will also hear from the parties if they so request. In addition, the rules of the ICC provide for the summoning of witnesses by the tribunal and hearing the experts appointed by the parties. The tribunal can summon its own experts after consultation with the parties.

There is no requirement for a formal hearing unless one of the parties requests it. The parties are entitled to legal representation. The tribunal itself decides at what point the hearing is concluded.

19 Ibid., p. 11.
20 Ibid., p. 12.

## THE AWARD AND COSTS

The tribunal must give a decision (an award) within six months of the conclusion of the hearing. The ICC Court can extend this time limit if need be. The tribunal is also empowered to give a consent award if the parties reach a settlement during the proceedings. The award is only available to the parties thus preserving the confidentiality of the dispute. Awards are published in very few cases and then only with the consent of the parties.

The court must approve each award and is active in its role in ensuring that awards are rendered in a form that minimises the risk of challenge in a court of law. The court is very active in fulfilling this part of its work. In 2006, the court approved 293 awards but in only 45 of these did it make no comments about either the substance of the award or the form of it.[21]

One of the major disadvantages with arbitral proceedings are the costs involved. Unlike court proceedings, the arbitrators' fees will have to be met by the parties. Arbitrators are highly skilled professionals in their various fields and accordingly their time is very expensive. The claimant is required to give security for any costs of the arbitration before it commences. Further, after the terms of reference are drawn up, an advance of costs is payable by each party.

The award itself will usually contain a decision as to how the total costs of the arbitration will be borne between the parties. These costs can be reviewed and fixed by the court of international arbitration if need be.

## ENFORCEMENT

One of the advantages of international arbitration is that there is an international convention signed by most countries of the world pursuant to which countries agree to enforce arbitral awards from other member countries' arbitral institutions. This is the Convention on the Recognition and Enforcement of Foreign Arbitral Awards 1958 ('New York Convention'). All of the EU member states are signatories to this convention. Thus, an award against a party from the EU can be enforced by the courts in the relevant EU country. There are limited grounds that a court can refuse to enforce an award under the convention. These include an invalid arbitration agreement under the law of the country where the arbitration took place; insufficient notice or inability of the losing party to present their case; the award was outside of the proper scope of the arbitration; the

[21] Ibid., p. 13.

arbitration was not conducted in accordance with the rules; the award is not binding on the parties; the subject matter is not capable of being subjected to arbitration; or it is against public policy to enforce the award. It can be argued that the degree of supervision that the ICC Court exercises over the arbitration process should minimise the possibility of a party using many of these grounds in an attempt to block enforcement of the award.

## MEDIATION OF INTERNATIONAL COMMERCIAL DISPUTES

Mediation involves a neutral third party attempting to find a compromise between parties who are in dispute. Due to the high costs of arbitration and procedural and other difficulties with litigation, mediation is increasingly a first option employed by parties in an attempt to negotiate a compromise. Most European countries have institutions that provide mediation services.[22] The ICC also provides conciliation and mediation services in addition to its more well-known arbitration service.

As with arbitration, each mediation body has its own set of rules of procedure. However, these tend to be fairly short given the flexible and more informal nature of mediation. The United Nations Commission on International Trade Law (UNCITRAL) has adopted the Model Law on International Commercial Conciliation 2002[23] which states may adopt to govern conciliation in international commercial matters.

In addition, in order to encourage confidence in mediation as a viable method for dispute resolution, most institutions require their mediators to abide by a code of conduct. There is a standard European code, the European Code of Conduct for Mediators.[24] Some institutions also have their own codes. In terms of formal regulation of mediation, there is an EU-level directive (the mediation directive)[25] requiring member states to take a number of steps that will promote the use of mediation as an accepted method for resolving international commercial disputes. The extensive preamble to the directive makes it clear that the European institutions consider mediation to be an effective and a relatively inexpensive method for dispute resolution.

22 For a list see <http://www.hg.org/arbitration-mediation-associations-europe.html>.

23 At <http://www.uncitral.org/pdf/english/texts/arbitration/ml-conc/ml-conc-e.pdf>.

24 At <http://ec.europa.eu/civiljustice/adr/adr_ec_code_conduct_en.pdf>.

25 Directive 2008/52/EC [2008] OJ L136/3.

There are a number of issues that arise in mediation. These are:

- commencing a mediation and selecting a mediator
- procedure that the mediator adopts pre-hearing
- the mediation hearing
- the settlement agreement and its enforcement
- costs.

## COMMENCING A MEDIATION

There are a number of reasons why parties to a commercial dispute might attempt to resolve the matter through mediation. There may be a provision in their agreement that requires mediation as a first step in the resolution of disputes. Alternatively, while they may have an arbitration clause in their agreement, they may have looked at the arbitration alternative and decided that mediation might be a more cost-effective way of dealing with the matter as a first option. They may have been recommended to use mediation by their legal advisers. If court proceedings have begun, it is possible that the court might have ordered the parties to undergo mediation before proceeding further or the parties themselves might have decided to try mediation rather than continuing down the litigation route. In these cases, court proceedings are stayed to await the outcome of mediation. If it is unsuccessful, then the parties will resume their court action.

The first step in mediation is to decide which institution will be most appropriate if this has not been provided for in the parties' contract. As noted, there are many available institutions and, as with arbitration, much will depend on the convenience of the parties as well as the reputation, rules of procedure and costs of the institution chosen.

### Case study

#### A mediation institution

The London-based Centre for Effective Dispute Resolution (CEDR) was established in 1990 with the support of the British Chamber of Commerce and Industry, law firms and public bodies. Its work involves not only assisting parties in actual meditations but also training of mediators and helping resolve other conflicts within society. The branch of the organisation that is involved in commercial mediations is known as

'CEDR Solve'.[26] It has its own set of procedural rules for the conduct of mediations, a draft agreement that parties enter into prior to commencing mediation and a code of conduct that all mediators must abide by as well as draft dispute resolution clauses that can be included in a commercial contract.

CEDR Solve has a team of administrative staff who are available for consultation by parties contemplating mediation. The staff are able to assist the parties to find a suitable mediator. They note on their website that they have access to over 3000 mediators with 50 mediators readily available for appointments to discuss mediation possibilities. As is the case with arbitration, the mediators are not employees of CEDR Solve but are independent persons who have trained as mediators and most often specialise in dealing with a specific class of dispute. They are also able to draw on a group of eminent persons – predominantly retired senior judges – to deal with high-profile disputes.

The range of disputes that CEDR Solve deals with is apparent from an examination of the case studies reported by two CEDR mediators in a general work on mediation.[27] Some examples include cases dealing with construction, energy projects, financial services, franchises, insurance, intellectual property, international trade and distribution arrangements, joint ventures, shipping, professional services, supply of goods and telecommunications. The amounts involved range from as little as US$250 000 to over US$400 million. Frequently, several million dollars is involved in the dispute between the parties, thereby belying the view that mediation is only suitable when the amount involved is small. CEDR Solve reports a settlement rate of 75–80% in mediations conducted through the organisation.[28]

The following discussion uses the CEDR procedure to illustrate how the mediation process works in practice.

## THE MEDIATION PROCESS – UP TO THE MEDIATION HEARING

Once the parties have agreed on a suitable mediator taking into account the mediator's expertise, the nature of the matter and what is at stake,

26 See <http://www.cedr.com/CEDR_Solve/>.

27 E. Carroll and K. Mackie, *International Mediation: The Art of Business Diplomacy*, 2nd edn., Kluwer Law International, Netherlands, 2006.

28 See http://www.cedr.com/CEDR_Solve>.

then the mediator will contact the parties with a draft mediation agreement. The CEDR Solve draft agreement will typically contain clauses setting out the following:

- the names of the parties and of the mediator
- a brief description of the dispute
- a short statement indicating the parties' assent to mediation as an attempt to settle the matter
- that the person signing on behalf of each party has authority from their organisation to bind the organisation
- that the mediator is independent of the parties
- that the mediation proceedings are to be kept confidential including not only communications during the mediation process but any settlement agreement
- that no outcome of the mediation is binding until a settlement agreement has been signed
- that any question regarding the validity of the settlement agreement is to be decided by English courts
- that the parties do not relinquish their rights to resort to litigation if the mediation fails[29]
- that the parties agree not to call the mediator as witness in any court proceedings should the mediation fail and the parties resort to litigation[30]
- that the mediators and CEDR Solve will not accept any legal liability for any matter concerning the mediation and its proceedings.

The parties will be required to sign this agreement at the commencement of the mediation hearing.

After the agreement is finalised, the mediator will then contact the parties to organise a suitable date and venue for the actual mediation hearing. It is usual in CEDR Solve mediations for there to be a lead time during which the parties will prepare a short summary of their case and gather relevant documents prior to there being an actual mediation hearing. The mediator will also need to become familiar with the parties' cases and may hold preliminary discussions with each of them. The mediator may reveal the parties' case summaries and documents to the other side provided they consent to this. The lead time will vary according to the nature of the matter and the convenience of the parties as well as of the mediator. A

[29] Article 8 of the mediation directive requires member states to provide that parties who use mediation should not be prevented from taking court proceedings if the mediation fails.

[30] Article 7 of the mediation directive requires member states to exempt mediators from being called as a witness if litigation ensues.

review of the case studies mentioned earlier suggests that the lead time can vary from a few weeks to several months with a common lead time being around two to four months.

## THE MEDIATION HEARING

The mediation hearing will typically take place over one or two days. It is important that the parties each send along a representative who is adequately prepared, is able to negotiate on their behalf, will stay for the entire length of the hearing and is authorised to enter into any settlement agreement. Experienced mediators have noted that the failure of the parties to do this is a frequent cause of the failure of mediation.[31]

At the hearing, the parties must sign the mediation agreement that was forwarded to them at the commencement of the process. The mediator is then likely to talk to the parties separately, at first, and then hold a joint meeting. They may then hold more separate and joint meetings in an attempt to see if a compromise is possible. During the whole process, including the hearing and the lead-up to it, the mediator will be bound by the CEDR Solve Code of Conduct for Mediators.[32]

The code requires mediators to act fairly, independently and impartially. They must disclose any possible conflict of interest that they may have including a prior business relationship with one of the parties, a financial interest in the outcome, or if they have prior confidential information about one of the parties. The mediator must withdraw if requested to do so by one of the parties because of an alleged breach of the code of conduct. Alternatively, the mediator themselves can decide to withdraw if the parties act in breach of the mediation agreement or act unconscionably or if the mediator forms the view that a settlement is not going to be possible. There is a provision in the code that requires a mediator not to unnecessarily prolong the mediation process, thereby making it incumbent upon the mediator to end the mediation if it is apparent a settlement will not be able to be agreed upon.

[31] Carroll and Mackie, op. cit., p. 63.

[32] The mediation directive requires member states to ensure that mediators are bound by codes of conduct. This directive must be implemented in the UK and, accordingly, CEDR Solve will have to abide by any provisions that affect its work. Having a code of conduct already in place means the CEDR already complies with this aspect of the directive.

## THE SETTLEMENT AGREEMENT AND ITS ENFORCEMENT

It is usual for the legal advisers for each party to draw up the terms of the agreed settlement for the parties to sign. If the matter is already the subject of court proceedings, it may be necessary to draw this up in a form required by the court where the proceedings have been stayed awaiting the outcome of the mediation. The court will then formally sanction the agreement entered into by the parties.

Mediation is often criticised because of the problem of enforcement. Despite this, some argue that because the parties have themselves arrived at a resolution of their problems, then they are not likely to later attempt to resile from their agreement. However, enforcement is enough of a concern for the EU mediation directive[33] to require EU member states to ensure that there are mechanisms in place whereby if one party to a mediation requests that the settlement agreement be made enforceable, then they should be able to have it formally sanctioned by a court and presumably subject to the same enforcement action as any other court judgements. As noted, if litigation is already in train then it will be necessary for the parties to obtain the court's sanction for any agreement to settle. This provision extends to any settlement at all from a mediation that a party to the mediation wants sanctioned by the court.

## COSTS

The CEDR Solve Code of Conduct for mediators requires mediators to notify the parties of the costs of mediation at the outset. The parties will generally share the cost of the mediation equally. However, costs appear to be reasonable. A review of the case studies mentioned earlier reveals that the costs do not depend on the amount involved. Mediation costs in a US$314 million claim only amounted to some US$10 000 and in a US$460 million claim to only US$8000. On the other hand, smaller claims can be equally as expensive depending on the amount of time that the mediator is required to put into the matter. However, these figures do not include each party's lawyer's fees.

[33] Article 6.

# Index